Ireland
TravelBook

Ninth Edition

Written by Susan Poole
Ninth edition verified by Louise McGrath
Series Editor: Sheila Hawkins
Project Editor: Marilynne Lanng

Published by AAA Publishing, 1000 AAA Drive, Heathrow, Florida 32746.
The *AAA Ireland TravelBook* was created and produced for AAA Publishing by AA
Media Limited, Fanum House, Basing View, Basingstoke, Hampshire, RG21 4EA, UK.

Cover photos
Front cover and spine: A spectacular complex of medieval buildings, County
Tipperary, Rock of Cashel, © SIME / eStock Photo.
Back cover: Poulnabrone Dolmen, County Clare, © age fotostock / SuperStock.

Cataloging-in-Publication Data is on file with the Library of Congress.

Color separations by Digital Department, AA Publishing.
Printed in China by C & C Offset Printing Co. Ltd.

A04764

Lights from the docks lining the riverbank are reflected in the River Liffey, Dublin, Leinster

Foreword

Pleasures are in store for you in the unique and beautiful country of Ireland; As you plan your trip to this magical land, this book will spark your imagination. Introduce yourself to Dublin, with its buzzing streets, stately Georgian buildings and haunting echoes of turbulent Irish history. Explore Belfast, which has rapidly been transformed into a vibrant European city with a modern outlook. Discover the wild and dramatic coastline of the west, the towering cliffs and the sandy beaches of Achill Island and the eerie limestone landscapes of The Burren.

This is a land that wears its personalities on its sleeve. The poetry of William Butler Yeats reverberates through Sligo. The lively celebrations for St. Patrick's Day honor Ireland's patron saint and put the country's citizens, as well as others, into a festive mood. Shadows of great authors such as James Joyce and Jonathan Swift fall on Dublin's streets, where the literary heritage still flourishes. Stories of Fionn MacCumhaill and other mythological heroes pervade the Irish psyche.

But Ireland's people, among the most smiling and welcoming you'll find anywhere, are its best attraction. Enjoy relaxing with them as they celebrate – at festivals and sporting events held all over the country.

Let the AAA Ireland TravelBook inspire your adventures. There are maps to help you get your bearings; descriptions and photos of places to see and things to do; and useful suggestions for eating, drinking and shopping – everything you need to get the most out of your trip.

Contents

Introduction to Ireland   **6**
Map of Ireland   6
Timeline   20
Survival Guide   22

■ **Connacht**   **27**
Introduction and Map   28

Galway   **32**
Introduction and Map   32
Essential Information   34

Galway Sights   **35**
Walk: Stroll Back in Time   37

Regional Sights   **38**
Feature: Journey Through
    Connemara   44
Drive: Yeats Country   50
Drive: Achill Island and
    County Mayo   55

■ **Leinster**   **59**
Introduction and Map   60

Dublin   **64**
Introduction and Map   64
Essential Information   69

Dublin Sights   **70**
Feature: Dublin Specials   75
Feature: Enjoy Exploring   78
Walk: South of the Liffey   86
Feature: Dublin's
    Literary Greats   88

Regional Sights   **90**
Drive: Boyne Valley   94
Drive: Castles and
    Ecclesial Gems   100
Feature: A Long Tradition
    of Gardens   108

■ **Munster**   **111**
Introduction and Map   112

Cork   **114**
Introduction and Map   114
Essential Information   116

Cork Sights   **117**
Walk: Cork's Mercantile
    Past   120
Drive: Island City,
    Magic Stone   122
Feature: Cork's Cultural
    Scene   125

Heather carpets the slopes of the Wicklow Mountains in the Sally Gap area

Regional Sights 126
Drive: Ring of Kerry 138
Feature: Medieval Castle
 Banquets and
 Traditional *Céilí* 144
Feature: Kerry's Festivals 147

■ **Ulster and
 Northern Ireland** 151
Introduction and Map 152

Belfast 155
Introduction and Map 155
Essential Information 159

Belfast Sights 160
Walk: Between Old and
 New 167
Drive: Strangford Lough 169

Regional Sights 172
Feature: American
 Connection 176
Feature: In St. Patrick's
 Footsteps 182
Drive: Fermanagh
 Lakeland 186
Feature: Fionn
 MacCumhaill 199

Hotels and Restaurants 201

Essential Information 213

Index 222

Key to symbols
🖫 map page number and coordinates
✉ address
☎ telephone number
🕐 opening times
Ⓢ nearest subway station
🚌 nearest bus/trolley bus/tram/funicular route
⛴ ferry
🍴 restaurant
Ⓟ admission charge
ℹ information
For conversion charts, see the inside back cover

Introduction to Ireland

Capturing the essence of Ireland in mere words is a daunting task. In 1842, William Thackeray wrote to an English friend: "I am beginning to find out now that a man ought to be 40 years in this country, and then he wouldn't be able to write about it!" Many a visitor would agree with him when struggling to reduce to words the emotional overload of Ireland's unique mix of scenic wonders and an irrepressibly romantic people brushed with a hint of magic. A varied and most welcoming country awaits you.

The Emerald Isle

The real Ireland only begins to come alive as you experience wonders such as the delicate play of light and shade on the mountains from Glengarriff in County Cork to Kenmare in County Kerry. Take the opportunity to pass

The stunning Mountains of Mourne sweep down to meet green pastures so evident in the north

through the lush greenness of County Waterford's byways or gaze in awe at the mystical moonscape of The Burren in Country Clare. See a grassy hillside change from the brightest hue of green to silver-gray in the changing light, or view a cloud-studded sky so enormous it makes eternity seem small. Stand on the rocky shore at Ventry on the Dingle Peninsula (Corca Dhuibhne), where legend says the "King of the World," Daire Donn, went down to defeat at the hands of Fionn MacCumhaill (see page 199) and his Fianna warrior band.

Above all, Ireland is the people who live among those scenic wonders and carry the legendary figures deep in their psyche. That ever-changing landscape and the unique charm of the Irish cry out for the poet; Many a bard has answered this call but fallen short of the mark. Poor Thackeray – no wonder he was so frustrated!

Geographically Speaking

To get the statistics out of the way: Ireland covers 31,557 square miles (about the size of New Hampshire, Vermont and Massachusetts combined), 302 miles at its longest point and 171 miles at its widest. It's the "last parish before America," the most westerly island of Europe, and its bowl-shaped contours are formed by a great limestone plain surrounded by mountains (Kerry's Carrauntoohil is the highest at 3,406 feet). The many jagged peninsulas create a dramatic coastline that measures almost 2,000 miles and encircles 9,000 miles of rivers (the 224-mile Shannon is the longest) and some 800 lakes, the largest of which is Lough Neagh (147 square miles).

From its early history, Ireland's 32 counties have been divided into the four provinces of Leinster, Munster, Connacht and Ulster (those "Four Green

Fields" of song and story). Since 1921, Ulster has been divided into the six counties that form Northern Ireland – Londonderry, Antrim, Armagh, Down, Fermanagh and Tyrone – and three that lie in the Republic: Donegal, Monaghan and Cavan.

All That Rain

You certainly wouldn't come to Ireland for a suntan. However, the Gulf Stream's warming currents create a friendly climate that deals in moderation rather than extremes – seldom more than 65 degrees in July, 40 degrees in January. That famous (or infamous) rainfall is heaviest and most frequent in the mountains of the west, and frequent enough in the rest of the country to keep at least 40 shades of green glowing. Of course, the country would not be called the "Emerald Isle" were it not for the rain. However, for more sunshine than showers, May is good just about everywhere except in the Midlands Region and the Southeast; June is apt to be even sunnier.

A Complex People

If it's hard to find words for Ireland itself, it's nearly impossible to capture the intricacies of the Irish personality. Complex they most certainly are – warm-hearted, witty, sometimes argumentative, often talkative, great at listening and, most of all, friendly. There's a certain panache about the Irish that so charms the visitor. True, they will seldom bowl you over with all that charm – if there's anything they're not, it's intrusive. But ask the first question, make the first comment, and you're off and running. Your American accent invites instant interest in where you live, where you're going and what you think of their country.

"The English gave us their language," the Irish will tell you with a sly grin, "then we showed them how to use it." There's perhaps truth in that – they have turned out a staggering number of

extraordinary writers, and most Irish men and women tend to embellish even everyday conversation with colorful phrases to make any writer weep with envy, stringing them together in yarns that may be wildly fanciful but are never dull, delivered in the most melodic, lilting rendition of the English language.

As for the celebrated Irish wit, more often than not it is directed at themselves, with a subtle blend of artful wording and a liberal dash of mischief. This all adds up to what the Irish call

craic, a sense of fun that blends seamlessly with daily life – from "tea and craic" (chat or news) to craic agus coel (music and fun).

There's more to the Irish, of course, than talk. There's the strong religious influence that passed from Celtic to Catholic rites without a hitch. You'll find Catholic shrines tinged with pre-Christian Celtic ritual, and holy wells thought to have been Celtic pre-Christian sites – they placed a special emphasis on pools and springs, believed to have been the gateway into the otherworld, Tir na nÓg (Kingdom of the Forever Young). You'll also see all kinds of offerings alongside religious icons placed in trees next to the water.

Today's Irish people are a testament to the country's past; their charm, wit, religious fervor, language and even the mix of brunettes, blonds and redheads are an evolved blend of Celtic, Viking, Norman and Saxon culture and identity.

View from Binevenagh, westernmost point of the Antrim Plateau, looking out over Lough Foyle

A Way with Words

When Irish monks began their laborious transcribing in the sixth century, they drew on an oral storytelling tradition that reached back into prehistory. Their first recorded stories came from glorious tales of fierce battles, passionate love affairs and heroic deeds that had been passed from generation to generation in both prose and poetry. *Táin Bó Cúailgne* (*The Cattle Raid of Cooley*), *Lebor na hUidre* (*The Dun Cow*) and *Lebor Laigen* (*The Book of Leinster*) preserve the exploits, triumphs and tragedies of such legendary figures as Fionn MacCumhaill (see page 199), Cuchulainn, Oisin and the beautiful Deirdre.

Brian Merriman's *Cúirt An Mheán Oíche* (*The Midnight Court*) is a masterful satire on the attitudes of Irish men to marriage, while the *Annals of the Four Masters*, written by Franciscan monks, and Geoffrey Keating's *Foras Feasa Ar Éirinn* (*History of Ireland*) deal with Irish history. Those early works were written in Irish, as was most Irish literature until the 17th century. During that same period, works on a much lighter note came from the witty poet Raftery and the roguish Owen Roe O'Sullivan.

By the end of the 17th century, the Anglo-Irish literary movement was well established. Irish writers Richard Brinsley Sheridan and Oliver Goldsmith penned English-style drawing-room comedies and English manners novels, while Jonathan Swift, then Dean of St. Patrick's Cathedral in Dublin, was verbally flaying the English with his knife-edged satires.

Maria Edgeworth joined the ranks of outstanding Anglo-Irish writers in the 1800s, along with Thomas Moore, Gerald Griffin, William Carleton and Oscar Wilde. Toward the end of that century, dramatist George Bernard Shaw and novelist George Moore began brilliant careers that were to spill over into the next, as did poet William Butler Yeats and playwright John Millington Synge. Edith Somerville and her cousin

Oscar Wilde (1854–1900)

Violet Martin were busy turning out comic sketches of Protestant life in rural Ireland, and Bram Stoker's *Dracula* was let loose on the literary public.

The 20th century brought about a veritable explosion of Irish literary talent, whose vitality never flagged, despite the oppressive Censorship Act that drove many Irish writers to foreign publishers. Sean O'Casey's controversial plays put him at the forefront of Irish dramatists; Samuel Beckett was awarded the Nobel Prize while living in exile; James Joyce (considered by many to be the greatest Irish writer of the 20th century) wrote knowingly of life in Dublin; and Brendan Behan enjoyed an all-too-short burst of literary fame.

Other writers who loom large on the Irish literary scene include playwrights Hugh Leonard, Brian Friel, Bernard Farrell and John B. Keane; novelists and short-story writers James Plunkett, Ben Kiely, Mary Lavin, John Banville, Edna O'Brien, Dermot Bolger and Elizabeth Bowen; and poets Patrick Kavanagh, Thomas Kinsella, John Montague and Seamus Heaney (also a Nobel Prize winner). As impressive as that long list is, it is by no means complete.

Today, scores more talented Irish writers are hard at work. So, browse the bookstores, pick up any titles you find intriguing, and who knows – you may well discover the next great Irish writer.

"And All Their Songs are Sad"

So said G. K. Chesterton about the Irish, having just asserted, "All their wars are merry." He may have been half right, but their songs are most assuredly not all sad. The Irish have celebrated, mourned, exalted, damned and lamented everything in their lives through music. Until the 1690s and the arrival of Englishman Oliver Cromwell, songs and ballads were composed entirely in Irish. After that, English was the only legal language, imposed as an attempt to help erase any remaining traces of nationalism. Even the Penal Laws were unable to do that, however, for the wily Irish praised their country under the guise of singing about their sweethearts: *Roisin Dubh* and *Kathleen Huallachain* spoke of loved ones, but every Irishman knew they really were odes to Ireland herself. Those traditional songs and airs are still played frequently today. If you listen closely to modern Irish ballads, you'll notice that a few are still concerned with celebrating, mourning or exalting some facet of Irish life.

Performances can feature a number of instruments: the harp, *uilleann* (elbow) pipes – played sitting down, some say developed to get around English law that forbade the playing of any instrument while standing in order to prevent the pipes from playing troops into battle – the *bodhrán* (a drum made of goatskin stretched tightly over a round wooden frame), the tin whistle, fiddle and accordion. These all mix in a unique harmony that can break your heart or send your spirits soaring.

In Ireland, native music has become trendy in recent years, and pubs often feature "trad" groups aiming in that direction. Even if a pub is not known for music, the lyrical Irish spirit frequently bursts forth as the evening progresses – be it the impassioned lyrics of Ireland's traditional songs, or perhaps the familar twang of American country music.

Culturlann na hEireann (pronounced "kultur-arn na-airan"), based in the Dublin suburb of Monkstown, organizes year-round traditional entertainment including *céilís* ("kay-lees," traditional set dancing) in hotels, pubs and at local branch meetings, all open to the public. During August, look for the Fleadh Cheoil ("flah kheoh-il") – a traditional music, song and dance festival held each year in a different town. Music lovers congregate in pubs, hotels, private houses and streets to play, sing or just listen to this special brand of music. The Fleadh Nua, run over nine days in late May, is one of many other showcases for the best in traditional music.

Listen to traditional Irish music entertainment in a pub in Dublin

Racing for the finish line at The Curragh, Co. Kildare, the heart of horseracing in Ireland

The Sporting Life

For the sports-minded, Ireland is a veritable banquet table. Every spectator sports event draws huge crowds, fanatically enthusiastic in cheering on their county soccer, rugby or Gaelic games teams. For fishermen there are rivers and sea coasts teeming with fish, top-notch golf courses for avid golfers and equestrian facilities for exploring the glorious landscape on horseback.

Horseracing is dear to the heart of the Irish, and each of the 250-plus race meets per year is a festive affair. It's a thrilling sight to see the famed Irish-bred horses round the last bend of a grass course against a backdrop of mountains. And it becomes even more exciting if you have a bet riding on a horse. Placing that bet is a very Irish experience, a matter of choosing the best odds offered by bookmakers who shout out competitive odds that change momentarily as they vie for punters

(bettors). If your horse comes up a winner, you'll be paid from a big satchel at the bookmaker's stand.

Probably the year's most popular race event is the Galway races in late July/early August, but people also flock to the Easter Monday meet at Fairyhouse (near Dublin) and Punchestown Steeplechases. Tourist offices can provide exact dates of meets around the country, but a "don't miss" for visitors is any race meet at a smaller course, where the atmosphere is not unlike a day at a county fair.

As far as team sports go, Ireland's greatest success has been in rugby. Organized across the whole of Ireland, the main teams are divided into its ancient provinces – Ulster, Leinster, Munster and Connacht, but the annual highlight is the Six Nations, when Ireland competes against England, Scotland, Wales, France and Italy.

Gaelic Games

Hurling is an ancient game unique to Ireland. Played by two 15-man teams of amateur players, it has a two-level scoring system that can be confusing, with goals and points depending on whether the little leather ball is hit past the goaltender and over the goal line or over the goaltender's head and between the upright goalposts. It is one of the world's fastest field sports, and the skill and speed of athletes wielding hurleys (paddle-like sticks) are amazing. Sunday afternoon matches are regular events all around the country, and it's great fun to mingle with the local fans.

While organized Gaelic football matches date back only about a century, the game undoubtedly evolved from fierce tribal rivalries. None of the fervor of participants or spectators has been lost in the shift. An amateur field game, it is played by two teams of 15, although this is an ancient game once used for training warriors. If you're looking for something similar, it is more akin to Australian rules football than soccer. Weekend local matches are great to watch, and for sheer excitement nothing quite matches that of the All Ireland finals in September when more than 90,000 fans in Dublin's Croke Park roar support for their county teams.

"Football" in Ireland refers to soccer – American football is only beginning to gain in popularity here.

Hands-on Sports

If there's such a thing as a fisherman's heaven, it must be Ireland! Irish waters are home to such freshwater fish (coarse fishing) as bream, dace, pike, perch and various hybrids in rivers, streams and lakes. Alternatively you may elect to stalk the famous Irish salmon from January through September in coastal rivers, their stillwaters and headwaters. Sea trout and brown trout are among other challenging game fish.

Sea anglers will find plentiful supplies of bass, whiting, mullet, flounder, plaice, pollack and coalfish from shore-casting off rocks, piers, promontories and beaches. Deep-sea fishing for shark, skate, dogfish, pollack, ling and conger is all around the coast, and there are plenty of vessels willing to take you out.

Other water sports include surfing, water skiing and windsurfing. Of course, there are lovely beaches for swimmers who don't need summer temperatures much above 70 degrees. For golfers, more than 360 superb golf courses dot the Irish countryside, and a growing number of hotels have a course or access to local courses. Ireland is gaining worldwide renown on the championship golf circuit. Caddies can be booked ahead at some of the larger courses, and you will find pull-carts or electric golf carts at most courses. Many courses have clubs for rent, but some do not. Irish golfing vacations can be arranged to include accommodations, golf clinics and special weekends with groups. Tourist offices can provide you with lists of locations and specific information about what's available at each course.

Equestrians of any age or level will find stables offering riding instruction, as well as trail riding, and guided point-to-point treks with overnight accommodations for the truly keen.

Hurling is a popular Irish sport

About the Past

The landscape of Ireland is haunted by its history. Ghosts lurk along every road, around every bend, behind every bush. Relics are sprinkled across the land, some left in ruins, others authentically restored. Visit the reconstructed crannog at Craggaunowen in County Clare, and Bronze Age men and women will almost materialize before your eyes. Great monastic crosses and ruined abbeys speak of early Christians, while Norman spirits inhabit ruined castles that squat along riverbanks, atop lofty cliffs and stand proud in lonely fields.

In the Beginning

The earliest inhabitants to have left traces of their existence in Ireland probably arrived from Scotland, England and Europe in 6000 or 7000 BC. It wasn't until about 2000 BC that Neolithic people arrived, bringing along farming expertise and beginning Ireland's long tradition of farming and cattle-raising. They cremated their dead and created communal burial chambers beneath stone cairns or inside earthen, tunnel-filled mounds like those at Newgrange (Brú na Bóinne) in the Boyne Valley. They were followed by Bronze Age metal workers and artisans, who fashioned the exquisite ornaments that fill today's museums and left a wealth of megalithic stone structures. They named Ireland after Ériu, the goddess of the land and one of the semi-divine Tuatha Dé Danann, and from this comes the modern derivation of Eire.

In the fourth century BC, tall, fair-skinned, red-haired Celts arrived, a fierce warlike people bearing iron weapons and military skills that soon established them as rulers of the land. A high king of Ireland ruled from Tara,

An abandoned cottage in fields near Rosmuck, Co. Galway

but the countryside rang with battle cries as regional kings embarked on expansionary expeditions, and the high king of the moment never sat easy on his honorary throne. Nevertheless, there was unity in the strong bonds of a common culture and traditions held together by a common language. Tribes honored traveling bards, above all the Druids, who memorized their legends and performed sacred ceremonies.

Saints and Scholars

The Romans rampaging in southern Britain never did get around to conquering Ireland, but in the fifth century a conquest of quite another nature took place. A pagan religion that had flourished for centuries surprisingly embraced the doctrines and rites of Christianity that landed on Irish shores with Patrick. Born Patricius in Britain as a Roman Empire citizen, in his youth the budding saint was kidnapped and had tended swine in Ireland as a slave. He escaped and went back to Europe, where he entered religious life before returning to his former captors as a missionary in 432.

Retaining just enough pagan customs to avoid hostile resistance, St. Patrick managed to transplant rites and superstitions into Christian soil without a murmur. The healing powers of many Irish "holy wells," for example, are those attributed to them by ancient Celts long before St. Patrick arrived on the scene. His firsthand knowledge of the Celtic love of the mystical, especially when applied to the natural world, perhaps inspired him to use the shamrock to symbolize the Holy Trinity, thereby make it Ireland's most enduring national symbol. Irish king after Irish king listened to the missionary and led his subjects into the new religion, although none went so far as to abandon such distinctly Celtic pastimes as intra-kingdom warfare and riotous revelry within his own court.

With the coming of Christianity, Celtic culture took a giant step forward.

The carved West Cross in the grounds of the church of St. Finghin, Clonmacnoise

Already deeply respectful of learning in its higher forms, the Irish devoted themselves to a cloistered life within great monasteries that taught all the learning of their time, both Celtic and Roman. As Europe entered its culturally deprived Dark Ages, Ireland's monastic universities kept the lights of theology, philosophy, astronomy, literature, poetry and science brightly burning. Artistic achievement hit new heights inside their walls, as the exquisitely illuminated manuscript, the *Book of Kells* demonstrates (see page 84). Up until the end of the eighth century, Ireland's Golden Age was the brightest beacon in the Western world.

Away from these seats of learning, monks also moved out to more remote parts of the country. There they lived austere lives of meditation, building the *clocháns* (beehive-shaped stone huts), still intact today, and marvelously engineered little stone churches such as Dingle's Gallarus Oratory (see page 131) – constructed entirely without mortar, and watertight for the past 1,500 years. The impressive stone Celtic crosses that dot the landscape had their origins in the seventh century.

Eventually, Europe's age of darkness retreated, helped by returning European scholars and Irish monks who had left home to carry their teachings into cathedrals, royal courts and universities.

Viking Invaders

Viking raiders came by sea in AD 795, making lightning-fast strikes along the coastline and taking away plunder and captives. Their superior mail battle dress and heavy arms made easy victims of even the most stout-hearted Irish. Their raids moved farther and farther inland, with rich monastic settlements yielding the most valuable prizes. Churchmen retreated from the danger to tall, round towers with the only entrance high above the ground. Today, you'll find one of the best preserved at the Rock of Cashel in County Tipperary.

After eventually turning to peaceful trading, the Vikings were soon intermarrying with native Irish folk and becoming as Irish as the Irish themselves, in a pattern that was to be followed by subsequent "conquerors." Vestiges of their city walls, gates and fortifications remain to this day; Reginald's Tower in Waterford Quay is thought to be one of the most perfect examples of this.

The Normans Enter

In 1014, Irish High King Brian Ború won a decisive victory against the Vikings. Ború ascended into the rarefied stratosphere of Ireland's most revered heroes, but his death was followed by a century and a half of kingly tug-of-war to establish one central authority. Dermot MacMurrough, king of Leinster, committed the grave error of stealing the wife of the king of Breffni, who promptly hounded him out of Leinster. MacMurrough persuaded England's King Henry II to send Norman troops to win back Dermot's lost throne. When Rory O'Conor, the last high king of Ireland was defeated, MacMurrough's

power began to rival that of King Henry. Alarmed, Henry elicited vows of fealty from many Irish kings who were anxious to hold onto their territories. For the next 350 years, territorial claims kept Anglo-Norman and Irish lords growling at each other as Normans acquired titles to more than half of the country, building most of those sturdy castles in which you'll sightsee, banquet or spend the night during your visit.

To Hell or Connacht

By the time Elizabeth I became queen, the Reformation was firmly entrenched in England and the staunchly Catholic Irish found themselves fighting for their religion with even more fervor than they had fought for their lands. Having lost several long and bloody battles, Irish chieftains went into hiding, their lands now confiscated by the English Crown and resettled by loyal English and Scottish Protestants.

Arriving in 1649 and driven by religious fervor as well as political motives, Puritan Oliver Cromwell's campaign across the country left a trail of destruction. The Irish who escaped were shipped as slave labor to English plantations in the Sugar Islands (a virtual "hell") or driven to the bleak, stony hills of Connacht. To his loyal soldiers Cromwell awarded vast estates in the fertile counties of the country. In the end, less than one-ninth of Irish soil remained in the hands of natives.

King Billy, the Treaty of Limerick and Penal Laws

Irish spirits rose once more when a Catholic, James II, claimed the English throne in 1688. Deposed by William of Orange – King Billy – James fled to Ireland in 1689, where the Irish took up arms in his defense. King Billy arrived to win a resounding victory at the Battle of the Boyne in 1690, after which James once more took flight. The Irish fought on until October 1691, when they signed the Treaty of Limerick, which allegedly allowed them to retain both their religion and their land. Parliament, however, instituted a series of measures so oppressive they became known as the Penal Laws. Catholics were stripped of all civil and political rights and forced to work hard on the estates of absentee, rich English landlords. Irish farmers paid extortionate rents for the mere privilege of building primitive huts and using a small plot of ground to raise the potato crops that kept their families from starving – just.

United Irishmen

Anglo-Irish Protestants gradually came to feel a much stronger allegiance to Ireland than to England and, demanding greater independence, got a token Irish Parliament in 1782. Forming the Society of United Irishmen to work for a totally independent Irish republic, and enlisting military aid from France, revolutionary Wolfe Tone led a fully fledged insurrection, known as the 1798 Rebellion. Disaster on the battlefield became even greater than the disaster happening in the halls of the English Parliament. In 1800 the Act of Union was passed and Ireland became an extension of British soil. It was Daniel O'Connell (affectionately named "The Liberator") who, on getting elected to the British Parliament in 1828, restored all Catholic civil rights, accomplished a partial repeal of the Penal Laws and embarked on a campaign for repeal of the Act of Union.

Just as members of the Young Ireland movement were beginning to be heeded, the terrible agricultural disaster of the potato blight gripped the country and the Irish goal became one of simple survival. By 1849 a population of nearly nine million people was reduced to little more than six million. Those who did not die of starvation and disease fled to the United States and Canada, but the vessels were so overcrowded and disease-infested that, for many, they became little more than floating coffins.

The Land League, Home Rule and Sinn Fein

By 1879 Irish tenant farmers were so frustrated by oppressive land rentals that they eagerly joined with Charles Stewart Parnell's Land League. Strikes were organized to "boycott" any landlord who evicted tenants – so called for Captain Boycott, against whom it was first used. Parnell's energetic campaign for Home Rule also granted limited independence, but it wasn't until the eve of World War I that such a measure was finally adopted by the British.

Outnumbered by Catholics, Unionists in Ulster feared Home Rule would become Rome Rule, and put up a strong armed resistance against the equally determined Irish Republican Army (IRA). The IRA were the military arm of Sinn Fein, a republican political party whose name is pronounced "shin fain," and means "ourselves alone." The country was fairly bristling with arms when everything was put on hold by the urgency of World War I and the need to fight a foreign aggressor.

The 12th-century church and tower of St. Finghin

The Winds of Change

The Irish have always treasured their cultural heritage, but at the end of the 20th century were using it as a base for swiftly moving changes in manners and mores of this dynamic era.

Up until the 1990s, hard times in Ireland spawned youthful emigration. In the wake of a hard-won reversal of fortunes, an ever-increasing number started returning. This, combined with the dramatic decrease in young people leaving, resulted in a large youthful population. Such a vibrant, well-educated and young workforce in turn lured more and more international companies to use Ireland as their gateway to European markets. With an economy labeled "The Celtic Tiger," the fastest growing in the European Union, the country was awash with signs of prosperity – until, that is, the global financial crisis of 2008 led to a recession that quickly brought Ireland's major banks to the brink of collapse and threatened the solvency of the Irish state itself. The dependence on international investment that contributed to the boom years made Ireland one of the worst-hit states in the euro zone, and across the country businesses of all kinds found themselves struggling.

It remains to be seen how Ireland will evolve in the current tough economic climate, but the Irish have centuries of flexibility and resilience to draw on, and their courtesy, compassion and zest for life remain.

On the social front, Ireland has embraced change with breathtaking speed: politically, male domination is fast disappearing, and the country had female presidents from 1990 to 2011.

All in all, Ireland's modernity belies the "quaint" label so often applied to it.

Nightlife in the busy Temple Bar area of Dublin, where cobbled streets and nightclubs exist side by side

Ireland in a Festive Mood

The festival season in Ireland runs from mid-March to mid-November, and planning a visit around one of these lively occasions is worth considering. The Irish Tourist Board can give specific dates for the time of your visit. In addition to those listed, you may come across others just as intriguing, such as Galway's International Oyster Festival, Lisdoonvarna's Matchmaking Festival and Cape Clear's International Storytelling Festival as you travel around the country during summer.

March 16–19

St. Patrick's Festival: Ireland's largest festival. Celebrations of this saint's special day (March 17) in cities, towns and villages, do not match the spirit of Dublin with its street entertainment, music, theater, dance, pageants and spectacular parade (featuring numerous American bands). Downpatrick, in County Down, hosts a more sedate event in the town where the saint is buried.

July

Orangefest: Annual commemorations of the 1690 Battle of the Boyne are marked across Northern Ireland with demonstrations (marches) by the Orange Order and other Loyalist groups. Events include Orangefest in Belfast city center on the 12th and battle re-enactments in Scarva, County Down, on the 13th.

Galway Arts Festival: A two-week colorful, vibrant eruption of theater, street entertainment, visual arts, music, literary and children's events. Floats created by Galway's street theater group, Macnas, are among the highlights.

August

Kilkenny's Arts Festival: Over 10 days the narrow streets and historic buildings of this medieval city make a perfect setting for classical music in St. Canice's Cathedral, visual arts in the ruins of Kells Priory and outdoor theater.

The Rose of Tralee Festival: Draws "roses" from around the globe for a lively five days (see page 147) of song and dance. A truly festive affair with an international flavor.

Fleadh Cheoil na hEireann: The venue for this festival changes each year, but regardless of locality it draws international musicians for a three-day, nonstop outpouring of traditional Irish music, song and dance. Scheduled concerts vie with spontaneous street sessions.

September

All Ireland Championships: Gaelic sports reach the peak of excitement when hordes of fans descend on Croke Park in Dublin for the GAA Football and Hurling All-Ireland Championship Finals.

Waterford International Music Festival: The city is awash with musical talent from around the world throughout the 13 nights of musicals – many of them straight from Broadway. And it's not just light opera – pub-singing competitions are also popular.

Mid-October, early November

Wexford Festival Opera: Three major productions and more than 40 smaller events are presented at this festival, unique in its emphasis on obscure, seldom-performed operas. Tickets must be booked well in advance.

Late October

The Cork Guinness Jazz Festival: Now running for more than 25 years, this long weekend event has been called "the greatest jazz party in the world." Performances by some of the world's most outstanding musicians pour out from Cork's pubs and concert halls.

The Belfast Festival: This lights up Belfast's Queen's University venues for two weeks with international theater, dance, film and literary productions, plus jazz and comedy.

Timeline

circa **3000** BC	Neolithic farmers construct sacred burial chambers at Newgrange and Knowth in the Boyne Valley. Bronze Age metal workers come seeking copper and gold.
600 BC	Celts arrive, bringing iron weapons and the Gaelic language.
AD **432**	Patrick begins his Christian conversion of Irish tribes.
circa **795**	Vikings plunder monasteries and found the cities of Dublin, Wexford, Waterford, Cork and Limerick.
1014	Brian Ború defeats the Vikings at Battle of Clontarf.
1169	Normans, led by Strongbow, begin England's long domination of Ireland.
1607	Leading Irish chieftains flee in the "Flight of the Earls."
1609	Plantations in Ulster begin as English and Scottish Protestants occupy Irish farms.
1649	Lord Protector Oliver Cromwell sweeps through Ireland to subdue the rebellious Irish.
1690	Catholic defeat at the Battle of the Boyne begins centuries of Catholic oppression under the Penal Laws.
1798	Insurrection led by Wolfe Tone, Robert Emmet and others quashed by English forces.
1800	The Act of Union is passed, handing direct rule of Ireland over to London Parliament.
1845–51	The Great Potato Famine causes widespread starvation; more than one million Irish emigrate to the United States.
1879	Charles Stewart Parnell and Michael Davitt found the Land League to secure tenant land ownership.
1905–08	Sinn Fein political party evolves, with Irish independence its primary goal.
1912	Home Rule goes into effect; Ulster Volunteers founded by loyalists; Irish Republican Army (IRA) established as military adjunct of Sinn Fein.
1916	Padraic Pearse, James Connolly and others lead Easter Rising; their execution unites Irish and world public opinion in support of Irish independence.
1921	Dominion status granted to 26 counties as Irish Free State; partition leaves six Ulster counties as part of the United Kingdom; civil war rages until 1923.
1937	New constitution put forth by Eamon de Valera.
1948	Some 26 of Ireland's counties become a republic, with no constitutional ties to Britain.
1968	Violence breaks out in Northern Ireland when several Catholic civil rights marches are attacked by Protestant loyalists.
1969	Start of "the Troubles": Continuing violence leads to Derry's Battle of the Bogside, riots in Belfast, the arrival of the British Army to restore peace, and Direct Rule from London.

1972	Twenty-seven civil rights protesters shot by the British Army in Derry, an event known as Bloody Sunday.
1973	The Republic of Ireland joins the European Economic Community (now the European Union, EU).
1986	Anglo-Irish Agreement gives Irish Republic limited input in Northern Ireland affairs.
1994	IRA declares an end to military operations; Loyalist paramilitaries issue similar cease-fire.
1996	IRA resumes campaign of violence as peace talks collapse.
1997	IRA declares new cease-fire and enters all-party peace talks.
1998	Good Friday Agreement affirmed by referenda in the Republic; Northern Ireland paves the way for a Northern Ireland Assembly; sporadic violence continues.
2002	The Euro becomes official currency of the Republic of Ireland.
2004	A no-smoking policy is introduced in all public places in the Republic of Ireland.
2007	The Northern Ireland Assembly is re-established at Stormont following elections in March 2007.
2010	Devolved power completed with the transfer of policing and Justice to the Northern Ireland Assembly.
2010–11	The global financial crisis takes its toll on the Republic of Ireland, resulting in an EU/IMF bailout.
2011	Taioseach (Prime Minister) Brian Cowen steps down after a vote of no confidence. Enda Kenny voted in at the head of a Fine Gael-Labour coalition. President Barack Obama and Queen Elizabeth II make historic visits to Ireland. Writer and politician Michael D. Higgins becomes President of Ireland.

A "Terrible Beauty is Born"

On Easter Monday of 1916, the whole question of Irish independence was put right back on the front burner. Leading a scruffy and poorly armed band of patriots, Padraic Pearse and James Connolly took occupation of Dublin's General Post Office in the name of a provisional government. Pearse read "The Proclamation of the Irish Republic to the People of Ireland," and for the next six days, the Post Office stood embattled under the ancient symbol of Ireland (a golden harp on a pennant of brilliant green) and the Sinn Fein banner of green, white and orange.

In the end the rebels surrendered, and Pearse, Connolly and 13 others were executed by firing squad. Irish loyalties became united behind their new republic and the ideal of Irish independence. It was at that moment – as the executioners' gunsmoke cleared in Kilmainham Gaol's yard – that the poet Yeats proclaimed "A terrible beauty is born."

In 1919 Sinn Fein set up the National Parliament of Ireland in Dublin: Bitter bloodshed followed. The 1921 Anglo-Irish Treaty later named 26 counties the Irish Free State. Six Ulster counties would remain, as they wished, an integral part of the United Kingdom. In 1948 Ireland was formally declared outside the Commonwealth, and was made a Republic.

Survival Guide

- Consider basing yourself in one spot for three or four days. Ireland is a compact country and lends itself to day trips from a central regional base. While you'll always be made welcome at any pub in the country, when you return a second night, you'll automatically become a "regular" and the locals will delight in hearing what you've done and seen during the day, as well as having "insider" tips to share for the next day.

- Plan to vary your accommodations between hotels, guesthouses and bed-and-breakfast homes. Ireland has an incredible array of high-quality places to stay. Accommodations with kitchens are also an attractive alternative – not only are they money-savers when it comes to meals, but trips to local grocery stores for essentials will add another dimension to your Irish experience.

- If you're traveling with children or if you exult in the glories of country life, stay in a farmhouse for a few days. Hospitality seems to take on an even keener edge out in the country, and most hosts will delight in showing you around a working farm. Children especially respond to close-up contact with farm animals.

- Keep your daytime activities flexible enough to stop and spend some time if you come across a street fair, cattle mart or horse fair. County Waterford's annual horse fair in Tallow is a great opportunity to watch such age-old practices as rural people bargaining for horses and sealing a deal with a handshake. Remember, in Ireland time is made for you, not you for time!

- Be sure to bring a raincoat, not only for Ireland's magical rain but also for the fluctuating temperatures.

- Plan at least one picnic. The Irish landscape beckons to picnickers to spread a lunch on a deserted beach, under a tree on the edge of a field, on a picnic table at a scenic overlook or looking out toward mountains. Or buy fresh produce in city-center markets, delis and bakeries to enjoy in a quiet park or square.

- Make your main meal a large lunch; lunch in even the most expensive restaurants costs a fraction of the same meal in the evening. Most pubs serve hot plates heaped with home-cooked meats and vegetables, as well as excellent cold salad plates of ham or chicken.

- Be sure to inquire about discounts at sightseeing attractions for families, senior citizens and students. They're not always posted and can amount to a considerable saving. Any identification will be helpful.

- Ireland's highways and secondary roads are improving, but especially in the west drivers should be on the lookout for potholes. When off the main roads, expect to encounter farmers driving cattle or sheep to and from fields in the early morning and

Gaelic Place-name Spellings

On March 28, 2005 a legal bill was passed to change the spellings of many place-names in Ireland from English to Gaelic. Most of the changes occur in areas of Ireland known as Gaeltacht, mostly in the west of the country, where the Celtic tongue is widely spoken and written. Road signs now show Gaelic spellings only, most prevalent in the counties of Galway, Kerry, Cork, Donegal, Waterford, Mayo and Meath. This process is ongoing and many more Gaelic spellings will be introduced over the coming years (see page 221 for the list of place-names that are already in use).

late afternoon – just stop the car and wait for the animals to pass.

- The plethora of Irish "roundabouts" (traffic circles) seems to present all sorts of difficulties for American drivers. The cardinal rule is: The driver coming from the right has the right of way. If you miss your exit, just go around again and be sure you're in the correct lane to exit.
- Both politics and religion are serious subjects in Ireland and you should be sensitive to people's beliefs. The best way to learn a little more about the past is by joining a guided tour; there are open-top bus tours, black taxi tours and Coiste Political tours in Belfast, run by people from both sides of the political spectrum. There are also historical tours in Derry and Dublin.
- Resist swimming off the beach when there's no one around, especially off the Atlantic beaches in the west where tides can often be strong and currents can be treacherous. Only swim at more populated beaches.
- Be aware that some conveniences you are accustomed to at home will not be on hand everywhere in Ireland, and some Irish customs may differ from those with which you are familiar.

Portrush Beach, Portrush, one of many scenic towns dotted along the Causeway Coast

Ireland

■ Connacht   27

■ Leinster   59

■ Munster   111

■ Ulster and
  Northern Ireland   151

Opposite: Tullymore Forest Park

Connacht

Introduction and Map 20

Galway 32

Introduction and Map 32

Sights 35

Walk: Stroll Back in Time 37

Regional Sights 38

Feature: Journey Through Connemara 44

Drive: Yeats Country 50

Drive: Achill Island and County Mayo 55

Opposite: Brightly painted boats rest on the shores of Lough Conn

Connacht

Connacht's counties – Galway, Leitrim, Mayo, Roscommon and Sligo – form a large portion of Ireland's West, a region of which Irish author James Joyce's poet-surgeon friend Oliver St. John Gogarty wrote,

There's something sleeping in my breast
That wakens only in the West;
There's something in the core of me
That needs the West to set it free.

That "something" undoubtedly springs from a long history of hardships stoically endured and rebelliously resisted.

Connacht's reputation as a remote and unforgiving place is reflected in the phrase "to hell or to Connacht". Reputedly Oliver Cromwell's comment to Irish Catholics after he had wreaked havoc across Ireland and banned all Catholic land ownership in the Act of Settlement of Ireland 1652, it implied that Connacht's westerly landmass wasn't fertile enough for Scottish and English settlers.

Within the boundaries of counties Galway and Mayo lie such distinct geographic divisions as Connemara, the Aran Islands (Oileáin Árann) and Achill Island (Oileáin Acla). Galway's landscape in the east is made up of flat, fertile plains that reach from Lough Derg and the Shannon Valley north to County Roscommon, while to the northwest, lumpy mountains push the mainland into a great elbow bent against the Atlantic. Connemara's stony landscape is bounded by a coastline

dotted with wonderful, uncrowded beaches. Lough Corrib stretches its 27 miles along an invisible line that marks the change. Some 30 miles offshore, the Aran Islands are an outpost of rugged, self-sufficient fishermen and their families. These people have kept alive many aspects of their ancient culture even as they move into and enjoy the easier lifestyles of modern Ireland. Pre-Christian stone forts rub shoulders with early Christian round towers, oratories and churches. The musical Gaelic language of their ancestors is that of today's islanders. Menfolk still fish the sea as they have done over the ages, while their womenfolk spin and weave and knit the clothing that is so distinctly theirs, all the while welcoming and providing for a steady stream of visitors who come by steamer or small aircraft.

Eastern County Mayo is flat; and it was near Cong, on the Plain of Southern Moytura, that a mythological battle raged between Tuatha Dé Danann and the Fir Bolg, ending in the first defeat

In the heart of Connemara – the peaks of the Twelve Pins seen from Roundstone Bay

of the Fir Bolg, who declined in power until they were crushed forever seven years later in Sligo. Today many visitors who come to Cong, however, are in pursuit of a different story: John Ford's 1952 film *The Quiet Man,* with John Wayne and Maureen O'Hara, was filmed here.

Northeast of Cong is the village of Knock, a shrine to the reported vision of the Virgin Mary in 1879 and which today is a pilgrimage site for thousands of Christians. West of here lies 13th-century Ballintubber Abbey, on the site of St. Patrick's Well, where the saint himself baptized his coverts. On the last Sunday in July each year, pilgrims follow a pre-Christian chariot route from here (later called St. Patrick's Causeway) that leads to the mountain of Croagh Patrick on the southern shore of Clew Bay. Many just climb the mountain, some venturing up barefoot as an act of penance (or hardiness).

A few miles north of Croagh Patrick is the vibrant town of Westport, popular as a holiday destination – partly due to its prolific number of public houses, many known for their traditional Irish music sessions.

Connected to the Irish mainland by a causeway, Achill Island (Oileáin Acla) presents a mountainous face to the sea, its feet surrounded by golden sandy strands. Along the western part of County Sligo are the heathery slopes of the Ox Mountains; the north holds high, flat-topped limestone hills like Yeats' beloved Benbulbin and the Sligo coastline attracts a young crowd who come to surf the Atlantic waves off its quiet, sandy beaches.

Out of season, Connacht is quiet and many tourist attractions are closed. If you don't want to drive, the best place to base yourself is in Galway city, which has plenty of year-round attractions and opportunities for excursions.

Autumnal browns and russets on the ferns surrounding Lough Gill and the Isle of Innisfree

Galway

Galway may have begun life as a small village grown from a fishing camp at the ford of the River Corrib, but over the centuries it has blossomed into a lively, thriving city that breathes new life into the entire region. It has become a center for arts, drama, music and all manner of creative activities that draw visitors from around the world, many of whom elect to stay as permanent residents in an environment that nurtures talent.

Galway grew up around a fortress built at the mouth of the river (then known as Gaillimh, or "stony river") by Turlough Mór O'Conor, King of Connacht (1106–1156) and later High King of Ireland. When the Normans arrived, they recognized the potential of the excellent harbor, developed a thriving maritime trade between Galway, Spain and France, and eventually enclosed the fine medieval town with stone walls. The 14 "Tribes of Galway" were composed of the town's most prosperous merchant families. At the height of the Great Famine in the mid-1800s, the city was filled with starving men, women and children who fought to board the infamous "coffin ships" in a desperate attempt to escape to America to try and begin a new life.

Today the fourth-largest city in the Republic of Ireland, Galway remains a prosperous commercial center, a delightful and interesting blend of ancient and modern that welcomes visitors with open arms. Traces of the city's history abound, with the oldest parts clustering around the harbor and riverside quays: the Spanish Arch, a gateway of the old city walls; Lynch's Castle, a 14th-century home now a branch of the Allied Irish Bank; and tiny cobblestone streets and narrow lanes. The Long Walk along the banks of the Corrib is a much-loved waterside promenade for all ages and Galway's version of Paris's "Left Bank" (the High Street and Quay Street quarter of old buildings) has been given a new life.

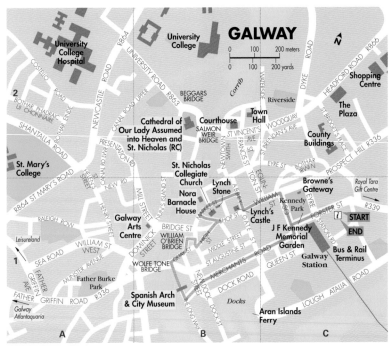

While all that ancient history is revered by Galway natives, they are busily creating a modern history that embraces the arts in all forms. Gaelic drama flourishes at An Taibhdhearc Theatre, while the Town Hall Theatre features avant-garde, new Irish and Anglo-Irish classic theater. Galway pubs ring with the sounds of traditional Irish music one night, rock 'n' roll the next, and aspiring (sometimes quite professional) musicians provide street entertainment.

Then there are the festivals: Galway's Arts Festival rages for two entertainment-filled weeks in July, with all sorts of stage plays, concerts and street entertainment, as well as a massive, offbeat parade.

At the end of July and the beginning of August, the week-long Galway Race Week draws the cream of the local and international horse-loving sets. When not at the track, horse owners, trainers and "punters" (bettors) are never idle – private parties warmly welcome complete strangers, and the track grounds are lined with food stalls and street entertainers. Meanwhile, Galway's pubs are at their liveliest.

In mid-August (weather permitting) there's the Blessing of the Sea, when a procession of fishing boats sails out to sea led by a priest-filled boat whose ecclesiastical passengers implore heavenly powers to grant safe and profitable voyages as the much-awaited herring season opens.

Hordes of Irish people from around the country descend in September to take part in the Oyster Festival, which they consider to be the festival to end all festivals. The Lord Mayor of Galway opens and eats the first oyster of the season, inaugurating a weekend of sheer, unashamed gluttony. Oyster-openers from around the world gather for lively competitions in opening the most oysters in the shortest time, and although some wash the bivalves down with champagne, the

---

Claddagh Rings

The design of these silver or gold rings originated in the Claddagh. Once a Gaelic-speaking fishing community outside Galway's city walls by the western mouth of the river, it is now a tidy suburb. Claddagh rings depict two hands holding a heart surmounted by a crown, symbolizing a promise, or a hope, of eternal love and friendship. The precious heirlooms were handed down through the family's female line and, depending which way around the ring was worn, showed whether a girl or boy was engaged or not.

---

overwhelming drink of preference is "the black stuff" (Guinness).

Galway is an upbeat, vivacious and enjoyable city that is good for shopping, especially if you're hooked on secondhand books and classy crafts. Besides its own variety of attractions, the city is a convenient base for exploring many local areas – Connemara, Lough Corrib, the beautiful Aran Islands and The Burren in County Clare.

Brightly painted houses line the harbor in Galway

Connacht

Essential Information

Tourist Information

Galway Discover Ireland Centre

(serving counties Galway, Mayo and
Roscommon), Áras Fáilte, Forster Street
☎ 091 537 700; www.discoverireland.ie/
places-to-go/visit-galway ⊕ Mon.–Sat.
9–5:45, Sun. 9–12:45 (later in summer).
The office will make reservations for
accommodations, excursions, ferry services
and bicycle and car rentals.
Be sure to get a city map – this ancient city
has narrow, winding streets, which often
change names every few blocks.

Urban Transportation

Galway's local bus service, running from the
Bus Eireann Travel Centre, Ceannt Station
(☎ 091 562 000; www.buseireann.ie) just off
Eyre Square, reaches most suburbs, including
Salthill and other neighborhoods. From here
there are good connections to almost
anywhere in the country. Bus Eireann runs
several worthwhile day tours from Galway and
Salthill: Connemara, The Burren and Cliffs of
Moher. Some are half-day trips; others last the
entire day. All are moderately priced, and you
can book a tour at the tourist office in Galway
or the railroad station.

The most central taxi stand is at Eyre Square.
You can also call to order a taxi from Galway
Taxis ☎ 091 561 111.

The first thing to be said about driving in
Galway city is – don't. The network of tiny
lanes, alleyways and passageways make city
driving a nightmare. Parking can also be a
problem – street parking operates a
pay-and-display system, and the few
multistory parking garages are expensive
and often fill up early in the day. Leave your
car at your hotel, take a bus into the center,
and walk.

There's a direct rail service between Galway
and Dublin. While there are connecting
services to other major destinations in the
country, they often involve time-consuming,
multi-change schedules. In Galway, trains
arrive and depart from Ceannt Station
(☎ 091 562 730) just off Eyre Square (down
from the Meyrick Hotel).

Several ferry companies operate regular
services to the outlying Aran Islands,
departing from Galway docks, a 90-minute
voyage, or Rossaveal (20 miles west of Galway
city on R336, the Barna road, with a shuttle
service to the ferry from the city), which takes
40 minutes. Make reservations at the tourist
office the day before your visit.

Airport Information

Ryan Air, Aer Lingus, Flybe and bmibaby all
operate out of Ireland West Airport Knock
(☎ 094 936 8100; www.irelandwestairport.
com) from several UK and European
destinations. Aer Arann Islands
(www.aerarannislands.ie) flies from
Connemara Airport (on Monivea road 4 miles
from Galway) to Kilronan, Inis Mór's main
port town.

Climate – average highs and lows for the month

Jan.	Feb.	Mar.	Apr.	May	Jun.	Jul.	Aug.	Sep.	Oct.	Nov.	Dec.
8°C	8°C	10°C	12°C	14°C	16°C	17°C	17°C	16°C	14°C	11°C	9°C
46°F	46°F	50°F	54°F	57°F	61°F	63°F	63°F	61°F	57°F	52°F	48°F
4°C	4°C	5°C	6°C	8°C	10°C	12°C	12°C	11°C	8°C	6°C	5°C
39°F	39°F	41°F	43°F	46°F	50°F	54°F	54°F	52°F	46°F	43°F	41°F

Galway Sights

Cathedral of Our Lady Assumed into Heaven and St. Nicholas

This Roman Catholic cathedral is a outstanding city landmark. Its green dome and tall spire visible from most of the city, the cathedral is often used by residents as a designated meeting place. Set beside the Salmon Weir Bridge on the River Corrib and constructed from native limestone with Connemara marble flooring, the Renaissance-style building, topped by a copper dome, is a showcase for mosaics, statues and stained-glass windows created by contemporary Irish artisans. It was completed in 1965 after seven years of construction.

Shoals of salmon leap the falls by the Salmon Weir Bridge as they swim upstream to spawn from mid-April to early July.

➕ B2 ✉ Gaol Road ☎ 091 563 577;
www.galwaycathedral.ie ⏰ Daily 8:30–6:30;
call for additional evening opening 🍴 Restaurant
🚌 2, 4, 5 🎫 Free (donations welcome)

Galway Arts Centre

This was once the townhouse of Lady Augusta Gregory (1859–1932), a wealthy widow who nurtured a generation of Irish writers and poets, and who co-founded the Abbey Theatre in Dublin (see page 66). Later, Galway Corporation took it over for office space. These days, it once more nurtures Irish artists and the Galway Youth Theatre, as well as presenting international artists through concerts, literary readings and ongoing exhibitions.

➕ B1 ✉ 47 Dominick Street ☎ 091 565 886;
www.galwayartscentre.ie ⏰ Mon.–Sat. 10–5:30
🚌 2, 4, 5 🎫 Concerts $$$; exhibits free

Galway Atlantaquaria

The National Aquarium of Ireland, one of Galway's top attractions, gives an amazing insight into the aquatic world off the west of Ireland, with an extensive and diverse collection of marine life. This is an all-weather attraction where you can have an underwater adventure without getting wet.

➕ Off map at A1 ✉ Seapoint Promenade, Salthill
☎ 091 585 100; www.nationalaquarium.ie
⏰ Mon.–Fri. 10–5, Sat.–Sun. 10–6, Mar.–Sep.;
Wed.–Sun. 10–5, rest of year 🍴 Restaurant
🚌 1 from city center or 15-minute walk 🎫 $$$

Galway City Museum

This striking museum is situated behind Galway's famous Spanish Arch. Displays on the first floor trace Galway's history from medieval times to the present day, while the third-floor exhibition explores Galway and the Wars of Empire. The second-floor exhibitions focus on contemporary Galway with an emphasis on arts in the city. There are great views of the city and the river.

➕ B1 ✉ Spanish Parade ☎ 091 532 460;
www.galwaycitymuseum.ie ⏰ Tue.–Sat. 10–5
🍴 Coffee shop 🎫 Free

Sails of the "hooker" tribute fountain in Eyre Square

Leisureland

Give the kids – and yourself – a break from sightseeing by setting aside some purely recreational time at Leisureland. There's a heated indoor pool, a tropical beach pool and treasure cove. Most popular of all is the 200-foot (65m) waterslide. Many other diversions, such as crazy golf and an amusement park, will keep you and the kids occupied.

➕ Off map at A1 ✉ Salthill ☎ 091 521 455; www.leisureland.ie ⏰ Daily 8 a.m.–10 p.m., Apr.–Oct.; hours erratic rest of year, call for details 🍴 Poolside restaurant 🚌 1 💰 $$$

Nora Barnacle House

This tiny 19th-century cottage was the girlhood home of James Joyce's lady love, later his wife and life-long inspiration, "rousse auburn"-haired Nora Barnacle. The tiniest museum in Ireland, it can be found in a quiet street close to the city center. Nora lived here with her family around the turn of the century until she left for Dublin in 1903.

Literary enthusiasts will enjoy perusing an interesting collection of photographs and other exhibits pertaining to the Joyces' connections with Galway (the Joyces were one of the ancient tribes that founded the city).

➕ B1 ✉ 8 Bowling Green ☎ 091 564 743 ⏰ Mon.–Sat. 10–5, mid-May to mid-Sep. Call ahead, hours can vary 🚌 City Centre 💰 $

Royal Tara Gift Centre

This distinctive Irish fine bone china used to be manufactured here by master craftspeople whom you could watch at work; it is no longer made here but you can still browse the finished pieces at your leisure. Set in Tara Hall, a lovely Queen Anne Georgian-style mansion, the center has a wide variety of crafts, including exclusive hand-painted pieces and a barrelmen collection. For bargains take a look at the imperfect pieces.

➕ Off map at C1 ✉ Tara Hall, Mervue ☎ 091 705 602; www.royal-tara.com ⏰ Mon.–Sat. 9–5:30, Sun. 10–5 🍴 Coffee shop 🚌 Half-hourly buses from Eyre Square to Mervue 💰 Free

St. Nicholas Collegiate Church

Legend tells that Christopher Columbus worshiped here in 1477 during a stopover on his way to discover the New World. That would be appropriate, since this church is dedicated to St. Nicholas of Myra, the patron saint of sailors.

Built in 1320 on the site of an earlier chapel, this is Ireland's largest medieval church still in constant use. Its unique shape came about when extensions were made during the 16th century. Cromwellian forces quartered here in 1652 destroyed many features; still intact, however, are tombstones from the 12th to 20th centuries, including a 12th- or 13th-century Norman crusader's tomb. Other outstanding relics are the unique free-standing holy water holder (*bénitier*) and a carved font from the 16th or 17th century.

In 2002, the Collegiate Church attracted controversy by carrying out Ireland's first same-sex "marriage," or Avowing Friendship ceremony, within its walls.

➕ B1 ✉ Market Street ☎ 087 237 5789; www.stnicholas.ie ⏰ Daily 10–7 (5 in Jan. and Feb.); check for services 🚌 City Centre 💰 Free (donations welcome)

A stained-glass window in the Collegiate Church

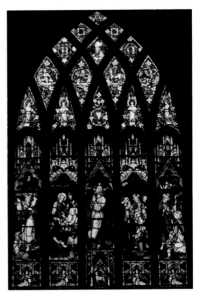

Walk
Stroll Back in Time

Refer to city map on page 32

There's hardly a street in Galway that doesn't retain facets of the city's history. Allow one to two hours.

Leaving the tourist office, head along Forster Street to Eyre Square.

At the far end of the square, the former Bank of Ireland, built it 1836, stands on the site of the priory of the Knights Templars dating back to 1312 or earlier. When the bank closed, a 17th-century mace and 18th-century sword were relocated to Galway City Museum.

Cross the street and into busy Eyre Square.

This is the setting for street entertainers. Originally called the Fair Green, it was presented to the town in 1710 by Mayor Edward Eyre. President John F. Kennedy spoke to the crowd here in 1963, and its name was changed to John F. Kennedy Park, although it's referred to locally as Eyre Square. It features a fountain with rustling sails symbolizing the dark brown sails of the Galway hookers (fishing boats) and *púcáns* of the Claddagh fishing fleet. Look for Brown's Doorway, removed from an old mansion dating from 1627 in Lower Abbeygate Street. Note also the "marriage stones" or carvings, which display the coats of arms of two families united in marriage.

Turn left at the top corner of the square and continue down Williamgate Street to Shop Street.

Lynch's Castle stands on the corner of Shop and Abbeygate streets, its stone facade bearing coats of arms (including those of the Earl of Kildare and King Henry VII), gargoyles and escutcheons.

Turn right into Abbeygate Street and take the first left into Market Street.

On a small wall beside St Nicholas Collegiate Church grounds, look for the Lynch Memorial Window, a black marble plaque over a blocked-up Gothic portal commemorating where, in 1493, Mayor James Lynch carried out "stern and unbending justice" when he condemned his 19-year-old son, Walter, to death after he pleaded guilty to murder. Walter was held in such high esteem, however, that the town executioner refused to carry out the execution. The sorrowing elder Lynch embraced his son and did the deed himself – thus, legend tells, bringing the term "Lynch law" into use.

Farther along the street, at No. 8 Bowling Green is Nora Barnacle House (see page 36).

Return to Market Street, turning right, then left into Churchyard Street (by the church). Turn right, then bear left past the intersection of Shop and Mainguard streets into High Street.

On your left you'll see the King's Head pub – some say haunted by King Charles I's restless spirit. Stop for a look at the magnificently carved 1612 chimneypiece and some refreshments.

Continue down High Street to Cross Street, turn right, then take a short left into Kirwan's Lane, which turns left and spills out onto Quay Street.

Continuing right, you enter the area known as Spanish Parade in memory of the merchant ships that once docked here. The air in the fishmarket across the road once rang with the sound of Claddagh women selling their wares.

By the river, a sculpture resembling a seabird commemorates Columbus's landing in 1477. Across Wolfe Tone Bridge is the Claddagh (see page 33), much changed since its beginnings as a tiny village on the far side of the square. The Galway City Museum (see page 35) is next door to the Spanish Arch, a fine example of medieval walling, through which you can reach the pleasant quayside Long Walk.

Turn left into Merchant's Road and walk to the end, turning left into Victoria Place and right into Forster Street to return to the tourist office.

Regional Sights

Key to symbols

✚ map coordinates refer to the region map on page 28 🎫 admission charge: $$$ more than €6, $$ €4–€6, $ less than €4

See page 5 for complete key to symbols

Aran Islands (Oileáin Árann)

Lying some 29 miles offshore, almost directly across the mouth of Galway Bay, the three inhabited Aran Islands are Inisheer (Inis Óirr, or eastern island), the smallest and nearest to the mainland (6 miles from Doolin, County Clare); Inishmaan (Inis Meáin, or middle island); and Inishmore (Inis Mór, or big island), 7 miles from the Connemara coast. Ferries dock at Kilronan (Cill Rónan), the only safe harbor. Bleak and virtually treeless and with no significant hills or mountains, these three remote islands are linked geologically with The Burren in County Clare. The sheets of gray rock are reminiscent of a moonscape (see page 134).

The cracked limestone islands are steeped in tales of the hardy fishermen and farmers who developed a culture of self-sufficiency that reaches back before recorded history. Traces of the past remain in one of the most dramatic stone forts in western Europe, Dún Aengus, while early Christians left tiny churches. Here you'll also still hear Gaelic.

Mere survival was an everyday challenge for those early inhabitants: for generations, fishermen braved the

Dún Aengus, the remains of a semi-circular stone fort, stands on the edge of a sheer cliff on Inishmore island

seas in frail wood-and-canvas *curraghs* (keel-less rowing boats). Those at home laboriously collected seaweed and sand, enriching the rocky soil to support enough produce to keep body and soul intact. They also built stout stone walls as protection from the strong Atlantic winds.

With the advent of electricity, modern plumbing and improved travel to and from the mainland, the centuries-old isolation of the islands has lifted and everyday life is easier. Day-to-day necessities arrive daily instead of monthly; larger, safer fishing vessels now augment the catches of *curraghs* that still sail to sea, but in more limited numbers. The traditional dress of the islanders is now reserved for special occasions. Probably the most important attack on isolation has been the arrival of tourism, with the consequent opening of island homes and restaurants to accommodate visitors.

Upon arrival at Kilronan pier on Inishmore, you'll be greeted by cars and minibuses for rent to explore the island, with delightful, informative narratives by your driver-guide. There are bikes for rent as well. While Gaelic is the everyday language, the courteous islanders will speak to you in English.

If you're a walker, this is the place for it, with stops to chat a bit with an old man smoking his pipe in an open doorway or a housewife hurrying along to the village. The Aran Way consists of three separate walks on each of the three islands: the Inis Mór Way (21 miles), the Inis Meáin Way (5 miles) and the Inis Óirr Way (6.5 miles). The highest point is Baile na mBrocht at 400 feet.

No matter how you choose to explore the island, don't miss the chief attraction, Dún Aengus. Dramatically perched some 300 feet above the sea, this 11-acre clifftop stone fort inhabits one of the most peaceful spots in Ireland. Don't miss either the cluster of ecclesiastical ruins known as the Seven Churches.

Stone walls around tiny fields in the Aran Islands

If you have a yen to visit Inisheer (Inis Óirr) or Inishmaan (Inis Meáin), ask any of the fishermen at the Kilronan pier and they'll arrange to take you over by *curragh* or another small boat. Both islands have fortresses, churches and folk museums. And if you're really taken with the islands, the tourist office in Galway lists several good accommodations. Occasionally you might see someone in traditional Aran dress, but it is a rare sight nowadays.

Several ferry companies serve the islands from Galway, Rossaveal and Doolin. Aer Arann Islands flies small aircraft to all three islands. All transportation services may be affected by weather and it is best to check schedules before your visit.

🚻 A1

Tourist information ☎ 099 61263 🕐 Daily 10–6, Jun.–Aug.; 11–5, rest of year; closed for lunch in winter

Aer Arann Islands ✉ Connemara Regional Airport, Inverin, Co. Galway ☎ 091 593 034; www.aerarannislands.ie

Doolin Ferries ✉ Doolin, County Clare ☎ 065 7074 455; www.doolinferries.com

Aran Island Ferries ✉ 4 Forster Street, Galway ☎ 091 568 903; www.aranislandferries.com

Connacht

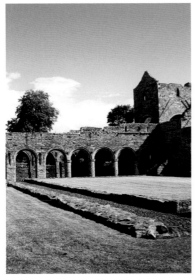

Twelfth-century remains of the Cistercian abbey at Boyle

Boyle

The Cistercian abbey that stands beside the rushing River Boyle in the heart of Boyle is the main reason to visit this quiet town. Dating from the late 12th century, it was founded as a daughter-house of Mellifont Abbey (see page 94). Unsuccessful in their efforts to keep the world's violence at bay, the abbey's monks were slaughtered and its walls torn down in the 17th century. The nave, with its Gothic and Romanesque arches, is in good condition, as are the choir and transepts. The restored 16th- to 17th-century gatehouse has an interpretive center.

In the beautifully restored King House, with its delightful setting overlooking the River Boyle, historical exhibitions give the 18th-century mansion, home of the earls of Kingston, a hands-on museum quality. Events from 1603 to 1957 are explained by the King family in one exhibit. In another you get to beat a regimental drum as you hear the exploits of the Connaught Rangers army regiment billeted here. In yet another, try your hand at building a brick vault.

You can see how difficult or easy it is to write with quill and ink, as well as join a clan feast in still another.

A short distance east of Boyle is Lough Key Forest and Activity Park, a lovely mixed woodland of 850 acres. Especially interesting is the bog garden, with heathers and other small peat-growing plants, and the dozen or so islands in the lake: Trinity Island holds the ruins of a McDermott castle and a medieval priory, and Church Island also holds the remains of a medieval priory. Wildlife thrives in the park's varied habitats. Other attractions include the Lough Key Experience, the Adventure Play Kingdom and the Boda Borg Challenge for older children.

Lovers of traditional music may want to make a pilgrimage to Keadue village (4 miles northeast of Lough Key). The blind harpist Turlough O'Carolan lies in Kilronan Abbey cemetery just west of the village. On the cemetery's arched gateway is inscribed: "Within this churchyard lie the remains of Carolan, the last of the Irish bards who departed this life 25th March, 1738. R.I.P."

Colorful rowing boats tied up alongside a jetty by the side of Lough Key

Nearby Tullyboy Farm is a great treat for children. Centered around an 18th-century farmhouse, this family-run working farm has the usual animals plus exotic breeds such as llamas, ostriches, Jacob sheep, and Angora and Anglo-Nubian goats. Soda bread is baked on the open hearth of the kitchen, and there's a vintage threshing mill for oats. As well as history to learn there are pony rides, a playground and a picnic area.

➕ C2

Tourist information ✉ The Courthouse, Market Street, Boyle ☎ 071 966 2145 ⏰ Mon.–Sat. 10–5:30, May–Sep.

Boyle Abbey ✉ N4 to Garrick ☎ 071 966 2604; www.heritageireland.ie ⏰ Daily 10–6, Easter–Sep. 🎟 $ (free while undergoing preservation work)

King House ✉ Main Street ☎ 071 966 3242; www.kinghouse.ie ⏰ Daily 11–4, Apr.–Sep.; pre-booked groups rest of year 🍴 Restaurant 🎟 $$$ ℹ Children's activities and crafts shop

Lough Key Forest Park and Activity Park ✉ N4, just east of Boyle ☎ 071 967 3122; www.loughkey.ie ⏰ Daily 10–6, Mar.–Oct.; Wed.–Sun. 10–4, rest of year 🍴 Tearooms overlook the lake 🎟 Boda Borg $$$; Lough Key Experience $$$;

Adventure Play Kingdom $$; parking $$ ℹ Combined ticket available

Kilronan Abbey ✉ 4 miles northeast of Lough Key

Tullyboy Animal Farm ✉ Tullyboy, 2 miles south of Boyle on N61, Boyle–Roscommon road ☎ 071 96 68031; www.tullyboyfarm.com ⏰ Mon.–Fri. 10:30–6, Sat.–Sun. noon–6, May–Aug.; Sat.–Sun. noon–6, Easter weekend–end Apr. 🍴 Café 🎟 $$$

Castlebar

The most notable attraction of Castlebar, the county seat of County Mayo, is the Museum of Country Life. In a carefully renovated 18th-century house, along with extensions, this is the first branch of the National Museum to be located outside Dublin.

Innovative displays, utilizing 50,000 items – household utensils, crafts, tools and clothing – reflect the everyday lives of Ireland's people and brilliantly illustrate the past 200 years of the country's history.

➕ B2

Museum of Country Life ✉ Turlough Park House ☎ 094 903 1755; www.museum.ie ⏰ Tue.–Sat. 10–5, Sun. 2–5 🍴 Restaurant 🎟 Free

Castlerea

Lying in the west of County Roscommon, Castlerea is the second biggest town in the county. The most impressive site here is Clonalis House, the home of the O'Conor Don, chieftain of the Clan O'Conor, one-time high kings of Ireland, traditional kings of Connacht and one of Europe's oldest families. Their ancestors can be traced back 60 generations to 1100 BC. Built in 1878 and now a hotel, the house is largely furnished with Sheraton and Louis XV pieces, and has a collection of artifacts including the harp of the bard Turlough O'Carolan (1670–1738), paintings, rare glass and china, the ancient O'Conor inauguration stone and Gaelic manuscripts.

B2

Clonalis House ✉ On the Roscommon–Castlebar road (N60) just west of Castlerea ☎ 094 962 0014; www.clonalis.com ⏰ Tours Mon.–Sat. 11–4, Jun.–Sep. 💷 $$$

Cong

Successive generations of Americans have loved Ireland as a direct result of the antics of John Wayne, Maureen O'Hara and Barry Fitzgerald as they romped through *The Quiet Man*, the epic 1952 movie that became a classic. The main village street scenes took place near the cross in the market square of Cong, and the nearby general store was transformed into Cohan's Bar to play its part in the movie. In 2008 a reconstruction of the bar was opened in the town, with regular screenings of the

Clonalis House, seat of the O'Conor Don, a family who gave Ireland two kings

movie inside. Many of the exterior shots were taken in the grounds of Ashford Castle – including the woodlands, the church, Squire Danaher's house and the salmon river with its arched bridge.

The interior of the Quiet Man Cottage is a replica of the cottage in the movie, complete with clothes and furnishings. There's also a local-interest archaeological museum upstairs.

The marvelous, fairyland architectural concoction that is Ashford Castle makes a superb luxury hotel much favored by international celebrities (President and Mrs. Reagan stayed here during their 1984 visit). No less marvelous are its grounds, with beautifully landscaped lawns sloping down to the island-dotted lake. The castle was originally built by the de Burgo family in 1228, and since then a French chateau-style mansion of the early 1700s and Sir Benjamin Guinness's additions in the mid-1800s have been incorporated – somewhat eccentric, to say the least.

At the heart of this picturesque little village is the ruined Royal Augustinian Abbey of Cong. This was built in 1120 by Turlough Mor O'Conor, high king of Ireland, and is the final resting place of Rory O'Conor, last high king, who died in 1198. Situated on the site of an earlier seventh-century St. Fechin community, this was an important ecclesiastical center for more than 700 years, and as many as 3,000 people once lived here.

Immediately east of Cong toward Cross lies the Plain of Moytura, where you'll find the Ballymagibbon Cairn. Dating from about 3000 BC, the 60-foot-high, 287-foot-circumference cairn was erected to commemorate a fierce mythological battle between the defending native Fir Bolg tribe and the semi-divine invaders, the Tuatha Dé Danann. According to myth, the Fir Bolg carried the day during the early fighting, and each warrior presented a stone and the head of a Danann to his king, who used the stones to build the cairn in honor of the grisly tribute.

Enter Cong's Augustinian abbey through this impressive stone doorway

On a happier note, nearby Moytura House, which is privately owned and not open to the public, was once the home of Sir William Wilde and his wife Speranza, parents of Oscar Wilde.

☩ B2

Tourist information ✉ Abbey Street, Cong ☎ 094 954 6542; www.congtourism.com ⏱ Daily 10–6, May–Sep.

Quiet Man Cottage Museum ✉ Circular Road, Cong ☎ 094 954 6089 ⏱ Daily 10–4, Apr.–Oct.; otherwise by appointment 💷 $$

Ashford Castle ✉ 0.5 miles outside Cong on the right of the Galway Road ☎ 094 954 6003; www.ashford.ie ⏱ Daily 10–5 (gardens only) 💷 $$

Journey Through Connemara

Life is simple in Connemara. Keep your eyes open for turf being cut and dried in the boglands April through June. Along the coastal road you may see donkeys with loaded creels transporting the dried turf to be stacked against the winter's cold. The Connacht Sheep Shearing Championships in May gives the chance to see it done the traditional way, with shearers from all over Ireland competing for the coveted title. Washed-up seaweed is traditionally harvested from the shore at the full and new moons. The biggest concentration of thatched cottages is between Ballyconneely and Roundstone and between Cleggan and the Clifden road by way of Claddaghduff, with thatchers usually at work in September and October.

At Roundstone and Cleggan, small trawlers fish year-round, with open lobster boats and *curraghs* setting out only in summer months. Allow time to stroll the two beautiful nearby beaches, Goirtin and Dog's Bay.

Roundstone is also the home of master *bodhrán* maker Malachy Kearns, whose workshop is in the IDA (Industrial Development Agency) Craft Centre. The *bodhrán* is a one-sided goatskin drum, and Malachy's artist wife, Anne, decorates the finished *bodhráns* with colorful Celtic designs.

The August Connemara Pony Show is in Clifden, where the spirited bidding for the sturdy little animals takes on an air of ritual in a country-fair atmosphere. Summer evenings bring traditional music in many hotel bars and pubs; check with the tourist office or the hotel's front desk.

One thing you won't want to miss in Clifden is the spectacular Sky Drive, a cliff road that forms a 9-mile circle around a peninsula and opens up vast seascapes. Boats are also available for deep-sea fishing expeditions for mackerel, blue shark, conger, cod, ling and many other varieties.

North of Clifden, Cleggan is the mainland departure point for Inishbofin Island, a place of tranquility, wide beaches and some stunning views.

Learn all about Connemara from prehistoric times to the present at the Connemara Heritage and History Centre at Lettershea, 4 miles east of Clifden. There is a spectacular 5,000-year-old burial site, a reconstruction of a *crannóg* (lake dwelling), ring fort and early Christian oratory.

A dramatic view of Kylemore Abbey as seen across Pollacappul Lough

South of the 19th-century Quaker village of Letterfrack is the 7,306-acre Connemara National Park, encompassing mountains, bogs, heaths and grasslands, and crisscrossed by nature walks through beautiful woodlands and hills. Irish red deer and herds of Connemara ponies roam these grounds, and birdwatchers will delight in the variety of winged species.

To the east of Letterfrack is magnificent Kylemore Abbey, in a picturesque setting of woodlands on the banks of Pollacappul Lough, the impressive neo-Gothic facade reflected in the lake's mirror surface. The stone mansion dates from the 19th century. It is now home to an order of Benedictine nuns who for many years ran an international girls' school, and still run a thriving pottery industry and a craft shop. Not to be missed is the beautifully restored Gothic chapel, reached by a footpath beside the delightful lakeside. The equally well-restored walled Victorian garden is the largest in Ireland and is accessed through a marvelous woodland walk.

Letterfrack's Ocean and Country Museum brings alive the Connemara coastal oceans through scenic and wildlife coastal cruises aboard the *Queen of Connemara*, sealife exhibits and an aquarium. On the grounds are sandy coves, picnic areas, children's play areas and a craft shop. And on Sunday afternoons, there are children's plays and Irish music sessions.

Tourist information ✉ Galway Road, Clifden ☎ 095 22622; www.connemara.ie
🕐 Mon.–Sat. 10–5, Jun.–Aug.

Roundstone Musical Instruments ✉ IDA Craft Centre, Roundstone ☎ 095 35808; www.bodhran.com 🕐 Mon.–Sat. 9:30–5:30 🍴 Café

Connemara National Park ✉ Letterfrack, Clifden–Westport road (N59) ☎ 095 41054; www.connemaranationalpark.ie 🕐 Visitor center: daily 9–5:30, Mar.–Oct.; park grounds open all year round 🍴 Tearoom 🎟 Free

Kylemore Abbey and Garden ✉ Near Letterfrack ☎ 095 52000; www.kylemoreabbeytourism.ie
🕐 Estate: daily 11–4:30, Jan.; 11–5, early Feb. to mid-Feb.; 10–5, mid-Feb. to mid-Mar.; 9–5:30, mid-Mar. to Apr. and Oct.; 9–6, May and Jun.; 9–7, Jul. and Aug.; 9–6, Sep.; 9–5, Nov.; 9:30–4:30, Dec. 🍴 Restaurant 🎟 $$$

Ocean and Country Museum ✉ Renvyle Peninsula, Connemara ☎ 095 43473 🕐 Daily 10–6, Mar. to mid-Oct. 🍴 Café 🎟 $$$

The restored 16th-century Dunguaire Castle catches the light at sunset

Gort

Gort is surrounded by history, which includes the seventh-century monastic settlement of Kilmacduagh, and five castles within a 5-mile radius. The poet William Butler Yeats bought Thoor Ballylee, a 16th-century castle keep, for just £35 ($56) in 1917 when it was not much more than a ruin. After restoring it to a habitable state, he summered here until 1929. Poems written about or at Thoor Ballylee are included in his book of poems *The Tower*. His life and times are vividly portrayed in an interesting audiovisual presentation.

The town is much associated with Yeats's contemporary, Lady Augusta Gregory (Dame Isabella Augusta *neé* Persse, born the 12th child in a family of 16 children), whose house at Coole was demolished in the 1940s. There must always have been creative inspiration in this tranquil setting, for this patron of the arts and founder of the Abbey Theatre in Dublin attracted many of Ireland's illustrious literary figures – writers W. B. Yeats, George Bernard Shaw and Sean O'Casey all drew encouragement from stimulating and appreciative conversations while visiting Coole House. Sadly, only ruins mark the place where the house once stood – the grounds are now a nature reserve. You can, however, take a look at the famous "Autograph Tree" for carved names of literary guests.

Such literati also had links with nearby Dunguaire Castle. In the early 1900s it was a country retreat for Irish writer Oliver St. John Gogarty, who held regular literary gatherings. The castle furnishings reflect its medieval beginnings, and the banquet and literary evening attractions are much more intimate than those at Bunratty and Knappogue. The entertainment reflects Ireland's bardic tradition and celebrates the richness of this country's literary and musical past.

🚩 B1

Tourist information ✉ Thoor Ballylee, Gort ☎ 091 631 436 🕐 Mon.–Sat. 10–6, May–Sep.

Yeats Tower (Thoor Ballylee) ✉ Signposted near Gort, half a mile off N18 (Galway–Limerick road) and half a mile off N66 (Gort–Loughrea road) ☎ 091 631 436 🕐 Closed for repairs. Possibly reopening in 2013 (call to check hours) 🍴 Tearoom 🍷 $$ 🛈 Picnic area

Coole Park ✉ 2 miles north of Gort, due west of N18 ☎ 091 631 804; www.coolepark.ie 🕐 Daily 10–6, Jul.–Aug.; 10–5, end Apr.–Jun. and first 2 weeks Sep. 🍷 Free

Dunguaire Castle ✉ Kinvarra, 10 miles northwest of Gort on the N18 Galway road ☎ 061 360 788; www.shannonheritage.com 🕐 Daily 10–5 (last admission 4:30), mid-Apr. to early Oct. 🍷 $$

Opposite: Read the runes inscribed on Sligo's monument to the poet W. B. Yeats

Sligo

Sligo (Sligeach, Shelly Place) grew up around a ford of the River Garavogue, which rises in Lough Gill and tumbles over swift rapids as it approaches its estuary. The town's strategic position gave it early prominence as a seaport, and as a fine religious center – today it is the cathedral town of both a Catholic and Protestant diocese. While many come to Sligo for the sights associated with the poet William Butler Yeats, it would be a mistake not to see the highlights of the old town itself.

Its streets are filled with quaint old storefronts and 19th-century buildings. The ruins of the Dominican Abbey on Abbey Street represent the town's only surviving medieval building. Kings and princes of Sligo were brought for burial here, and the abbey often suffered raids during the 1641 rebellion, eventually closing after being damaged by fire. Ghost stories surrounding the ruins are said to have provided part of the inspiration for Bram Stoker's *Dracula*.

The altar here is one of the few surviving medieval altars in Ireland.

On Adelaide Street, the Cathedral of the Immaculate Conception is a massive limestone structure of Renaissance Romanesque style. St. John's Cathedral on John Street dates from the mid-1700s and was designed by the same architect as Leinster House (see page 80), the seat of the Irish government in Dublin.

The Town Hall on Quay Street dates from 1865 – a graceful building in the Italian Renaissance style that legend says stands on the site of a 17th-century Cromwellian fort. At Teeling and Chapel streets, the Courthouse incorporates part of an earlier courthouse. In 1832, when cholera swept over Sligo, the building housed coffin builders.

The impressive Pollexfen Ships Building at the corner of Adelaide and Wine streets originally belonged to the owners of the largest shipping company in Sligo. It was Yeats' grandfather who, on owning the large stone building, added the tower as a lookout point for his ships returning to port.

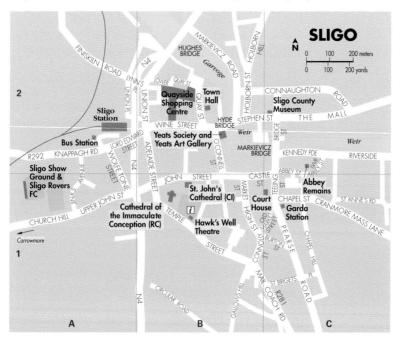

There's no shortage of nighttime entertainment in Sligo. The Hawk's Well Theatre was the first built for this purpose in western Ireland, and it places a strong emphasis on Irish playwrights. Productions are performed by leading Irish theater companies, with occasional evenings of poetry, musical concerts and traditional song, dance, drama and comedy. It's fairly easy to find traditional music and ballads in Sligo pubs. However, since such events are often non-schedule, be sure to check with the tourist office for information about where is likely to have musical entertainment.

For Yeats' devotees, it comes as no surprise that Sligo offers much information and memorabilia. For two weeks in late July or early August, Sligo breathes, eats and sleeps the incomparable poet as the Yeats International Summer School presents seminars, lectures, workshops, readings and dramas that draw throngs of scholars from around the world. However, the ultimate source of information on W. B. Yeats can be found at the Yeats Society, headquartered in the red-brick 1895 Yeats Memorial Building on Hyde Bridge. Inside, the plethora of exhibits relating to the poet include his complete works in first editions and his 1923 Nobel Prize for Literature. The new Yeats Arts Gallery, which has replaced the former Sligo Arts Gallery, displays work by local artists, rotating them every two to three weeks.

Sligo has intrigued painters as much as writers, and Yeats had no family monopoly on fascination with this countryside – his painter brother, Jack Yeats, sought to capture it on canvas, and there's an extensive collection of his paintings and drawings.

County Sligo encompasses some of Ireland's most wondrous scenery – the sort of sea and mountains and far-flung vistas that shaped Yeats's life and work. From boyhood stays in Magheraboy with his grandparents to the end of his life when he was laid to rest in Drumcliff churchyard, Yeats's imagination was fired by legends of ancient heroes who lived out their sagas in this part of Ireland and left the countryside strewn with mementos of their passing; cairns, dolmens, passage graves and prehistoric relics continue to bear silent witness to the lives that so engaged him.

Places associated with Yeats are marked by simple signposts inscribed with appropriate verses, but before rambling through Yeats Country, go by the tourist office or a Sligo bookshop and pick up the excellent booklet *The Yeats Country*, which tells you which poems were written about which places. The Yeats Country drive on pages 50–52 also takes you to some of these spots: beautiful Lough Gill, where you'll find his Lake Isle of Inisfree; the cairn at Knocknarea's summit where, according to Yeats, "passionate Maeve is stony-still." His words about this mystical, magical part of Ireland cannot be bettered, and you will find yourself recalling them again and again.

Scattered over the county are traces of the prehistoric races who lived here during three periods: Late Stone Age (Neolithic, 2500–2000 BC); the Bronze Age (2000–500 BC); and the Early Iron Age (500 BC to AD 500). In the immediate vicinity of Sligo town is Carrowmore (south near Ballysadare), Ireland's largest and most impressive group of megalithic tombs. Covering 1.5 square miles, it is filled with stone rings, dolmens and passage cairns (see page 52).

✚ C3 (regional map on page 29)
Tourist information ✚ B1 ✉ Temple Street
☎ 071 91 61201; www.sligotourism.ie ⏰ Daily 9–5:30, Apr.–Oct.; Mon.–Fri. 9–5, rest of year
Yeats Society and Yeats Arts Gallery ✚ B2
✉ Yeats Memorial Building, Hyde Bridge
☎ 071 91 42693; www.yeats-sligo.com
⏰ Mon.–Fri. 10–5; artists open gallery occasionally at weekends 🎫 Free
Hawk's Well Theatre ✚ B1 ✉ Temple Street
☎ 071 91 61518; www.hawkswell.com ⏰ Box office: Mon.–Fri. 10–5:30, Sat. noon–6 (8 on performance days)

Drive
Yeats Country

Duration: 1–2 days

Steeped in echoes of prehistory and the poet William Butler Yeats, you'll find in this corner of Ireland a happy unison of wooded lakes, bare mountaintops and Atlantic seascapes. This 98-mile tour starts from the tourist office on Temple Street in Sligo.

Take the N4/N15 northwards to Drumcliff.

Under bare Ben Bulben's head
In Drumcliff churchyard Yeats is laid
An ancestor was rector there
Long years ago; a church stands near,
By the road an ancient cross,
No marble, no conventional phrase;
On limestone quarried near the spot,
By his command these words are cut:
Cast a cold eye
On life, on death,
Horseman, pass by!

Yeats's poem describes Drumcliff completely, and his grave can be found easily in the Protestant churchyard. Yeats died in 1939 in the south of France and was buried in a cemetery overlooking the Mediterranean Sea. His remains were brought home to his beloved Sligo in 1948 and placed here, as he wished, in the shadow of Benbulbin. The road runs through a monastic site to the church where the poet's grandfather was rector.

Continue on the N15 and almost immediately take a turn left on Orchard Grove for 4 miles to Lissadell.

Yeats was a regular visitor to the Greek-revival style Lissadell House. The slightly forbidding classical facade hides the romance captured in his poem in memory of the Gore-Booth sisters, Eva (of whom he was particularly fond) and Constance, which begins thus:

The light of evening, Lissadell,
Great windows open to the south,
Two girls in silk kimonos, both
Beautiful, one a gazelle.

Constance became the Countess Markievicz, a leader in the Easter Rising of 1916 and the first woman to be elected to Westminster, although she never took her seat. The 1830s limestone mansion has many attractive interior features, including a charming music room, a dining room with intriguing murals and a striking two-story entrance hall with Doric

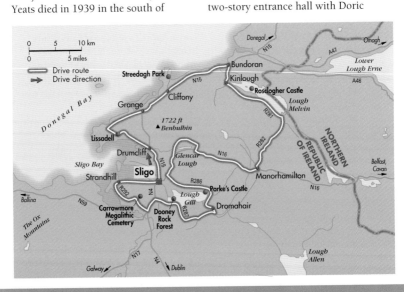

columns and a beautiful double staircase. Unfortunately, since 2009 Lissadell House has ceased operating as a tourist attraction and is no longer open to the public. The house is set in fine parkland near the sea, and seals can be spotted basking on the sandbanks.

Drive through the parkland (access during daylight hours only), rejoin the road and turn left, then right at the fork. Soon after that, turn right and continue to the village of Grange. Turn left to rejoin the N15 for Bundoran.

Contrasting with the placid towns and coastal villages of the northwest, the busy seaside resort of Bundoran offers many attractions, a good beach and cliff walks. Southwest of Bundoran, at Streedagh, a small park commemorates the place where three vessels of the Spanish Armada foundered in 1588. Members of the crew who struggled ashore from the overladen ships found little help on land.

Take the R280 off the N15 bypass for 3 miles to Kinlough.

This attractive village is at the north end of Lough Melvin and is good for coarse and salmon fishing. On the shore is the ruin of Rosclogher Abbey, and on an artificial island are the remains of the MacClancy Castle (known as Rosclogher Castle), where nine survivors of the Armada were given refuge.

Follow the R281 east along the Lough Melvin shore for 8 miles, then turn right onto the R282 south for Manorhamilton.

This unassuming village in County Leitrim stands in an area of mountain valleys with lofty peaks, lush slopes, steep clefts and gray cliff walls. It's overlooked by a ruined castle that was built at the meeting of four mountain valleys by the Scottish 17th-century planter Sir Frederick Hamilton, who gave his name to the village.

Take the N16 for Sligo. After 7 miles turn right onto a very steep unclassified road signposted for Glencar Lake.

Glencar is a beautiful lake; the steep valley slopes are clothed with mixed

Benbulbin, near Sligo, at sunset

woodland, a profusion of rare plants and luxuriously heathered mountaintops. Glencar Waterfall, white with spray, cascades down from a rocky headland and is immortalized by Yeats in his poem "The Stolen Child."

Continue on past the end of the lake until the road rejoins the N16. Turn right toward Sligo, then left to Park's Castle Visitor Centre on R286.

Although its name comes from the English family who moved in during the 1620 plantation of this part of Ireland, the restored Parke's Castle is a fortified manor house that was originally the home of the O'Rourke clan, rulers of the kingdom of Breifne. The audiovisual show not only tells this story (including how the Parke family unashamedly dismantled a neighboring castle for materials to use in their own), but also includes information on other points of interest in the area. From Parke's Castle, there is a superb view over Lough Gill, and to the southwest is the Isle of Innisfree for which Yeats yearned – "where peace comes dropping slow" – and to which you can take a cruise from Parke's Castle (including an especially evocative one at sunset). If you explore the lake, you'll find a sweat-house, medieval Ireland's answer to the sauna.

Connacht

Continue on the R286, then at the end of the lake turn right onto the R288 for Dromahair or Carrick-on-Shannon, then turn right on the R287 for Sligo. After 2.5 miles turn right again, following the R287 past the sign for Innisfree to Dooney Rock Forest, before rejoining the N4.

This corner of Lough Gill reveals forests and paths to satisfy any enthusiastic walker as well as great views of the lough. Dooney Rock Forest bears the vestiges of a once-important oak forest. Here you can see the "twining branches," two linked oaks. Yeats wrote of "The Fiddler of Dooney," who made folk "dance like the waves of the sea." The poem has inspired a Fiddler of Dooney competition for the champion fiddler of Ireland. It's held in Sligo in October.

Cairns Hill Forest Park marks the two cairns on Belvoir and Cairns peaks. A legend holds that these cairns are the burial places of the warriors Omra and Romra. Omra fell in love with Romra's daughter Gille (meaning beauty). When a mortal battle ensued after the lovers were discovered by Romra, Gille drowned herself, and Lough Gill was formed from the tears of her nursemaid.

Travel south on the N4, then turn right on the R292 (by the bus station) for Rathcarrick and Strandhill.

Huge Atlantic breakers crash onto the beach at Strandhill – a favored place for surfing championships. If you prefer calmer waters drive to Culleenamore. The town nestles beneath the cairn-capped Knocknarea mountain. This is the great Misgaun Maeve, an unopened cairn about 200 feet in diameter and 80 feet high that archeologists believe covers a vast passage grave, but legend insists is the burial monument to Maeve, the warrior queen of Connacht. If you climb to the summit of Knocknarea, Sligo tradition is to add a stone to the cairn as a protection against the fairies.

Among the fields below Knocknarea at Carrowmore is one of Europe's largest concentrations of megalithic tombs. Visitors are inevitably moved by this sacred burial place of more than 100 passage graves. The earliest tombs are said to predate the more famous passage grave at Newgrange by about 700 years. To explore properly, wear shoes suitable for uneven terrain.

Take the R292 for 5 miles back to Sligo.

Lissadell House ✉ Drumcliff, off N15 (main Sligo–Donegal road) 8 miles north of Sligo

Parke's Castle ✉ Five Mile Bourne, Co. Leitrim, on the north shore of Lough Gill ☎ 071 91 64149; www.heritageireland.ie ⊙ Daily 10–6, Easter–Sep. 🍴 Tearoom 💳 $

Carrowmore Megalithic Cemetery ✉ Carrowmore Visitor Centre. Signposted on N15 from Sligo, N4 from the south ☎ 071 91 61534; www.heritageireland.ie ⊙ Daily 10–6, Easter–Sep. 💳 $

A painted wooden fishing boat rests on the shore of Lough Gill, Co. Sligo

Strokestown and Roscommon

Many Irish towns and villages reveal their Georgian origins in wide streets, but Strokestown, said to have the widest main street in Ireland, is exceptional in that it was originally modeled on Vienna's Ringstrasse. The town is little more than an adjunct to Strokestown Park House, one of Ireland's finest great houses, which lies beyond the Gothic triple arch on this main street. Dating from the early 1700s, the 45-room Palladian house incorporates parts of an earlier tower house, and the reception rooms, galleried kitchen and some bedrooms and nurseries are furnished in its original style. The restored walled "pleasure garden" invites a stroll.

Elaborate vaulted stables in the south wing of the house hold the fascinating Irish Famine Museum. Strokestown Park was the seat of the Pakenham Mahon family from the 1600s to 1979, and archives that were purchased with the house shed light on the heart-wrenching plight of the Irish poor during the devastating years of the potato famine. They also form an authentic platform for the museum's critical view of contemporary world poverty and hunger.

South of Strokestown, the county town of Roscommon also lies to the west of Lough Ree and has many fine old buildings, including several churches, the Old Military Barracks, the Court House and the Old Jail, which had an 18th-century female executioner called "Lady Betty." Condemned to death herself, allegedly for murdering her own son, she volunteered to step into the breach when the hangman was ill on condition that her life be spared. Betty was subsequently appointed for the job with a salary and accommodation at the jail, where she remained for about 30 years. She dispatched her clients from a hinged board outside her third-floor window, and was said to then draw charcoal portraits of the bodies.

Overlooking the town, ruins of drum towers are all that remain of the

Ruins of Roscommon's Norman castle

13th-century castle that once stood here. After changing hands between the O'Kelly and O'Conor clans over the centuries, it finally fell into those of Cromwellian troops, who left behind the destruction of all but the towers. The remains of Félim O'Conor, 13th-century king of Connacht, rest in the ruins of a Dominican priory in a tomb decorated with effigies of gallowglasses (soldiers of fortune).

Three miles southwest of Roscommon, the ruins of Fuerty, a Franciscan church, mark the setting for the slaughter of 100 priests by a local tyrant. Among the interesting headstones in the graveyard is that of a blacksmith, with carvings depicting an anvil, bellows and tongs, and that of a shepherd with his crook and sheep.

✚ C2

Tourist information ✉ John Harrison Memorial Hall, Roscommon ☎ 090 66 26342; www.visitroscommon. com ◷ Mon.–Sat. 10–6, Jun.–Sep.

Strokestown Park House, Garden and Irish Famine Museum ✉ Strokestown, on N5 (Dublin–Castlebar road) ☎ 071 96 33013; www.strokestownpark.ie ◷ Daily 10:30–5:30, mid-Mar. to Oct. (tours at noon, 2, 4:30); 11:30–4, rest of year (tours at 2:30) 🍴 Restaurant 💷 $$$

Westport

With an octagonal center and lime trees lining both sides of the river, Clew Bay at its feet and a wealth of grand Georgian buildings, Westport is one of western Ireland's most charming market towns and is designated a Heritage Town of Ireland. The Thursday morning market at the James Street parking lot brings the farmers into town, and there is a frenzy of buying and selling clothes, produce, meats and novelties. It's even more lively when the annual arts festival takes place in October, with live music, visual arts, and theater.

Westport's main sight is Westport House, a lovely old 1731 Georgian mansion set in fine parkland near the quay. It sits on the grounds of an earlier O'Malley castle, the dungeons of which are now visited by children who are happily "terrified" by horrors installed for their entertainment. Lord and Lady Altamont are in residence here, and over the years they have turned their estate into a stylish virtual museum of Irish memorabilia and craftsmanship, with a magnificent drawing room, two dining rooms, a long gallery and grand entrance hall. Up the marble staircase, four bedrooms hold such treasures as state robes and coronets and 200-year-old Chinese wallpaper. On the grounds there's an animal park, amusements, rides and opportunities for boating and fishing on the lake and river.

Between Louisburgh and Westport, Clew Bay opens before you as the road passes through stony, barren hillsides and touches the bay at several points. The 16th-century pirate queen Grace O'Malley (Granuaile) roamed these waters freely, darting in and out of the bay to attack merchant ships that sailed the coastal waters. When summoned to London by Queen Elizabeth I in 1575, she refused to bow in submission, proudly proclaiming herself "Queen of Clew Bay." The square tower near the harbor on Clare Island was her refuge and stronghold, and splendid views of Clew Bay and the mountains of Connemara and Mayo undoubtedly explain her deep love of the island, which also has a 15th-century abbey and an ancient promontory fort on its southern cliffs. Regular mailboat sailings from Roonagh Pier (4 miles west of Louisburgh) carry present-day visitors to Clare Island year-round.

Five miles west of Westport, Croagh Patrick, Ireland's holy mountain, rises to 2,510 feet. St. Patrick is believed to have fasted at the summit for 40 days. Each year pilgrims climb the stony paths, some in their bare feet, on the last Sunday in July for a 4 a.m. Mass at its top.

✚ A2

Tourist information ✉ James Street ☎ 098 27766; www.westporttourism.com 🕐 Mon.–Sat. 9–6, May–Oct.; Mon.–Fri. 9–6, Sat. 9–1, Nov.–Jan.

Westport House ✉ Westport ☎ 098 25430 or 098 27766; www.westporthouse.ie 🕐 House and gardens: daily 10–6, week before and after Easter, Jul. and Aug.; 10–4, Mar. to mid-Jun., Sep and fall mid-term break (end Oct.); attractions open variable times within above opening hours 🍴 Tearoom 💶 $$$

Golden light bathes a fishing boat and its reflection on the lough near Westport

Drive
Achill Island and County Mayo

Duration: 2 days

The ghost of pirate queen Grace O'Malley will follow you on this 207-mile tour that travels to Achill Island, Ireland's most scenic island and home to one of O'Malley's many strongholds.

Starting from Westport's tourist office on James Street, take the N59 north for 8 miles to Newport.

Picturesque little Newport, which dates from the 17th century, faces Clew Bay and is sheltered by mountains. Its neo-Romanesque Catholic church was built in 1914 and features a superb stained-glass window of the Last Judgment designed by Harry Clarke. Four miles west, Rockfleet Castle,

sometimes called Carrigahowley Castle, was one of Grace O'Malley's strongholds, where the indomitable pirate queen came to live permanently after her second husband died in 1583.

Follow the N59 west to Mulranny, then the R319 to Achill Island, 28 miles.

Connected to the mainland by a bridge, Achill Island is the largest of Ireland's islands. Only 15 miles long and 12 miles wide, it is a scenic mix of soaring cliffs, golden beaches, heathery boglands and tiny villages. Fishing for shark and other big-game fish is excellent, and you'll find boats and guides for rent. The Atlantic Drive is spectacular, climbing from gently rolling mountain foothills, past stretches of sandy beaches, and through charming villages with excellent views of the sea, Clew Bay and the mainland. Yes, it's easy to see why Grace O'Malley fell in love with Achill's unspoiled wildness and profound peace. Beside Kildownet Castle are the ruins of a small 12th-century church. At the center of holiday activities is Keel, which has a fine sandy

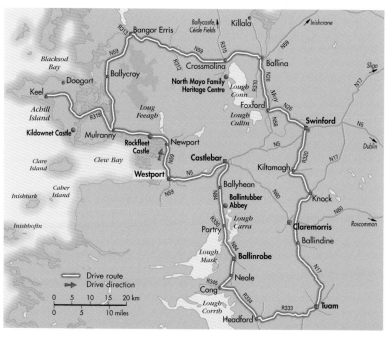

beach and a small harbor with fishing and sightseeing boats for rent. Viewed from a boat, the sea-carved rocks below the Menawn cliffs at the eastern end of the beach take on fanciful shapes. At Doogort, nestled at the foot of Slievemore, the fascinating Seal Caves cut far into the cliffs.

Take the R319 back to Mulranny, then turn north on the N59 for the drive to Crossmolina, passing through Ballycroy and Bangor Erris (where the N59 turns sharply east).

At Crossmolina, on the shores of Lough Conn, is the huge genealogical data bank of the North Mayo Family Heritage Centre, where ancestors can be traced by searching through church registers, wills, leases and school rollbooks. The center displays a collection of farm implements and household items from rural life of long ago.

Northward via the R315 to Ballycastle is Céide Fields. More than 5,000 years old, it's the oldest enclosed farm system in the world, revealed virtually intact underneath the bogs. The 12-square-mile site holds relics of Stone Age rural life and includes stone walls that surrounded the ancient community and megalithic tombs. A 20-minute presentation in the visitor center precedes a guided tour.

Return to Crossmolina and continue on the N59 to Ballina.

Founded in 1730 on the River Moy, Ballina is County Mayo's largest town. An important fishing center, it celebrates a week-long salmon festival each July. Stood beside the 1892 Cathedral of St. Muiredach, with its fine stained-glass window, are the ruins of a Franciscan abbey built about 1427. Eight miles north of Ballina via the R314 is Killala, which has a wealth of antiquities, inluding one of the finest round towers in the country.

On the east side of Killala Bay is the pleasant 3-mile beach resort of Inishcrone (take the N59 from Ballina northeast then turn left onto the R297),

whose most noted attractions are bath houses that specialize in curative hot, seaweed-enriched soakings.

Take the N26 south to Foxford.

Foxford is famous for its woolen mills, set up by a nun in 1892 as a means of providing work for the area's many unemployed. Since then, it has grown into one of the country's leading mills, producing world-renowned blankets, tweeds and rugs. View the visitor center's multimedia presentation of the mill's history, then go on the industrial tour.

Continue on the N26 through Foxford on to Swinford. Follow the R320 south to Kiltimagh, then turn southeast on the R323 for 5 miles to reach Knock.

The little church in the village of Knock has become a shrine, for it was here in 1879 that an apparition of Our Lady was seen at the Church of St. John the Baptist. Now officially designated a Marian Shrine, the magnificent basilica built on the grounds has welcomed visitors from around the world, including Pope John Paul II and Mother Teresa of Calcutta. More than 1.5 million pilgrims visit the shrine annually to attend one of the seven daily Masses. The 32 pillars in the ambulatory were contributed by all the counties of Ireland and the four medieval-style windows are replicas of cathedral windows in each of the four provinces. On the south side of the basilica, the Knock Folk Museum portrays life in rural Ireland at the end of the 19th century.

Take the N17 south to Tuam.

A thriving commercial and agricultural center under James I's charter of 1613, Tuam was altered to include a diamond-shaped town "square" on which all roads converged. Tuam claims Ireland's first industrial museum, the Mill Museum – an operational corn mill with mill wheel and other industrial exhibits. St. Mary's Cathedral, founded in 1130 and rebuilt in the 19th century, is a fine example of Gothic-revival architecture and incorporates a 12th-century chancel with magnificent windows. The town's well-adorned but incomplete 12th-century high cross stands in its grounds. **Leave Tuam on the N17 southwest. After 3 miles, turn west on the R333 for 9 miles to reach Headford. Take the R334 northwest for just over 6 miles, then turn left to Cong via the R346.**

The little town of Cong was the setting for the popular 1950s movie *The Quiet Man*. That, however, is the least of its claims to fame. More notable are the ruins of the Royal Abbey of Cong and the impressive Ashford Castle (see page 43). **At Cong take the R345 northeast to the R334 and turn left for Ballinrobe. Take the N84 north to Castlebar.**

Partry lies between Cong and Castlebar, and 4 miles north you will find the restored Ballintubber Abbey. This is the only church in the English-speaking world with a history of uninterrupted services since the seventh century. What makes this all the more remarkable is the fact that Catholic Mass has been celebrated within its walls since 1216, despite years of religious suppression, two burnings and the assault of Cromwellian troops. During these times,

suppliants sometimes had to kneel before the altar in secret, and under open skies when there was no roof. **Take the N5 road southwest, back to Westport.**

North Mayo Heritage Centre ✉ Enniscoe, Castlehill, Ballina, 2 miles south of Crossmolina (off R315) on Lough Conn ☎ 096 31809 🕐 Museum, shop and tearoom: Mon.–Fri. 9–6, Sat.–Sun. 2–6, Apr.–Oct.; genealogical center: Mon.–Fri. 9–4 💶 Museum $$; genealogical center free

Céide Fields ✉ About 22 miles west of Ballina, 5 miles northwest of Ballycastle on the R314 ☎ 096 43325 🕐 Daily 10–6, Jun.–Sep.; 10–5, mid-Mar. to May and Oct.–Nov. 🍽 Tearooms 💶 $$

Foxford Woollen Mills ✉ St. Joseph's Place, Foxford, about 20 miles north of Castlebar en route to Ballina ☎ 094 92 56104; www.foxfordwoollenmills.com 🕐 Mon.–Sat. 10–5, Sun. noon–5, May–Oct.; Sun. from 2, Nov.–Apr. 🍽 Restaurant 💶 $$$ ℹ Shop, art gallery

Knock Shrine and Knock Folk Museum ✉ Knock ☎ 094 938 8100; www.knock-shrine.ie 🕐 Basilica: daily 24 hours; museum: daily 10–6, May–Oct.; daily 2–4, rest of year 💶 Basilica free; museum $$

Ballintubber Abbey ✉ Claremorris, on the N84 Cong–Castlebar road ☎ 094 90 30934; www.ballintubberabbey.ie 🕐 Daily 9 a.m.–midnight 💶 Free (donations welcome)

This cottage on Achill Island has a stunning view across sandy Keel Beach

Leinster

Introduction and Map 60

Dublin 64

Introduction and Map 64

Sights 70

Feature: Dublin Specials 75

Feature: Enjoy Exploring 78

Walk: South of the Liffey 86

Feature: Dublin's Literary Greats 88

Regional Sights 90

Drive: Boyne Valley 94

Drive: Castles and Ecclesial Gems 100

Feature: A Long Tradition of Gardens 108

Opposite: View over the grounds of Powerscourt Gardens toward Great Sugar Loaf Mountain

Leinster

Leinster

The 12 diverse counties that make up the Leinster region – Carlow, Dublin, Kildare, Kilkenny, Laois, Longford, Louth, Meath, Offaly, Westmeath, Wexford and Wicklow – have collectively borne witness to most of the complex historical events that have shaped modern-day Ireland. At its center is cosmopolitan Dublin, increasingly taking its place on the world stage as a major capital city. It is the largest city in the country, and growing in popularity as a holiday destination.

Long before Norsemen arrived around AD 840 to found Dubh-Linn (Black Pool) on the banks of the Liffey as an important trading port, prehistoric and pre-Christian settlers set up whole communities along glacial folds that edged ancient lakes. Over the centuries, lakes became bogland and nature brushed rolling hills and miles of tilled fields with all of Ireland's famed "forty shades of green" as they merged softly into the marshy browns of the bogs. The resultant landscape is pockmarked with the remains of ancient burial sites, religious buildings, castles and other tangible records left by each wave of early invading peoples who

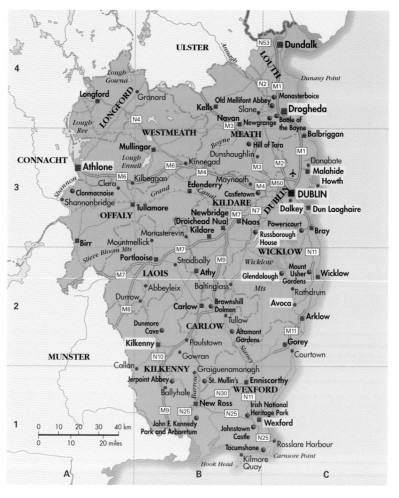

stayed on to become inhabitants. It was, in fact, from the fearsome *laighens* (iron-bladed spears) of invading Celts that Leinster took its name.

Leinster might well be called the "Royal Province" of Ireland. It has been a seat of power from the days of the prehistoric clans who constructed the great burial mound at Newgrange, to the high kings of Ireland who held court on the Hill of Tara (both, in fact, once part of the fifth "royal" province of Meath, or Mide), and from the warring days of the Celtic, Viking and Norman conquerors to appointees of English kings and queens.

In such a setting, it is little wonder that a legacy of myths and legends endures to this day, legends that blend magically with this region's long factual history, and that have been passed from generation to generation by bardic poets and storytelling *seanashai*. Tales still abound of gods, goddesses and the heroic deeds of Fionn MacCumhaill (see page 199) and his valiant band of Fianna warriors, as well as the military and romantic exploits of the high kings.

It was just northeast of Dublin at Clontarf that the Vikings were finally defeated in 1014 by Brian Ború, some say the greatest of Ireland's high kings. Englishman Oliver Cromwell arrived in 1649 and proceeded to cut a swath of slaughter from Dublin to Drogheda that claimed thousands of lives. Meanwhile, the long-lasting effects of William of Orange's overwhelming victory at the 1690 Battle of the Boyne, which so profoundly changed the course of Irish history, are echoed in headlines today.

Set amid County Wicklow's beautiful mountain scenery, Glendalough and its twin lakes reflect the tranquility of its

Ruins are all that remain of Slane's old abbey, which was once associated with St. Patrick

ecclesiastical past. To the south of The Pale's fortifications (a barrier originally created to divide English settlers from their Irish counterparts), County Wexford already bore the scars of Viking occupation when Cromwell's rampaging forces passed this way. The arrival of the Normans in 1169 and the revolutionist uprising of 1798 also left their imprint on that beleaguered county. The Normans gravitated to the countryside of counties Carlow and Kilkenny, building Kilkenny town (which for a time outdid Dublin as an administrative center) beside a pre-existing Irish settlement, and appropriating the most scenic spots for their distinctive castles.

Legend has it that County Kildare's Hill of Allen hosted Fionn MacCumhaill and his followers during winter months. Today it is the international set who flock year-round to its horse stud farms, which consistently turn out winners on international racetracks as well as on Kildare's own track, The Curragh. Counties Louth and Meath still wear the mantle of royalty, from the little town of Kells, birthplace of the magnificent *Book of Kells*, to the stirring Hill of Tara, and from Ireland's first Cistercian monastery, Mellifont Abbey, founded in 1142, to the enigmatic burial mound at Newgrange that predates both the Egyptian pyramids and England's Stonehenge.

Away from the coast, vestiges remain of Athlone's military might from the days when it stood guard over County Westmeath's lake-dotted landscape and Ireland's most important waterway, the River Shannon. Neighboring County Longford has nurtured writer Oliver Goldsmith and several other literary figures. Clonmacnoise on the banks of the Shannon in County Offaly is still a place of pilgrimage for thousands of visitors who come to glimpse the splendor of its ecclesiastical heyday, when its monastic community (founded in 548) presided over one of Europe's most important centers of learning. The remains are remarkably well-preserved.

The vast flatness of Ireland's great central plain is interrupted only by the Slieve Bloom Mountains rising in the northwest corner of County Laois.

While Leinster is a repository of history, it is also acknowledged to be Ireland's most progressive and rapidly

Heather carpets the slopes of the Wicklow Mountains in the Sally Gap area

changing region. In the last two decades, Dublin has grown significantly as a tourism destination, European financial center and commercial port. The swiftness of its growth and the thousands of residents who commute to the capital city daily from surrounding Leinster counties have brought some problems of traffic and housing, but do nothing to lessen the appeal of a city with a pace of life that belies its easy-going, gentle landscape.

Dublin

Dublin might rightly be called the birthplace of the "Celtic Tiger" that brought such prosperity to Ireland in a brief period at the end of the 20th century. The country has attracted investments from leading international industrial, commercial and financial firms, with a concentration in and around Dublin that has swelled the capital's numbers to about one-third of the country's population of more than four million.

As fast-moving as Dublin's growth and social change have been, the city has managed to hold onto and value the treasures of its past. Side by side with its modern developments, Dublin still reflects the blemishes and beauty spots left by a colorful history. Over the centuries, the ancient city has been called many things. Baile Atha Cliath (Town of the Ford of the Hurdles) is its Irish name (a wicker bridge – the hurdles – once spanned the river). Norsemen called it Dubh-Linn (Black Pool) when they founded the present city on the banks of the Liffey in 840.

By any name, Dublin is one of Europe's loveliest capital cities, with proud Georgian buildings (a style popular from the early 1700s to the mid-1800s, during the reigns of George I to George IV), elegantly groomed squares of greenery (Fitzwilliam, Parnell, Merrion), and acres of shaded leisure space (St. Stephen's Green and Phoenix Park). Its heart beats to the rhythm of the Liffey, and its horizons extend to Howth Head to the north, around the curving shores of Dublin Bay, to the slopes of the Wicklow Mountains to the south.

Little remains of medieval Dublin, but it's easy to trace its outlines and see how the modern city has grown around it. To the south of the Liffey you'll see Christ Church Cathedral's square tower – almost the exact center of the original city. To the east, Grattan Bridge stands near the "black pool" that marked its eastern boundary and served as a Viking trading port. Little Ship Street follows the course of the River Poddle (now underground), once a city boundary on the river's south bank, and the quays along the north bank marked another outpost of the original city.

The Millennium Bridge spanning the River Liffey, with the dome of the Customs House in the distance

There were few major changes to the original Dublin until magnificent Georgian buildings began to appear in the 18th century. The Victorian age arrived in the mid-1800s, leaving traces of its architecture that can still be seen today in railroad stations, banks, pubs, markets and hospitals. Between 1916 and 1922 Dublin was scarred by the ravages of violent uprising, but careful rebuilding has managed to erase most of the damage.

In the 1960s came the first "office revolution," when, in a fit of progressive zeal, the grand old city came close to demolishing many of its finest legacies. Fortunately, citizens halted this destruction at an early stage, so you may today walk through a mix of historic and modern structures.

The Liffey, which flows from west to east, divides the mile-long city center into "northside" (to Parnell Square at the northern end of O'Connell Street) and "southside" (to St. Stephen's Green at Grafton Street's southern end).

Of the Liffey's 20 or so bridges, O'Connell Bridge is the primary link

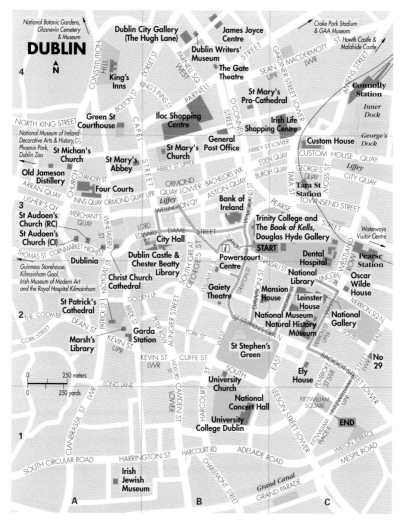

between north and south. North of the river, O'Connell Street is an extension of the bridge and the location of landmarks such as the historic General Post Office, statues of Parnell, Father Matthew and Daniel O'Connell and a monument, the Spire (officially known as the Monument of Light), erected in 2002 on the site of the former Nelson's Pillar – as well as a leading hotel, Clery's (one of Dublin's oldest department stores) and a jumble of fast-food eateries.

Once the center of social life in the city, O'Connell Street had deteriorated over the years, but has now undergone a massive cleanup and redevelopment to restore its charms. It is still advisable, however, to exercise big-city caution when walking there after dark.

To the south of O'Connell Bridge, Westmoreland Street extends for only one block before becoming College Green, a broad intersection outside the entrance to Trinity College. College Green then quickly becomes Grafton Street, Dublin's most fashionable shopping street. It is reserved for pedestrians only and features good (and some not-so-good) street entertainment. At the southern end of Grafton Street

is the cool, green oasis of beautiful St. Stephen's Green, a peaceful refuge from city streets.

The Liberties (so named in medieval times because its residents were exempt from the long arm of the law) is one of Dublin's oldest neighborhoods. It has been home to some of the city's most colorful and strongly independent characters, as well as a distinctive, easily recognized accent. Its boundaries lie west of Upper Kevin Street, beginning at The Coombe, its main thoroughfare (named for the valley, or coomb, of the River Poddle), and run west to somewhat indeterminate borders. Nearby are such historic landmarks as St. Patrick's Cathedral, Christ Church Cathedral and Dublin's oldest pub, the Brazen Head (see page 78), which witnessed much United Irishmen activity in the 18th century.

You will find some of the best examples of Dublin's famed Georgian architecture, a legacy of 18th-century residents, clustered around Merrion and Fitzwilliam squares and adjacent streets. Doorways whose fanlights are embellished with ornate wrought-iron decorations, cast-iron foot scrapers,

Theater and the Performing Arts

The Abbey Theatre on Lower Abbey Street began in 1903 when Augusta, Lady Gregory, W. B. Yeats and J. M. Synge determined to perform Irish plays with Irish casts. The theater has provided a voice for such writers as J. M. Synge and Sean O'Casey, even though this has sometimes rattled ultra-conservative Irish audiences. The original Abbey was quite small. When it burned down in 1951, it was 15 years before its modern, functional replacement was completed.

The National Concert Hall is an intimate venue for varied presentations by the National Symphony Orchestra, the Irish Chamber Orchestra and a host of visiting international luminaries.

On a much larger scale, The O2 (formerly known as The Point), which reopened in late 2008 after a major renovation, is well equipped to host leading international rock stars, classical ballet companies and full-scale musical stage shows in the heart of Dublin's docklands.

The Gaiety Theatre on South King Street is the venue for the two-performance seasons of the Opera Ireland repertory company. The Bord Gáis Energy Theatre is the new kid on the block. Located in the renovated Docklands on the south side of the Liffey, it hosts top London and Broadway shows as well as other touring productions.

ℹ You can pick up most concert and theater tickets at the Ticketmaster desk in the tourism center on Suffolk Street or go online at www.ticketmaster.ie

Docks line the banks of the River Liffey towards the Sean O'Casey Bridge in Dublin

doorway lamps, knockers and railings give each red-brick townhouse its own distinction. South of the Grand Canal, only a short walk from the city center, Ballsbridge is Dublin's most upscale residential section and the setting for several fashionable hotels and restaurants. So many embassies, including that of the United States, are located in this area that locals have dubbed it "Embassy Row."

Temple Bar, Dublin's lively center of popular culture and entertainment, is the result of a massively funded and carefully planned development of a city-center section where narrow lanes and alleys had at one time become glaring examples of neglect and urban decay. Named for the river walkway (once known as a "bar") of Sir William Temple, whose family owned much of this site from 1554 to 1628, this area is bordered by Essex, Wellington and Aston quays to the north, Lord Edward Street and Dame Street to the south, Westmoreland Street to the east and Fishamble Street to the west. With its narrow lanes recobbled and ancient buildings restored, Temple Bar is Dublin's 21st-century bohemia. Its

eclectic collection of art galleries, street entertainment, avant-garde shops, trendy restaurants and trendier pubs gives this area a vibrant, youthful air. The development of Temple Bar has continued into Cow's Lane.

"Dubs" ("jackeens" in the vernacular) are a breed, or rather, several breeds apart, with an increasingly cosmopolitan population mix. True Dubs will tell you, however, that unless you're born and bred in the city, you remain a *culchie* (country person) no matter how long you make the city your home. Arrogant? Not really – the tags are applied with good humor and a dollop of sharp wit, and are as often directed at themselves as at those other "blow-ins." Proud? Without doubt. Dubliners are happily convinced their city is not only the centerpiece of Leinster, but of Ireland and the entire universe as well.

Still, anything even remotely connected with reverence – including their own claims to their beloved city – is simply nonexistent in their makeup. Take, for example, when the Dubs christened a fountain – whose reclining female figure was meant to represent Anna Livia, Joyce's poetic name for the

Liffey River – "The Floozie in the Jacuzzi." Or the wonderfully realistic figures of two housewife shoppers at the north end of the Ha'penny Bridge tagged "Hags with the Bags." Or the statue of Sweet Molly Malone at Nassau and Grafton streets, now universally known as "The Tart with the Cart." Any new statue or monument erected by the city fathers is certain to fall prey to this brand of Dublin wit.

It's sometimes hard to hear Irish music, as it pours from the irrepressible Irish spirit, finding its voice in its own environment. With a very few exceptions, that's something you almost always have to stumble onto when the music and song are totally unplanned. In Dublin, however, that spontaneous spirit in all its passionate glory is alive and well at the headquarters of Cultúrlann na hÉireann in Monkstown (☎ 01 280 0295). There's traditional entertainment here most nights of the week, but to hear some of the best musicians, go on Friday or Saturday. Fiddlers fiddle, pipers pipe, whistle-players whistle, dancers take to the floor, and singers lift their fine Irish voices in informal musical sessions.

Cabaret in Dublin is served up with distinctly Irish seasonings: "Danny Boy" and "The Rose of Tralee" are favorites of many audiences, both for Irish people and visitors alike. You'll find an Irish comic telling Irish jokes, pretty, fresh-faced *colleens* dancing, singing and playing the harp, an Irish tenor or baritone, and youngsters stepping a lively jig or reel. It's Irish entertainment on the light side. No purists, these – but they're lots of fun and the performances are usually well above average. Most performances are held in hotels, and you can opt for dinner and the show or come for the show alone. The most popular cabaret is at the Burlington Hotel in Ballsbridge (May–Oct.), which has been running almost 35 years.

For many Dubliners, the best possible start and finish to a Dublin evening is a visit to their favorite pub. With "Enjoy Exploring" (see page 78) as a guide to pubs, you can opt for your own "local" during your stay or embark on a pub crawl for an entertaining sampling.

Excursions

If time is at a premium, the quickest way to see major attractions is by organized bus tours. Any of the Dublin Tourism centers can furnish details of what's available during your visit and make tour reservations.

The 90-minute open-top bus (covered double-deck bus on rainy days) tour is a delightful way to view the highlights of Dublin's major sightseeing attractions. The tour is a photographer's dream and includes Trinity College, the Guinness Brewery, St. Patrick's and Christ Church cathedrals, elegant Georgian squares, historic Phoenix Park and other points of interest.

With the all-day ticket for Dublin Bus Hop-On, Hop-Off tour, you can stay aboard for the 90-minute tour of 23 stops at major attractions, or you may elect to leave the bus at a stop of special interest and catch a later bus to complete the tour. Buses operate frequently, so you won't have a long wait for ongoing segments of the tour.

Dublin Bus also operates a three-hour North Coast and Castle tour that visits the 12th-century Malahide Castle along a scenic coastal drive to the village of Howth, and on to Howth Head for great views of Dublin Bay. The South Coast and Gardens Tour, lasting four-and-a-half hours, takes you through scenery sometimes called Dublin's Riviera. The route includes Dun Laoghaire's yacht-filled harbor, Joyce's Tower at Sandycove, Killiney Bay, Bray and Greystones, before turning inland to visit the Wicklow Mountains, Enniskerry and Powerscourt.

Other companies offer trips to Kilkenny and Glendalough, Newgrange and the Hill of Tara. If you want to go it alone, you could opt for a train to Belfast for the day from Connolly Station.

Essential Information

Tourist Information

Dublin Tourism ✉ Suffolk Street
☎ 1850 230 330 ⓘ Mon.–Sat. 9–6:30,
Jul.–Aug.; Mon.–Sat. 9–5:30, rest of year.
Sun. and bank holidays 10:30–3, all year
Dublin Airport ☎ 01 814 1111
ⓘ Daily 8–8; 8–6, Dec. 24 and 31
Ferry Terminal, Dun Laoghaire
☎ 01 204 7700 ⓘ Mon.–Sat. 9:30–5:30
Upper O'Connell Street (walk-in office only)
ⓘ Mon.–Sat. 9–5

ℹ Dublin Tourism's money-saving Dublin
Pass Card can reduce charges to 27 major
attractions. The Dublin Tourism website is a
useful source of information for many aspects
of your visit: www.visitdublin.com.

Urban Transportation

Dublin Bus services the city and outlying
areas, making it easy to seek accommodations
beyond the center. The main bus station,
"Busáras," is on Store Street. Buses marked
"An Lar" will be headed for the city center.
Buses run from 6 a.m. to 11:30 p.m. There is a
limited Nitelink bus service Mon.–Sat.; confirm
times with Dublin Bus. For more information,
call Dublin Bus ✉ 59 Upper O'Connell Street
☎ 01 873 4222; www.dublinbus.ie.

The electric train suburban service that runs
from Howth to Greystones stops at some 30
stations en route. Called the Dublin Area Rapid
Transit (DART), the service is fast, silent and
convenient, since departures are every five
minutes during peak hours, every 15 minutes
at other times. Service begins at 6:30 a.m. and
ends at about 11:30 p.m. Some 19 feeder bus
lines link up with the DART. Timetables can be
obtained at most of these stations. For
information, contact DART, Pearse Street
Station, Dublin 2 ☎ 01 703 3504.

Opened in 2004, the fast and efficient Luas
tram system operates two lines from Dublin
center out to the suburbs.

Taxis cannot be hailed from the street, but
may be called by telephone, and they operate
from stands at all bus and train stations and
many city-center locations, including Grafton
Street, Lower O'Connell Street, College Green
and St. Stephen's Green. They're listed in the
telephone directory under "Taxi-cab ranks."
Rates are set by law, and all taxis are metered,
with a small extra charge for each additional
passenger and each piece of luggage. There's
also a small additional charge between the
hours of 8 p.m. and 8 a.m.

Driving is best avoided. Public transportation
is efficient and frequent. Parking can be
difficult. Remember, once you reach the city
center, most places are going to be within
walking distance.

Dublin's two ferry terminals are Dun
Laoghaire Ferryport (☎ Stena Line
01 204 7777; www.stenaline.co.uk)
and Dublin Ferryport (☎ 0818 300 400;
www.irishferries.com), with bus and taxi
services meeting ferries at both.

Airport Information

Dublin International Airport is located
7.5 miles north of the city center.

The Airlink bus goes to and from the airport
from Busáras, the central bus station on Store
Street, north of the Liffey. Alternatively the
Aircoach makes several stops in the city. Taxis
are readily available at the airport.

Climate – average highs and lows for the month

Jan.	Feb.	Mar.	Apr.	May	Jun.	Jul.	Aug.	Sep.	Oct.	Nov.	Dec.
8°C	8°C	10°C	12°C	14°C	17°C	19°C	19°C	17°C	14°C	10°C	8°C
46°F	46°F	50°F	54°F	57°F	63°F	66°F	66°F	63°F	57°F	50°F	46°F
3°C	3°C	4°C	5°C	7°C	10°C	11°C	12°C	10°C	8°C	5°C	4°C
37°F	38°F	39°F	41°F	45°F	50°F	52°F	54°F	50°F	46°F	41°F	39°F

Leinster

Dublin Sights

Key to symbols

➕ map coordinates refer to the Dublin map on
page 65 🏛 admission charge: $$$ more than €6,
$$ €4–€6, $ less than €4
See page 5 for complete key to symbols

Bank of Ireland

This magnificent semicircular building facing onto College Green was built in 1729. It was the highlight of Ireland's wonderful years of freedom at the end of the 18th century, when Dublin reached the peak of its architectural achievement. Architect Edward Lovett Pearce designed the recessed south-facing "piazza" of Ionic columns (*circa* 1729–39) and the rooms behind it. James Gandon added the curving, windowless screen and the east-facing Corinthian portico between 1785 and 1789, and a corresponding portico was added to the west side years later.

The structure started life as the seat of the Irish Parliament, which gained its legislative independence in 1782. When the Act of Union was passed in

The south transept in Christ Church Cathedral

1800, Henry Grattan (whose statue stands across the way), although quite ill, rose to bid an eloquent farewell to the independent parliament. After the parliament was dissolved, the building was acquired by the Bank of Ireland in 1802 on the condition that the lower house be demolished to avoid any possible *coup d'etat*. The House of Lords is still intact, resplendent with two fine 18th-century tapestries by Jan van Beaver – one that portrays King James II at the 1689 Siege of Derry and the other that shows King William of Orange at the 1690 Battle of the Boyne – topped by a 1788 crystal chandelier made up from 1,233 intricate crystal pieces.

➕ B3 ✉ 2 College Green ☎ 01 677 6801 🕐 House of Lords: Mon.–Fri. 10–4 🚌 All city center (An Lar) buses 🏛 Free ℹ House of Lords tours on Tue. (except public holidays) at 10:30, 11:30 and 1:45

Chester Beatty Library and Gallery of Oriental Art

There are more than 22,000 cultural items in this extraordinary collection, given to the Irish nation by American-Irish engineer Sir Alfred Chester Beatty (1875–1968) in 1956. Biblical materials include papyri dating from the second to fourth centuries, and the Islamic collection contains more than 270 copies of the *Koran*. Rare books, illuminated manuscripts and miniature paintings originate from an impressive range of ethnic groups.

➕ B3 ✉ Clock Tower, Dublin Castle, Dame Street ☎ 01 407 0750; www.cbl.ie 🕐 Mon.–Fri. 10–5, Sat. 11–5, Sun. 1–5; closed Mon., Oct.–Apr. 🚌 49, 77, 77A (from Eden Quay) 🏛 Free

Christ Church Cathedral

Christ Church Cathedral dates back to 1038, when King Sitriuc erected a wooden structure, which was replaced with stone following the Norman invasion in 1169. Anglo-Norman leader Strongbow lies here, with a memorial in the cathedral nave. King Richard II came in 1394 to knight four Irish kings

The Custom House on Custom House Quay is illuminated at night and is best seen from across the water

after they pledged allegiance to the British Crown. James II prayed here in 1689 before the Battle of the Boyne, and King Billy came back to offer thanks for his victory in that battle. The south transept, the oldest part of the upper church (1180), contains many examples of late Norman and early Gothic architecture, and there are fine 16th- to 19th-century sculptures. You'll find statues of English kings, medieval carvings and oddities such as a mummified cat and rat, thought to have become trapped during a chase through organ pipes. Linked to the cathedral by a covered stone bridge is Synod Hall, which holds the Dublinia exhibition (see page 76).

✚ A3 ✉ Christchurch Place ☎ 01 677 8099; www.cccdub.ie ◉ Mon.–Sat. 9:30–6, Apr., May, Sep. and Oct.; Mon.–Sat. 9:30–6, Jun.–Aug.; 9–5:30, Nov.–Mar.; Sun. 12:30–2:30 and 4:30–6, Jun.–Aug.; 12:30–2:30, Sep.–May 🚌 78A (Aston Quay) or 50, 51B, 65, 90 (Eden Quay) 💷 $$ ℹ Prayers for peace in Ireland 12:45 Mon.–Sat.; Eucharist and sermon 11 a.m. every Sun.; call for times of other services

Croke Park Stadium and GAA Museum

The Gaelic Athletic Association is Ireland's largest sporting organization. Located at Croke Park, the home of Ireland's national games of hurling and football, this museum explores an integral part of Irish life and heritage. Touch-screen technology and high-definition interactives bring the games to life.

The museum is a good introduction to Gaelic sports, while the stadium tour provides first-hand history and background by a knowledgeable guide.

✚ Off map at C4 ✉ Cusack Stand, Croke Park, St. Joseph's Avenue ☎ 01 819 2323; http://museum. gaa.ie ◉ Mon.–Sat. 9:30–6, Sun. 10:30–5, Jul.–Aug.; Mon.–Sat. 9:30–5, Sun. 11;30–5, rest of year. Tour times: Mon.–Fri. 11, 1 and 3, Sat. hourly 10–3, Sun. 11–3, Jan.–May and Sep.–Dec.; Mon.–Sat. hourly 10–4, Sun 11–4, Jun.–Aug. (except on match days 🍴 Cafe 🚌 3, 11, 11A, 16, 16A 💷 $$

Custom House

The first large-scale commission for leading Irish architect James Gandon, the gracious 1791 Custom House is an outstanding example of Georgian architecture. Its facade is made up of arched arcades with a Doric portico at its center, topped by a green copper dome crowned with a statue of Commerce. A series of carved allegorical heads representing the 13 rivers of Ireland and the Atlantic Ocean decorate the building, alongside other sculptures and coats of arms. After dark, floodlights that illuminate the Custom House provide one of Dublin's most impressive nighttime sights, especially when viewed from the opposite bank of the River Liffey.

✚ C3 ✉ Custom House Quay ⏲ Not open to the public 🚶 Five-minute walk from O'Connell Bridge

Douglas Hyde Gallery

Funded by Trinity College and the Arts Council of Ireland, this is one of Ireland's leading contemporary art galleries. The diverse collection of temporary exhibitions displays thought-provoking art that embraces both emerging and well-established Irish and international artists. There are tours and lectures available.

✚ B3 ✉ Trinity College (Nassau Street entrance) ☎ 01 896 1116; www.douglashydegallery.com ⏲ Mon.–Fri. 11–6, Thu. 11–7, Sat. 11–4:45 🚌 All city center (An Lar) buses 💶 Free

Dublin Castle

Dublin Castle is built on the site of an earlier Danish fortress. The only remaining portions of the original castle (built between 1208 and 1220) are a piece of a curtain wall and two towers. You can get a pretty good idea of the original outline from the upper castle yard, dubbed "The Devil's Half Acre" by Dubliners when this was the nerve center for centuries of repressive British

Dublin Castle is a jumble of architectural styles, from 13th-century to modern

Dublin

rule. British viceroys resided in the opulent state apartments (now restored). It was from here that the injured James Connolly, patriot leader of the 1916 uprising, was taken by stretcher to Kilmainham Gaol to be executed.

Sumptuous furnishings, huge Waterford crystal chandeliers, tapestries, hand-tufted Donegal carpets mirroring the ceiling plasterwork and Robert Adam fireplaces abound, revealing the palatial lifestyle led by the viceroys. One of the most impressive rooms, St. Patrick's Hall, is adorned with banners and coats of arms beneath an ornately painted ceiling and is now used for the inauguration of Ireland's presidents. The throne room contains a massive throne believed to have been brought to Dublin by William of Orange after his victory at Boyne.

Other points of interest are the Church of the Most Holy Trinity (formerly the Chapel Royal), the 13th-century Record Tower, used by the Tudors as a prison, and the memorial outside the main gate honoring those Irish killed here during Easter Week of 1916, standing on the spot where heads of Irish kings once were displayed publicly on high spikes. The complex also houses the Chester Beatty Library (see page 70).

✚ B3 ✉ Dame Street ☎ 01 645 8813; www.dublincastle.ie or www.heritageireland.ie 🕐 Mon.–Fri. 10–4:45, Sat.–Sun. 2–4:45 🍴 Café/ Restaurant 🚌 49A, 56A, 77, 77A (from Eden Quay) 💰 $$ 🛈 Apartments may be closed for functions

The Dublin City (Hugh Lane) Gallery

Occupying one of Dublin's finest Georgian mansions, the Dublin City Gallery is the permanent home for Sir Hugh Lane's art collection, which was donated to the gallery in 1908. There's an extensive collection of 20th-century Irish art; French Impressionists Manet, Monet, Renoir and Degas; and ever-changing temporary exhibitions of works by international contemporary artists. The recreation of Francis Bacon's studio contains some 7,500 examples of the artist's work.

✚ B4 ✉ Charlemont House, Parnell Square North ☎ 01 222 5550; www.hughlane.ie 🕐 Tue.–Thu. 10–6, Fri.–Sat. 10–5, Sun. 11–5 🍴 Café 🚌 3, 10, 11, 16, 19, 46A 💰 Free

Dublin City Hall

One of Dublin's finest neoclassical buildings, dating from 1779, Dublin City Hall contains a multimedia exhibition ("The Story of the Capital") tracing the evolution of the city from 1170 to the present day. The story is told through displays of civic regalia, including the Great City Sword and other treasures, with computer interactives, archive films, models and costumes.

✚ B3 ✉ Cork Hill ☎ 01 222 2204; www.dublincity.ie 🕐 Mon.–Sat. 10–5:15 🍴 Coffee shop 🚌 49A, 56A, 77, 77A (from Eden Quay) 💰 $$

The copper-topped rotunda of the Four Courts was completed in 1796

Dublin Writers' Museum

Ireland's wealth of internationally recognized literary talent (including four Nobel prize winners) is celebrated in this superbly restored Georgian house that holds books, letters, portraits and personal belongings from the likes of Shaw, Wilde, Yeats, Swift, Joyce and Beckett. There are examples of magnificent stucco in this late 18th-century building. The colonnaded main salon, now the Gallery of Writers, has busts and paintings of famous names, a decorative ceiling and boisterous friezes. Children's literature is allotted its own room, with frequent visiting exhibitions and readings. The Irish Writers' Centre nurtures contemporary writers next door by providing meeting and work space.

✚ B4 ✉ 18 Parnell Square North ☎ 01 872 2077; www.writersmuseum.com ⏱ Mon.–Sat. 10–5, Sun. 11–5 🍴 Chapter One restaurant in basement 🚌 10, 11, 13A, 16A, 19A; 10-minute walk from DART Connolly Station 💰 $$$ ℹ Extensive bookshop with a mail-order service; self-guiding audio tour also available

Dublin Zoo and Phoenix Park

Established in 1831, Dublin Zoo encompasses 60 acres on the grounds of Phoenix Park. It is noted for breeding lions and other large cats, having successfully bred the first lion cubs in captivity in 1857. Picturesque landscaping and gardens surround two natural lakes alive with pelicans, flamingos and scores of ornamental ducks and geese, and there are spacious outdoor enclosures.

You can see rhinos and giraffes in the African Savanna, Asian elephants on the Kaziranga Forest Trail, the zoo's group of gorillas in the Gorilla Rainforest, endangered bats and rare birds in Roberts House, snakes, tarantulas and crocodiles in the House of Reptiles, and saki monkeys and pygmy marmosets in the South American House. There's also a Family Farm where kids can meet a variety of animals face to face.

Beautiful Phoenix Park, with its main entrance on Parkgate Street, is referred to by Dubliners as "The" Phoenix Park. It is one of Europe's largest enclosed city parks, and within its 1,652 acres are the residences of Ireland's president as well as that of the American ambassador. In addition to Dublin Zoo, the lofty trees provide shade for humans during the day and shelter for a free-roaming herd of deer after dark. Walkways lace the grounds, where ornamental gardens are joined by plantings of indigenous shrubs and trees. The 205-foot obelisk erected in 1817 commemorates the Duke of Wellington, a Dublin native, and the beautiful Papal Cross marks Pope John Paul II's 1979 visit to Dublin.

Dublin Specials

During special events, the entire city enters into the festive spirit. You should check with Tourism Ireland about specific dates during your visit. Advance reservations for inner-city accommodations are vital, and prices may become a little inflated.

St. Patrick's Festival
For generations, celebrations of Ireland's patron saint were confined to March 17, but since 1996 Dublin's festival has been lasting almost a week. A theme is selected each year, and with more than 5,000 performers (including U.S. marching bands), it has grown into Ireland's largest annual celebration. The undisputed highlight is the Festival Parade, but each day is filled with street events that include a Monster *Céilí* in St. Stephen's Green, colorful carnival events along the quays, magic, comedy and puppet performances, mini-parades and spectacular fireworks.

🛈 For full details on future festivals, contact St. Patrick's Festival, St. Stephen's Green House, Earlsfort Terrace, Dublin 2, or visit their website at www.stpatricksfestival.ie

Bloomsday
For many visitors, Bloomsday, which commemorates the June 16, 1904 setting of James Joyce's *Ulysses*, is reason enough to come to Dublin. At least a week before June 16 each year, Joyce fans and scholars are busily attending readings, lectures and dramatic performances. The day itself, however, is anything but a serious, head-scratching analysis of the book: Streets are thronged with people in period costumes re-enacting events from the classic tale; pubs visited by the novel's central character, Leopold Bloom, go all out with special meals and readings. There's an air of revelry as Dubliners celebrate turn-of-the-20th-century life in their beloved city and accord the writer a celebrity that eluded him during his lifetime.

Dublin Horse Show
The social highlight of the year, for five days in August the showgrounds of the Dublin Royal Society are packed with sophisticated international visitors who mingle happily with Irish horse-lovers. In some of the finest jumping enclosures in the world, virtually nonstop jumping competitions are a backdrop for auctions that net enormous sales figures for horses with impeccable pedigrees. The Aga Khan Trophy competition is Friday's main event, and on Sunday, the International Grand Prix of Ireland ends the week. Festivities include army band concerts, floral displays, a Ladies' Day fashion competition and art exhibits (www.dublinhorseshow.com).

Dublin Theatre Festival
Two weeks at the end of September and the beginning of October are devoted to the Dublin Theatre Festival (www.dublintheatrefestival.com). Every theater in the city, as well as university campuses and community halls, are filled with a series of first nights of innovative Irish drama and major overseas theater and dance companies. The festival provides a lively platform for Irish playwrights, new plays are performed and theatergoers have a rare opportunity to meet the participating actors and directors.

➕ Off map at A3 ✉ Phoenix Park ☎ Zoo: 01 474 8900; www.dublinzoo.ie.; Park Visitor Centre: 01 677 0095 🕐 Zoo: Mon.–Sat. 9:30–6, Sun. 10:30–6, Mar.–Sep.; Mon.–Sat. 9:30–dusk, Sun. 10:30–dusk, rest of year; Park Visitor Centre: daily 10–6, mid-Mar. to Oct.; Wed.–Sun. 9:30–5:30, rest of year 🍴 Several eateries 🚌 10 (from O'Connell Street), 25, 26, 66, 67, 68, 69 (from Pearse Street); Heuston Luas 💶 $$$
ℹ Zoo: play area, pet care area, discovery center

Dublinia and The Viking World

Across the footbridge from Christ Church Cathedral is a medieval setting that recreates Dublin life from the time the Anglo-Normans arrived in 1170. The exhibition is in the beautifully preserved former Synod Hall. An audio headset guides you on a "Journey Through Time" among lifesize reconstructions of those long-ago times. The exhibitions are interactive and include the "Viking Dublin Exhibition," where you can experience the sights and sounds of a real Viking street, and the one-of-a-kind "History Hunters" exhibition.

➕ A3 ✉ St. Michael's Hill, Christ Church ☎ 01 679 4611; www.dublinia.ie 🕐 Daily 9:30–5, Jun.–Jul.; 10–5, Mar.–May and Aug.–Sep.10–4:30, rest of year. Closed Dec. 24–26 🚌 50 (from Eden Quay), 78A (from Aston Quay), Four Courts Luas 💶 $$$

Four Courts

The Chancery, King's Bench, Exchequer and Common Pleas are the four courts for which James Gandon designed this building in 1785. Political turmoil delayed its opening until 1796, and it was finally completed in 1802. Scars and bullet holes on portico columns are a result of a heavy bombardment in 1922 during Ireland's civil war, when anti-treaty forces occupied the building. An explosion destroyed irreplaceable historical records and left the building a burned-out shell. Beautifully restored, this massive Georgian edifice facing the Liffey functions again, although it now hears only civil cases.

➕ A3 ✉ Inns Quay ☎ 01 872 5555 🕐 Visits are only when courts are in session 🚌 All city center (An Lar) buses; Four Courts Luas 💶 Free

General Post Office

The imposing General Post Office, with its Ionic portico and fluted pillars, was built in 1814. In 1916 its classical entrance provided a dramatic platform from which Padraic Pearse hoisted the Irish tricolor for the first time and proclaimed to his fellow Irish citizens and the world at large that Ireland would from that date on claim its independence (see page 21). After intense shelling, the building was set on fire and its interior gutted. Now completely restored, the central hall holds a statue of Ireland's ancient mythical warrior hero, Cuchulainn, a memorial to the men who fought here. On the marble base is inscribed the Proclamation of the Irish Republic.

➕ B4 ✉ O'Connell Street ☎ 01 705 7000 🕐 Mon.–Sat. 8:30–6 🚌 All city center (An Lar) buses 💶 Free

Glasnevin Cemetery and Museum

Ireland's largest cemetery, Glasnevin opened in 1832 as a burial place for people of all faiths. Today it is on the tourist trail as it is something of a national pantheon of renowned Irish folk. Follow one of their printed guides or a historian-led tour to visit the graves of politicians and rebels like Daniel O'Connell, Michael Collins, Eamon de Valera and Countess Markievicz, as well as writer Brendan Behan and mining mogul/art collector Chester Beatty.

Glasnevin Museum opened in 2010 to give a fuller insight into political, historical and artistic Ireland through the lives of the people buried in the cemetery here. It is divided into three exhibitions: The City of the Dead explores burial practices and religious beliefs; The Milestone Gallery has an interactive timeline giving details of the most famous people buried in the cemetery; and the Prospect Gallery offers information on funeral monuments and historic graves.

➕ Off map at A4 ✉ 11 Finglas Road ☎ 01 882 6500; www.glasnevintrust.ie 🕐 Daily 8–4:30; tours

2:30. Museum: Mon.–Fri. 10–5, Sat.–Sun. and public holidays 11–5 🚌 13, 19, 19A, 40, 40a 🎫 $

Guinness Storehouse

The sprawling Guinness Brewery, set on some 60 acres south of the Liffey, was the largest brewery in the world in the mid-19th century and today still exports more beer than any other company in the world. The rich, dark stout it has produced since 1759 is truly the "wine of Ireland." As you begin the Storehouse tour, an escalator whisks you to the heart of the building into what is described as a large glass pint. Within the structure you journey through the production process of a pint of Guinness. Old machinery is utilized to present entertaining displays and audiovisuals give an insight into the history, manufacturing and advertising of Dublin's famous product. You end your visit in the rooftop Gravity bar, which has excellent views, to try a free glass of the "black stuff."

✚ Off map at A2 ✉ St. James's Gate ☎ 01 408 4800; www.guinness-storehouse.com ⏰ Daily 9:30–7, Jul.–Aug.; 9:30–5, rest of year 🍴 Café, bar 🚌 51B, 78A (from Aston Quay), 123 (from O'Connell Street); James Street Luas 🎫 $$$ ℹ Free parking

Irish Jewish Museum

The former Dublin synagogue now houses a fascinating museum, yet the upstairs in this building is virtually unchanged and could be used to conduct a service without much delay. Irish and Jewish documents, photographs and relics of Jews in Ireland for the past 500 years are displayed here. Belfast-born and Dublin-educated Chaim Herzog opened the museum in 1985 when he was president of Israel.

✚ A1 ✉ 3–4 Walworth Road, off Victoria Street, South Circular Road, Portobello ☎ 0857 067 357; www.jewishireland.org ⏰ Tue., Thu. and Sun. 11–3:30, May–Sep.; Sun. 10:30–2:30, rest of year 🚌 16A, 19, 19A, 122 🎫 Free (donations welcome)

Irish Museum of Modern Art and the Royal Hospital Kilmainham

Built in 1684 as a home for retired soldiers, the Royal Hospital in Kilmainham is one of Ireland's finest 17th-century buildings. These days it houses the Irish Museum of Modern Art, with more than 1,200 woodcuts, etchings and engravings by Irish and international artists such as French Impressionists Manet, Degas and Renoir, and old masters Rembrandt, Hogarth and Goya alongside lesser-known artists.

✚ Off map at A2 ✉ Royal Hospital, Military Road, Kilmainham ☎ 01 612 9900; www.imma.ie ⏰ Tue.–Sat. 10–5:30 (except Wed. 10:30–5:30), Sun. noon–5:30 🍴 Café 🚌 51B, 79 (from Aston Quay), 123 (from O'Connell Street); Heuston Luas 🎫 Free ℹ Pre-booked tours Tue.–Fri. 10, 11:45, 2:30, 4

Barrels of Guinness are displayed in the Guinness Storehouse, ready to be shipped all over the world

Enjoy Exploring

There are more than 1,000 pubs in Dublin, each with its own personality. Those listed here are among the most interesting, but don't confine yourself to these – drop into the nearest establishment anytime you're overcome with a terrible thirst, and you'll likely go home raving about your own favorites. Irish pubs are quite happy to serve soda (minerals) as well as the hard stuff. It's the *craic* that matters most and is a national art.

The Brazen Head

The oldest drinking place in Ireland may have been licensed by Charles II in 1666, but it drew its name from a beautiful redhead who couldn't contain her curiosity during a civil disturbance, stuck her head out of a window, and promptly lost it to an English sword. The entrance is tucked away at the back of a courtyard down an alleyway on the west side of Bridge Street. It's dimly lit inside with low ceilings, brass lanterns and uneven floors. Patriots Robert Emmet, Wolfe Tone and Daniel O'Connell often came here to drink.

Doheny and Nesbitt

This is the place for people-watching. Doheny and Nesbitt, 5 Lower Baggot Street, has earned a special place in the affections of Dubliners in its 130 years of dispensing drink. Mirrored partitions along the bar and ceilings add to the setting and provide drinking "snugs" (enclosed nooks). Journalists, politicians, artists, locals and visitors often fill bars to overflowing.

The Stag's Head

Another long-standing favorite of Dubliners is the Stag's Head, tucked away in Dame Court. Here since the 1870s, it wears its age with grace, its stained-glass windows and skylights, gleaming wood and mounted stag's head reflecting the soft patina of time. One of James Joyce's regular haunts, it also serves an excellent pub lunch.

Mulligan's

This is as much a conversation pub today as it was when it was favored by James Joyce and other Dublin notables. Mulligan's on Poolbeg Street has

The popular Doheny and Nesbitt Pub on Lower Baggot Street in Dublin

been a Dublin institution since 1782, and the 19th-century gas lights are among its original trappings. Said to serve the best pint of Guinness in town.

Davy Byrnes

For James Joyce fans, Davy Byrnes, 21 Duke Street, still draws those who come looking for the "moral pub" described in *Ulysses*. True, the 1890s wall murals are still here, but the atmosphere these days is likely to be more that of a modern-day cocktail lounge than what Leopold Bloom encountered.

McDaids

Brendan Behan staked out a spot for himself, his pint and his typewriter in McDaids, 3 Harry Street, a dark, high-ceilinged pub that became his second home. Literary luminaries such as Patrick Kavanagh and Flann O'Brien also drank here, and many current wordsmiths have followed suit.

The Old Stand

Patronized by what sometimes seems to be at least half of Ireland's rugby team, as well as other athletes, The Old Stand at 37 Exchequer Street is a center for sports conversation.

Ryan's

Ryan's, 28 Parkgate Street, is a real gem. Located in the Phoenix Park area, it is worth a visit just for the decor: superb antique mirrors, brass lamp fittings mounted on the bar counter, a magnificent old oak and mahogany central bar with a unique double-faced mechanical clock and partitions of ornate, beveled-mirrored dividers. Heads of state and celebrities from the movie and theater worlds regularly mingle with natives to enjoy the great atmosphere.

Kavanagh's

Adjacent to what was once the main gate to Glasnevin Cemetery, Kavanagh's (also known as the Gravediggers) at 1 Prospect Square, has been here for over 150 years and has accumulated an inexhaustible fund of stories about gravediggers who would bang stones against the pub's wall and then wait for drinks to be passed through an opening and placed on their waiting shovels.

James Joyce Centre

Of all the literati to grace the Dublin scene during the 20th century, James Joyce has earned the greatest reputation, so it is fitting that this lovely 18th-century Georgian house is devoted to the writer and his work. Take time to browse in the extensive library and gaze at the portraits of those featured in the master's work. You can see the original doorway rescued from the now demolished No. 7 Eccles Street, the imagined residence of the *Ulysses* hero, Leopold Bloom. The center is also a starting point for an 80- to 90-minute walking tour of the Joycean sites.

➕ B4 ✉ 35 North Great George Street ☎ 01 878 8547; www.jamesjoyce.ie ⏰ Tue.–Sat. 10–5, Sun. noon–5 🍽 Café 🚌 3. 10, 11, 16, 19 💷 $$

Kilmainham Gaol

In the years between its opening in 1796 and its closure in 1924, Kilmainham Gaol has held political leaders of rebellions in 1798, 1803, 1848, 1867 and 1916. President Eamon de Valera was confined within its walls in 1916 and again in 1923 and was its final prisoner. Though the cells hold no prisoners now, corridors evoke a strong sense of patriots held here such as Robert Emmet, Charles Stewart Parnell, and Padraic Pearse and James Connolly and the 13 people executed with them for their part in the Easter Rising in May 1916. As a museum documenting the Irish struggle for independence, a visit to Kilmainham Gaol is a moving experience. Access by guided tour only.

➕ Off map at A2 ✉ Inchicore Road, Kilmainham ☎ 01 453 5984 ⏰ Daily 9:30–5, Apr.–Sep.; Mon.–Sat. 9:30–4, Sun. 10–5, rest of year 🍽 Tearoom 🚌 51B, 79; Suir Road or Heuston Luas 💷 $$

Leinster House

Since 1925, this 1745 mansion has been the home of Ireland's Parliament (Oireachtas na hÉireann), composed of the Dáil (the Lower House) and the Seanad (the Senate). Look for the memorial on Leinster Lawn that commemorates Arthur Griffith, Kevin O'Higgins and Michael Collins, all among the founders of the Republic of Ireland. Leinster House is flanked on either side by the National Gallery and the Natural History Museum. Visits are usually by organized tour only but in recent years it has flung its doors open for Open House events each fall, and taken part in September's Culture Night with entertainment on the grounds.

➕ C2 ✉ Kildare Street ☎ 01 618 3781 ⏰ Visits by reserved tour only, usually Mon.–Fri. 10:30, 11:30, 2:30, 3:30; also 7 and 8 p.m., Tue. and Wed. 🚌 All city center (An Lar) buses 💷 Free

Marsh's Library

Jonathan Swift and James Joyce are among Dubliners who have made great use of the 25,000-volume literary collections housed in Marsh's Library, the first public library in Ireland. Built beside St. Patrick's Cathedral in 1701 by Archbishop Narcissus Marsh, its beautiful interior remains unchanged since it opened, with dark oak bookcases and unique wire cages in which readers were locked when studying rare books. Some books were actually chained to the

Old and valuable books are found in Marsh's Library

The Beit Wing of the National Gallery of Ireland on Merrion Square

shelves. The four collections cover a wide range of subjects (theology, ancient history, music, law, travel and medicine) and include about 300 manuscripts, including *The Lives of the Irish Saints*, which dates to 1400.

➕ A2 ✉ St. Patrick's Close ☎ 01 454 3511; www.marshlibrary.ie 🕐 Mon., Wed. and Thu.–Fri. 9:30–1, 2–5, Sat. 10–1 🚌 50, 54A, 56A (from Eden Quay) 💰 $

National Gallery

In his youth, George Bernard Shaw spent many inspirational hours in the National Gallery and expressed his appreciation by bequeathing royalties from his plays for its upkeep. The doors first opened in 1864 with only 125 paintings, a collection that has grown to around 2,500. There's a major collection of works by Irish artists, and European masters such as Rembrandt and Rubens are well represented. Caravaggio's *The Taking of Christ* (*circa* 1602) receives plenty of attention; it was discovered hanging on the wall of a Jesuit house in Dublin. Also look for the collection of portraits of renowned Irish figures such as Lady Lavery and the Countess Markiewicz. Representing works up to the 19th century, the gallery has

computer facilities with information about its paintings. The Millennium Wing, opened in 2002, houses a center for the study of Irish art, temporary exhibition galleries and an archive dedicated to Jack B. Yeats.

Due to refurbishment of the Dargan and Milltown Wings, visitors can only access the museum via the entrance on Clare Street. The gallery aims to keep most highlights on display in the Millennium and Beit Wings while work is underway.

➕ C2 ☎ 01 661 5133; www.nationalgallery.ie 🕐 Mon.–Sat. 9:30–5:30, Thu. 9:30–8:30, Sun. noon–5:30; closed Good Friday and Dec. 24–26 🍴 Two restaurants 🚌 All city center (An Lar) buses 💰 Free ℹ Tours Sat. at 3 and Sun. at 2, 3 and 4

National Library of Ireland

Those with an interest in Irish studies or tracing Irish ancestry will find the National Library an invaluable resource. Opened in 1890, the library's thousands of volumes include first editions, and works of Irish writers. James Joyce fans will recognize the library as the Chapter Nine setting in *Ulysses*.

➕ C2 ✉ Kildare Street ☎ 01 603 0200; www.nli.ie 🕐 Mon.–Wed. 9:30–9, Thu.–Fri. 9:30–8, Sat. 9:30–1 🍴 Café 🚌 All city center (An Lar) buses 💰 Free

Detail on the main door, National Museum of Ireland

National Museum of Ireland – Archaeology and History

Opened in 1890, the museum's collections have artifacts spanning the centuries from 2000 BC to the 20th century. The archeological section includes relics from the Iron Age to the 15th century. Prehistoric and Viking Ireland, Ireland's Gold, Medieval Ireland, Roman World and Ancient Egypt collections breathe life into each era. Don't miss the eighth-century, jewel-encrusted Celtic Tara Brooch, one of the museum's most prized possessions and considered the finest of its kind.

➕ C2 ✉ Kildare Street ☎ 01 677 7444; www.museum.ie 🕐 Tue.–Sat. 10–5, Sun. 2–5 🍴 Café 🚌 All city center (An Lar) buses 💷 Free

National Museum of Ireland – Decorative Arts and History

Collins Barracks, built in 1701 and occupying 18 acres north of the Liffey, is the oldest military barracks in Europe. When the National Museum purchased the large, rather austere building in 1994, its decorative arts, weapons, furniture, costumes, silver, ceramics and glassware collections were moved from their Kildare Street home and installed in these more spacious rooms. The radical Protestant barrister Wolfe Tone,

who set up the United Irishmen in Belfast, was held prisoner here and his pocketbook from that time is among the items on display.

➕ Off map at A3 ✉ Benburb Street ☎ 01 677 7444; www.museum.ie 🕐 Tue.–Sat. 10–5, Sun. 2–5 🍴 Café 🚌 25, 25A, 66, 67, 90; Museum Luas 💷 Free ℹ Audiovisual room and community education room

Number Twenty-Nine

So perfectly has this four-story townhouse been restored to its late 18th-century comfort and elegance that you may feel you're an invited guest of the middle-class family who occupied it back then. From top to bottom, every item is authentic to the period, whether genuine antique or a meticulous reproduction by Irish artisans. The living rooms are the epitome of respectability, and the upper-floor bedrooms, especially the nursery – where you can admire an enormous dolls' house – exude charm.

➕ C2 ✉ Lower Fitzwilliam Street (entrance on corner of Upper Mount Street) ☎ 01 702 6165; www.esb.ie/no29 🕐 Tue.–Sat. 10–5, Sun. noon–5; closed 2 weeks at Christmas 🍴 Tearoom 🚌 7, 10, 45 (from city center) 💷 $$

Old Jameson Distillery

Back in the sixth century, *uisce beatha* (pronounced "ish-ke ba-ha") which translates as "the water of life," was the name given to Ireland's blended whiskey. It was in due course anglicized to "fuisce" before evolving into "whiskey." The Jameson Distillery, housed in an old warehouse that once used to mature whiskey, features an audiovisual history of the making of Irish whiskey, an interesting museum that includes a copper-pot still, distillery model and other implements of the trade. With any luck, you'll be chosen as one of four tasters to sample various brands. Luck or no luck, everyone gets a sample at the end of the tour, in JJ's bar. When you bend an elbow, don't forget to turn to your neighbor and raise your glass in the traditional Irish toast, *slainte* (pronounced "slawn-che") – meaning "good health."

➕ A3 ✉ Bow Street, Smithfield ☎ 01 807 2355; www.jamesonwhiskey.com 🕐 Mon.–Sat. 9:30–6, Sun. 10–6 🍴 3rd Still Restaurant 🚌 68, 69, 79, 90; Smithfield Luas 💲 $$$

Oscar Wilde House

In the northwest corner of Merrion Square resides the wonderful statue of Oscar Wilde languishing on a rock. Dressed in a velvet smoking jacket, Wilde appears incredibly lifelike and is especially haunting when illuminated at night. Across the road the house he lived and was educated in as a child between 1855 and 1876, with its exceptional cornices and architraves, is a fine example of the Georgian architecture so typical of this part of Dublin. Now owned by the American College Dublin, students study on the top two floors while the first floor is used for private functions, art exhibitions and cultural events.

➕ C2 ✉ 1 Merrion Square ☎ 01 662 1896; www.amcd.ie/about-us/history/oscar-wilde-house 🕐 House not open to visitors 🚌 Cross-city buses

St. Audoen's Church of Ireland and Roman Catholic Church

The Celtic Church of St. Columcille stood on this site before the Normans replaced it in 1190, dedicating it to St. Ouen (eventually corrupted to its present spelling). The three bells in its tower are reputed to be the oldest still in Ireland (1423), and there's a pre-1309 Christian gravestone known as the "Lucky Stone," which supposedly possesses strange powers. Of note is the 1190 west doorway and the 13th-century nave. The churchyard park is bordered by part of the old city walls, and steps descend to St. Audoen's Arch, the only surviving gateway of the old city.

The Roman Catholic church next door is a much younger building, dating from 1847, and much more intact than its neighbor. The fine interior is accessible by a side door. The two giant clam shells, relics of a Pacific Ocean voyage, are used as holy water containers.

➕ A3 ✉ Cornmarket, High Street ☎ 01 677 0088; www.heritageireland.ie 🕐 Daily 9:30–5:30, end Apr.–Oct. 🚌 21A, 78A, 78B 💲 Free

St. Michan's Church

St. Michan's Church dates to the 17th century, its square tower all that remains of an earlier Danish church that stood on this site. Through some strange process not fully understood, elements from the soil and the air in the crypt combine to perfectly preserve remains that have lain here for centuries. Mummified bodies, which include those of a 15th-century nun and the Sheare Brothers (patriots executed for treason during the 1798 rebellion), can be viewed through a small hatch. Their co-conspirator in that rebellion, Robert Emmet, was comforted by St. Michan's rector in the last hours of his life, and his remains are reputed to be buried in the churchyard.

➕ A3 ✉ Church Street ☎ 01 872 4154 🕐 Mon.–Fri. 10–12:45 and 2–4:45, Sat. 10–12:45, Mar.–Oct.; Mon.–Fri. 12:30–3:30, rest of year 🚌 83; Smithfield Luas 💲 $$

Banners in St. Patrick's Cathedral (see page 84)

St. Patrick's Cathedral

St. Patrick is said to have baptized Christians on this site, and there's been a church here since AD 450. The present building, the largest church in the country, replaced the earlier structure in 1191. From 1320 to 1520, this was Ireland's first university. In the 17th century Oliver Cromwell's troops used it as a stable, while Huguenots worshiped here from 1666 to 1816. Reminders of its long history bombard your view on all sides, from Celtic gravestones to centuries-old Irish regimental banners to memorials for some of Ireland's most famous citizens, including Carolan, last practitioner of the Irish bardic tradition. The tomb of the cathedral's best-known dean (1713–1745), Jonathan Swift (author of *Gulliver's Travels* and witty, satiric essays), can be found in the south aisle near that of his beloved "Stella." Christians of all denominations are welcome at all church services.

✚ A2 ✉ St. Patrick's Street ☎ 01 453 9472; www.stpatrickscathedral.ie ⏰ Mon.–Fri. 9–5, Sat. 9–6, Sun. 9–10:30, 12:30–2:30 and 4:30–6 (Nov.–Mar. open until 2:30 on Sun. only); no tours during services on Sun. 10.45–12:30, 2:45–4:30 🚌 50, 54A, 56A (from Eden Quay) 💷 $$

St. Stephen's Green

Since 1690, peaceful St. Stephen's Green, at the foot of Grafton Street, has been preserved as a bucolic respite from the hustle and bustle of city streets. It is beautifully landscaped with a lovely artificial lake and a network of pathways threading their way through colorful flower beds. There are numerous statues and busts of famous Irish men and women dotted about, including impressions of James Joyce, Robert Emmet, Wolfe Tone and Sir Arthur Guinness. The park is surrounded by some of the finest buildings in Dublin, dating back to the city's Georgian prime. Architectural gems include the fashionable Shelbourne Hotel, with statues of Nubian princesses and their ankle-fettered slaves decorating the

An eye-catching statue outside the Shelbourne Hotel

front, and the neo-Byzantine interior of the atmospheric Roman Catholic University Church. Dublin office and shop workers often head for the Green for a picnic lunch, and visitors also gravitate to its peaceful tranquility in the very heart of the city.

✚ B2 ⏰ Mon.–Sat. 8–dusk, Sun. 10–dusk 🚌 All city center (An Lar) buses; St. Stephen's Green Luas

Trinity College and the *Book of Kells*

Trinity College was founded by Queen Elizabeth I in 1592 on a 40-acre site in the heart of the city "to civilize Ireland with both learning and the Protestant religion." Catholics were allowed entry as well as free education – provided they converted to Protestantism. The roll of honor is impressive: Edmund Burke, Jonathan Swift, Oliver Goldsmith, Bram Stoker, Wolfe Tone, William Congreve, J. M. Synge and Samuel Beckett all passed through these hallowed portals.

Walk through the gates and you're in a world of cobbled squares and red-brick buildings from the early 1700s called the Rubrics, the college's oldest surviving structures. The lofty vaulted Long Room and Colonnades Gallery in the Old Library hold some of Ireland's most important antiquities, including the magnificently illustrated *Book of Kells* (created *circa* AD 800). The richness of color and design throughout this four-volume, handwritten, Latin transcript of the four gospels is stunning. "The *Book of Kells*, Turning Darkness into Light" is a major exhibition in the Old Library that explains the context of the book and highlights the rare manuscript. Also on display are the beautiful ancient books of Durrow and Armagh.

Since 1801 Trinity College has had – like the British Library in London and the Bodleian in Oxford – the right under copyright law to claim a free copy of all British and Irish publications, and now houses a vast collection of nearly three million volumes in eight buildings. Even on a stringent selection basis, nearly half a mile of new shelving is required each year to house newly acquired publications, which are now kept off-site.

✚ B3 ✉ College Green ☎ 01 896 2320; www.bookofkells.ie 🏛 Old Library: Mon.–Sat. 9:30–5, Sun. 9:30–4:30 (Sun. noon–4:30, Oct.–Apr.); closed 10 days over Christmas and New Year 🚌 All city center (An Lar) buses 💰 Campus free; Old Library $$$

Over 200,000 ancient books are on display in the the Long Room Library, Trinity College

Walk
South of
the Liffey

Refer to route marked on city
map on page 65

Dublin is a small, vibrant city that's
a delight to explore on foot. From
broad O'Connell Street on the
northside to the leafy green spaces of
St. Stephen's Green on the southside
and the tiny lanes of Temple Bar, you
can soak up the atmosphere of a city
steeped in history, firmly in step
with today and yet looking forward
to tomorrow. Allow about three
hours for this walk.

Begin at the tourist office on Suffolk Street,
turn left onto Andrews Street, then right
down Trinity Street to Dame Street. Cross
Dame Street to the Central Bank Plaza and
Cope Street into Crown Alley (behind the
bank) to reach Temple Bar.

Chances are that something will be
going on in Temple Bar. Allow time to
wander the maze of tiny 18th-century
cobblestone streets that only a few years
ago were lined with ancient, dilapidated
warehouses. Urban renewal has brought
an amazing cultural vibrancy to this
area, with street entertainment that
includes jazz, ethnic and rock concerts,
street theater, art exhibits and The Ark,
an arts center and theater for children.
Look for the Temple Bar Gallery and
Studios and some of Dublin's most
interesting shops, quirky boutiques and
equally interesting restaurants, cafés
and pubs (see page 67). Crown Alley
takes you to Temple Bar Square (site of
many open-air entertainments and
sidewalk artists) and Merchants Arch,
through which you will see the
rejuventated, cream-colored Ha'penny
Bridge, which exacted a half-penny toll
from pedestrians from 1816 to 1919.

Walk left along Temple Bar Street to
Parliament Street, turn left and walk to the
City Hall.

The Corinthian-style City Hall was built
between 1769 and 1777 as the Royal
Exchange, and it is now the venue for
meetings of Dublin City Council. Its
impressive entrance rotunda displays
statues of Daniel O'Connell and other
Irish leaders, and the corporation's coat
of arms and motto are represented in the
floor mosaic. During the 1780s, this was
a meeting point for volunteer rallies, and
during the 1798 rebellion it was used by
government troops as barracks and
torture chambers. The roadway outside
City Hall was once the entrance to the
medieval city through the Dame Gate.

Turn left onto Dame Street, cross the road
and turn right into Upper Castle Yard where
you'll see a gate into Dublin Castle.

Dublin Castle (see page 72) really
doesn't look much like a castle these
days. That's because of drastic 18th-
century renovations that left intact only
a few of the original towers (1204) and
no trace of the curtain wall's massive
towers, drawbridge or portcullis.
Surviving today are the record tower and
the Bermingham tower (14th century).
Dubliners will point out with a wry
smile that Van Nost's statue of justice
atop the upper castle yard gate was
placed with its back to the city's citizens.
The elegant state apartments are open to
the public, as are 10th-century Viking
defenses, exposed by renovation work in
1990, and the impressive Chester Beatty
Library (see page 70).

Walk east along Dame Street, continue east
on Dame Street to meet College Green.

The Bank of Ireland, a magnificent
Georgian structure, only became a bank
in 1800 after the Irish Parliament
legislated its own death when it passed
the detested Act of Union. The elegant
former House of Lords is open to the
public for tours (see page 70). Opposite
the bank is Trinity College (see page 84)
and you'll find the beautifully decorated
Book of Kells in the Old Library building

View over the River Liffey towards Ha'penny Bridge and the Bachelors Walk area of Dublin

(to the right of the Campanile, which is in front of you as you enter from College Green). While Catholics were barred from attending Trinity College until 1966 unless they obtained dispensation or converted to Protestantism, women (non-Catholics, of course) were admitted as early as 1903. On the corner of Grafton Street, the Provost's House is a superb Georgian mansion.

From College Green, walk south on Grafton Street, a pedestrian avenue lined with fashionable stores. The lovely bronze statue near the corner of Nassau and Grafton streets depicts Molly Malone of the "Dublin's Fair City" song. The figure has been irreverently (but affectionately) dubbed the "Tart With the Cart." Turn right at Johnson's Court, a narrow lane, and proceed to the Powerscourt shopping center.

Set in a 1774 townhouse built by Lord Powerscourt, this shopping center is a far cry from its modern counterparts. Both the house itself and the courtyard have been only slightly modified to accommodate a wide variety of small stores and restaurants.

Return to Grafton Street and walk south.

At the foot of Grafton Street, St. Stephen's Green is a landscaped oasis of greenery and calm in the heart of the city and is a favorite sunning and lunching spot for Dubliners. Once known as "Beaux Walk," the north side of the Green now houses some of Dublin's most prestigious private clubs.

Turn left on St. Stephen's Green North, then left onto Dawson Street for Mansion House.

In January 1919 the first assembly of Dáil Éireann (the Irish Parliament) met in this beautiful 1710 mansion, now the official residence of the Lord Mayor of Dublin. It is used mainly for receptions and exhibitions and is not open to the public.

Return to St. Stephen's Green North and take the next left onto Kildare Street. Leinster House (see page 80) is on your right. From the north end of Kildare Street, turn right onto Nassau Street, which becomes Leinster Street, then Clare Street, then Merrion Square.

Take a look at the blue plaques on many of the Georgian houses that line this square, one of Dublin's finest. They commemorate notable former residents such as W. B. Yeats and Daniel O'Connell. **Continue south along the west side of the square, which becomes Merrion Street, then turn left onto Lower Baggot Street. Turn right onto Fitzwilliam Street and on your right is Fitzwilliam Square.**

A pocket of well-preserved Georgian architecture, this square, although among the city's smallest, is worth browsing to appreciate elegant fanlights above front doors, elaborate iron bootscrapers and other ingenious details such as glass recesses for lamps. The studio of one of Ireland's most famous artists, Jack B. Yeats, brother of W. B. Yeats, was in No. 18.

Dublin's Literary Greats

For such a small country, Ireland has contributed an inordinate number of articulate, sharp-witted writers, and Dublin has been home to many of the best of them.

Samuel Beckett

Born in Cooldrinagh in Foxrock, Dublin in 1906, Samuel Beckett was a prolific poet, novelist and playwright who produced a body of work considered to be the greatest influence on mid-20th-century European drama. His most memorable play is undoubtedly *Waiting for Godot*, quickly followed by such bleakly horrifying comedies as *End Game*.

Brendan Behan

Brendan Behan was born in Dublin in 1923. He became involved with the IRA by the age of 15 and was sentenced to jail for 14 years in 1942. He was released in a 1946 amnesty and set about chronicling his prison experiences in plays like *The Quare Fellow* and *The Hostage* in a bluntly honest, irreverent style that often angered fellow Dubliners. He died in 1964 and was laid to rest in Glasnevin Cemetery.

James Joyce

The house at 41 Brighton Square West, Rathgar, was the birthplace of James Joyce in 1882. A museum devoted to Joyce memorabilia now occupies the Martello Tower in Sandymount, where he lived for a time in 1904. The tourist board has prepared a "Ulysses Map of Dublin," but the meanderings of Joyce's character Leopold Bloom can be traced from the book as unerringly as if Joyce had written a guidebook to the city rather than his *Ulysses* masterpiece. Bloomsday is celebrated every June 16.

Iris Murdoch

Born in Dublin to an Anglo-Irish family in 1919, Iris Murdoch wrote a series of highly successful intellectual novels. Several deal with conflicting loyalties of families such as her own, most notably *The Red and the Green*, published in 1965 and set in the turbulent 1916–23 period of Irish life.

Sean O'Casey

Sean O'Casey was born in 1880. Self-educated, he was deeply involved with the labor movement and the Irish Citizens Army. His first play to be accepted by the Abbey Theatre was *The Shadow of a Gunman*, a highly controversial work that caused consternation among ultra-conservative audiences. Later, *The Plough and the Stars* was to cause the most dramatic row in Ireland for years. When the Abbey refused to produce *The Silver Tassie*, O'Casey left Ireland and remained abroad until his death in 1964.

Cornelius Ryan

You'll know Cornelius Ryan, who was born in 1920 at 33 Heytesburn Street (off the South Circular Road), for his outstanding World War II accounts *The Longest Day* and *A Bridge Too Far*. He died in Washington, D.C. shortly before the latter was published in 1976.

George Bernard Shaw

Best remembered as the dramatist whose prolific output includes *St. Joan*, *Man and Superman* and a wealth of other plays, George Bernard Shaw was born at 33 Synge Street in 1856. He continued to write right up until his death in 1950. Shaw's birthplace has been restored to the way it was when he lived here and is open to the public.

Abraham Stoker

Although Abraham (Bram) Stoker, born in 1847 at 15 Marino Crescent in Clontarf, wrote a dozen novels, his literary immortality is assured by his masterpiece *Dracula*, which has moved into the world's folklore.

Jonathan Swift

The house at 7 Hoey's Court, where Jonathan Swift was born in 1667, stood very near St. Patrick's Cathedral, his last resting place after some 32 years as the cathedral's most famous dean. Trinity College (see page 84), where Swift studied, also echoes with memories of the great irreligious satirist, poet and novelist who penned such masterpieces as *Gulliver's Travels*. He died in 1745, leaving funds to found St. Patrick's Hospital for Imbeciles, the first institution of this kind in Ireland. His body of work reflects a compelling mixture of compassion and rage at mankind's behavior.

Oscar Wilde

Born at 21 Westland Row in 1856, many critics consider Oscar Wilde's finest work to be *The Ballad of Reading Gaol* (an account of his years in prison on a charge of homosexuality). His brilliance in challenging conventional thinking and espousing sometimes bizarre new ideas shines through such other works as *The Importance of Being Earnest* and his gripping novel *The Picture of Dorian Gray*.

W. B. Yeats

The birthplace of W. B. Yeats (1865) was 5 Sandymount Avenue, and from 1928 to 1932 he resided at 42 Fitzwilliam Square. Aside from his poetry and *The Celtic Twilight* about "romantic Ireland," one of Yeats's most important contributions to Irish culture was his involvement in the founding of Dublin's Abbey Theatre (see page 66). He was often seen in Toner's pub on Lower Baggot Street in Dublin.

Leinster

Regional Sights

Key to symbols

➕ map coordinates refer to the region map on
page 60 admission charge: $$$ more than €6,
$$ €4–€6, $ less than €4

See page 5 for complete key to symbols

Athlone and the Shannon

Straddling the River Shannon, the historic town of Athlone is a premier center for cruising and fishing in the heart of Ireland. The river marks a change in character between the two halves of the town, with narrow streets of old buildings grouped around the castle on the west bank and 19th- and 20th-century developments on the east. Athlone has always been an important crossing on the Shannon (*Áth Luain* means the Ford of Luan) and Athlone Castle, dating from 1210, was positioned as a powerful defense of this strategic ford of the river.

During Oliver Cromwell's rampage through Ireland, the castle was the focus of sieges of the town in 1690 and 1691. At the end of the 18th century, the ruined walls were heavily reconstructed when there was a threat of a Napoleonic invasion. A presentation in the visitor center details the siege history, and there are exhibits about the castle, the town and the power resources of the Shannon. The Museum of the Old Athlone Society in the castle keep includes medieval gravestones and mementos of the great Athlone-born tenor, John McCormack.

South of Athlone along the river is one of Ireland's holiest sites, Clonmacnoise, where St. Ciaran founded a monastery in 548. It was plundered by Irish chieftains, Vikings and Anglo-Normans, and Cromwell's forces desecrated it beyond restoration. Today you'll find among its ruins a cathedral, eight churches, two round towers, the remains of a castle, more than 200 monumental slabs and three replica sculptured high crosses. (The original crosses have been moved

to the visitor center to stop further deterioration.) There are guided tours during the summer, and an excellent presentation at the visitor center.

East of Athlone on the N6 road is Locke's Distillery. Established in 1757, Locke's was one of the first licensed distilleries in the world and operated for nearly 200 years before it closed in 1957. Restored as a museum, it uses the original machinery to demonstrate whiskey-making techniques.

The River Shannon is the longest river in Ireland. Rising in a humble pool in County Cavan, it carves a ponderous course to Limerick through the flood plains and water meadows of several counties straddling the Leinster–Connacht border. At first the landscape around the river appears monotonous – a shallow saucer of endless arable and pasture land broken by lakes, rivers and canals – and there are few memorable vistas. The smallish watery counties forming the geographical heart of Ireland are often portrayed as places to get through on the way to somewhere more interesting and facilities for visitors are limited compared with popular western or southeastern spots. However, these lakeland counties offer a less stereotyped picture of Ireland.

The Shannon is not only an important navigable waterway, but also a popular recreational base for fishing and boating activities, scenic interest and wildlife habitats. Visitors are welcomed with true Irish hospitality, with no pressure to buy sweaters or shamrock table linen!

➕ A3

Tourist information ✉ Civic Centre, Church Street
☎ 090 644 2100; www.athlone.ie Mon.–Fri. 10–1
and 1:30–5, Easter–Oct.; also Sat. 10–1:30, Jun.–Aug.
Athlone Castle ✉ St. Peter's Square ☎ 090 644
2130; www.athloneartandheritage.ie Daily 10–4:30,
May–Oct. $$
Clonmacnoise ✉ 4 miles north of Shannonbridge
on R357, Co. Offaly ☎ 090 967 4195;
www.heritageireland.ie Tours only, daily 10–7,
Jun.–Aug.; 10–5:30, Nov. to mid-Mar.; 10–6, rest of
year 🍴 Coffee shop $$

Dalkey Castle, a fortified 14th-century town house, is just 7 miles from Dublin city center

Locke's Distillery ⊠ Main Street, Kilbeggan, Co. Westmeath ☎ 05793 32134; www. lockesdistillerymuseum.com ⏰ Daily 9–6, Apr.–Oct.; 10–4, rest of year 🍴 Restaurant 💰 $$$

Avoca

Avoca, a pretty hamlet of neat white cottages in a wooded setting, is the home of Ireland's oldest hand-weaving mill dating from 1723, whose weaves, colors and patterns have won worldwide acclaim. The Avonmore and Avonbeg rivers combine to become the Avoca River here, inspiring 19th-century poet Thomas Moore's tribute "Meeting of the Waters." A path leads down to the river bank and a clearing, which holds a bust of the poet; the tree stump on which he sat while composing his famous lines is marked with a plaque.

Just 4 miles north toward Rathdrum, in one of County Wicklow's most beautifully forested areas, is Avondale House. Charles Stewart Parnell, a heroic and tragic figure among Ireland's most prominent nationalist leaders, was born and lived much of his life in this 1777 mansion. Much of his patriotic fervor undoubtedly came from his mother, an American with strong anti-British leanings. His political career was crowned by land reforms achieved by his leadership of the Land League. His popularity, however, was dealt a death blow when he was named corespondent in a divorce action against his long-time mistress Katherine (Kitty) O'Shea, and he never recovered politically. There's a

small museum filled with mementos of his life (1846–91) and an interesting gift shop. A walk in the adjacent forest park provides a restful interlude.
➕ C2

Avoca Handweavers ⊠ Old Mill, Avoca ☎ 0402 35105; www.avoca.ie ⏰ Daily 9–6, May–Oct.; 9:30–5:30, rest of year 🍴 Café 💰 Free
Avondale House and Forest Park ⊠ 1 mile south of Rathdrum ☎ 0404 46111; www.collte.outdoors.ie ⏰ Daily 11–5, mid-Apr. to Oct. (subject to change) 🍴 Restaurant 💰 $$$

Dalkey

Originally a fishing village at the southern end of Dublin Bay, Dalkey is one of the Leinster coast's most charming spots. In recent years it has become a stylish address for several stars. Nothing new, really – George Bernard Shaw lived for a time in a cottage on Dalkey Hill, and writers Flann O'Brien and Hugh Leonard (still a resident) have also called Dalkey home.

Off the coast from Collemore Harbour, 22-acre Dalkey Island is inhabited these days only by a few wild goats, but there is evidence that people lived here as early as the fourth century BC. It's a wonderful get-away-from-it-all spot, and even better if you bring a picnic. During summer it is possible to rent a boat from Bulloch Harbour to take you to the island. The Heritage Centre, located in restored Dalkey Castle, offers Living History tours with live actors, and its helpful staff can steer you to other points of interest in the area and arrange guided walks with prior notice.

Killiney Bay has been likened to the Bay of Naples, and it is best viewed from Victoria Park, a short walk from Dalkey along the Vico Road. A beautiful public beach leads to Killiney Hill and Victoria Park. Panoramic views of the bay add to the tranquility of the park's open green spaces, which are interspersed with rocky outcroppings perfect for hiking up if you want an even better view.

✚ C3

Tourist information ✉ Dublin Tourism, Suffolk Street ☎ 1850 230 330 🕐 Mon.–Sat., 9–7, Sun. 10:30–5, Jun.–Aug.; Mon.–Sat. 9–5:30, Sun. 10:30–3, rest of year

Dalkey Castle and Heritage Centre ✉ Castle Street, Dalkey ☎ 01 285 8366; www.dalkeycastle.com 🕐 Mon.–Fri. 9:30–5, Sat.–Sun. 11–5 🚉 8, DART Dalkey Station 💳 $$

Drogheda

Drogheda stands at the lowest bridging point of the River Boyne, just a few miles from the site of the famous Battle of the Boyne in 1690. Something of the historic medieval town can still be seen in the hilly streets, though little remains of the old town walls. Its most famous sight is the head of 17th-century Christian martyr Saint Oliver Plunkett, held in a shrine at St. Peter's Roman Catholic Church.

To the west of Drogheda lies the Boyne Valley, and while it is filled to bursting with historical landmarks, none is more significant than this stretch along the Louth and Meath border. It was here that William of Orange defeated James II, changing the course of Irish history dramatically. The visitor center at the restored 18th-century Oldbridge House gives an account of the battle with audiovisual presentations, maps and life-sized exhibits. There are also arms and artifacts from the time, battle trails around the grounds and a modern café overlooking the formal gardens.

The Boyne Valley is strewn with some of Ireland's most important archeological monuments, more than 40 in all, and the Brú Na Bóinne (Palace of the Boyne)

Visitor Centre in Donore unfolds their story before you set off to explore this remarkable landscape. It is also the required starting point from which to tour the two most impressive megalithic tombs, Newgrange and Knowth. The visitor center operates a minibus service to and from these wonders. The numbers for each tour are strictly limited, but the experience is well worth the wait.

Newgrange was probably built by the first settlers who came to Ireland from the European continent more than 5,000 years ago. This makes it possibly 1,000 years older than Stonehenge and the Egyptian pyramids. We know almost nothing about them or what the ornamental spirals and other decorations at this massive burial mound symbolize. We don't even know for whom the structure was built, whether holy men, chieftains or kings. What we do know is that they were skilled builders, for the corbeled roof above the burial chamber has kept out the dampness of 40 centuries, the 62-foot-long passage still serves quite well as an entry to the 19-foot-high chamber, and the stone at its entrance remains an enduring testament to prehistoric craftsmanship. This amazing 36-foot mound includes 200,000 tons of stone and a six-ton capstone. Stones as large as 16 tons each came from as far as County Wicklow.

Archeologists are constantly carrying out research at Newgrange in an effort to unravel such mysteries as the reason a roof box above the doorway is so placed that the sun's rays reach the burial chamber only at 8:58 a.m. on the shortest day of the year, and then for exactly 17 minutes!

At busy times you will have to arrive early in the day to ensure admission to Newgrange. Archeological work continues in the Boyne Valley, which means that some sites may be closed. Knowth, about a mile northwest of Newgrange, is still under excavation. Here there are two passage tombs, with another 17 smaller tombs in the immediate vicinity. Like Newgrange's, the enigmatic passage tomb artwork at Knowth is some of the finest in Europe.

✚ C4

Tourist information ✉ Mayorality Street ☎ 041 983 7070; www.drogheda.ie 🕐 Mon.–Sat. 9:30–5:30, Sun. noon–4:30

Brú Na Boînne Visitor Centre ✉ Donore, Co. Meath ☎ 041 988 0300; www.heritageireland.ie 🕐 Daily 9:30–5:30, Feb.–Apr.; 9–7, Jun. to mid-Sep.; 9–6:30,

May and mid- to end Sep.; 9:30–5:30, Oct.; 9:30–5, Nov.–Jan.

Knowth 🕐 Daily, May–Oct.; call tourist office for details. Last tour for Knowth and Newgrange departs one hour, 45 minutes before closing 🚌 Newgrange/ Knowth $$$; visitor center $

Battle of the Boyne ✉ Oldbridge, Drogheda, Co. Meath ☎ 041 980 9950; www.battleoftheboyne.ie 🕐 Daily 9:30–5:30, Mar.–Apr.; 10–6, May–Sep.; 9–5, Oct.–Feb. 🍴 Café 💲 $

The mid-18th-century St. Peter's Roman Catholic Church, Drogheda, houses the shrine of St. Oliver Plunkett

Leinster

Drive
Boyne Valley

Duration: 1–2 days

This historic 84-mile drive through Ireland's past passes through pleasant countryside rich in megalithic and early-Christian monuments.

Starting from the tourist office at Drogheda, take the R132/N1 for Belfast. After 5 miles turn left under the M1 motorway, following signposts for Boyne Drive, Monasterboice. After half a mile, turn left again.
Monasterboice was once a large monastic community. Pick your way between ancient and modern graves to see two of the finest high crosses in the country. (At the time of writing, these crosses were considered to be under threat from weather erosion, and could be moved to a visitor center.) These free-standing carvings in stone were of a quality unparalleled anywhere in Europe at the time they were erected, even more impressive when you realize that the very high round tower is a reminder that these remarkable works of art were created in the midst of Viking attacks.

The West Cross stands close to the round tower, while the 17-foot-high Cross of Muiredach – so called because of the inscription on the base, "A prayer for Muiredach by whom this cross was made" – is smaller and more perfect. The messages on these crosses follow coherent themes of God's grace to man and the parallels between Old and New Testaments. On Muiredach's Cross, look for stories of Adam and Eve, Cain and Abel, the Last Judgment and the crucifixion of Christ.

An event of religious significance of more recent times was the visit of Pope John Paul II in 1979, and the point where he celebrated Mass is marked on the main Belfast-to-Dublin road.

Continue past Monasterboice. After a mile, turn right for Old Mellifont Abbey. Continue for another mile, then turn left on the Drogheda road, R168, drive for one more mile, and turn right for Old Mellifont Abbey.
To walk in the footsteps of monks who founded Old Mellifont Abbey here on the banks of the Mattock River in 1142 is to drink in the peacefulness of a setting that invites meditation. The chapter house and ruins of the cloister still remain from the structures built in the 13th century, but only the foundations are left of the original building. An octagonal lavabo once

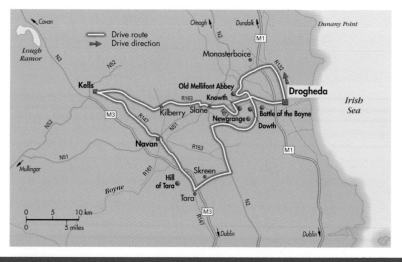

equipped with water jets and basins is the most interesting structure.

Return to the crossroads and turn right. After 2 miles turn right. Bear left at the intersection, and turn rght at the T-junction (Lynch's Cross). After a mile turn right on to the N51, then after 2.5 miles, turn left and follow signs for Newgrange (see page 92).

Irish architecture may have begun in the Boyne Valley in 3000 BC, when a people who had only stone and wood for tools created the most impressive monuments of their kind in Western Europe. Little is known of these people or of those interred in these prehistoric tombs, but excavations have shown that they cultivated crops and cleared areas of forest.

The mound at Newgrange, constructed with water-rolled pebbles, is retained by a curb of great stone blocks lying end to end, topped by white quartz and granite boulders. The passage is lined with huge stones, and the central cross-shaped chamber is roofed with a vault untouched in 5,000 years. Standing around the mound is an incomplete circle of stones.

At Dowth – where you cannot enter the site but can walk around – a larger passage tomb has two chambers, while Knowth has two passage tombs surrounded by 18 smaller ones. Knowth was used beginning in the Stone Age, and in the early Christian era was a seat of the high kings of Ireland. The significance of the Boyne Valley tombs is that here artwork combines with the engineering feats of the passage tombs of Ireland. Spirals, lozenges, zigzags, sunbursts – figures cut in stone with stone implements – decorate the monuments.

Return by minor roads to the N51 and turn left for Slane.

Slane occupies an attractive curve on the River Boyne and is overlooked by the Hill of Slane, where St. Patrick is said to have announced Christianity's arrival in Ireland. Legend or fact, the summit of

Standing stone outside the mound at Newgrange

Slane Hill would certainly have been ideal for that purpose, with its sweeping views of the Boyne Valley. From the viewpoint on the hill, the pleasant village of Slane can be seen running steeply down to the banks of the river. Just to the east is the cottage of the poet Francis Ledwidge, who died during World War I.

Slane Castle on the banks of the Boyne is the home of the Mount Charles family. Badly damaged by fire in 1991, the castle has been restored and tours are available in summer. The magnificent amphitheater in front of the house is used once a year as a spectacular stage for the largest open-air rock concerts in Ireland.

Take the N51 for Navan, and after a mile turn right on the R163 for Kells.

In the sixth century, St. Colmcille founded a monastic settlement on this site. Kells, or Ceanannus Mór, became one of the great religious centers of

Western Europe. This is where Ireland's most celebrated illuminated medieval manuscript, the famous *Book of Kells*, was written, now on display in the library at Trinity College, Dublin (see page 84). Facsimiles of the book are on display in the Kells Heritage Centre.

St. Columba's Church at the top of Market Street now stands on the monastery's original site. There are four high crosses and a round tower in the grounds, and visitors are welcome to attend services.

Take the R147/N3 (via Navan) for Dublin, and after 6 miles turn right at the sign for Tara. The Hill of Tara commands majestic views over the fertile plains of Meath and beyond. From the time that pagans worshiped here, Tara has figured in Irish history and legend. The high kings were seated here and it was the center of political and religious power before the arrival of Christianity. A *feis* (festival) at royal Tara was held at harvest or at the crowning of a king.

Detail of the Muiredach Cross, Monasterboice

Burial mounds here go back some 4,000 years, and there are earthworks dating from the Iron Age. All else of Tara's regal trappings must be left to your imagination as you view this low hillside. A presentation at the visitor center in St. Patrick's Church will give you a fuller understanding of its importance.

Five chariot roads led here from all parts of Ireland. The Rath of the Synods is an elaborate 2,000 year-old earthwork. The Mound of the Hostages, a Stone Age passage tomb that stands inside the royal enclosure, is an Iron Age hill fort and encloses the Royal Seat, a ring fort. On Cormac's House is the *Lia Fáil* (Stone of Destiny), used in the inauguration of the Irish high kings. Also here are the banquet hall, the enclosure of King Laoghaire (who is said to have been buried upright), the Sloping Trenches and Grainne's Enclosure. A statue of St. Patrick recalls his profound influence, but it was the coming of Christianity that led to the decline of Tara.

Return to the R147/N3 and turn right. After 2 miles turn left, following signs to Skreen Church and Cross, go straight through two intersections and follow an uneven road for 4.5 miles, then turn left toward Drogheda. After a mile turn left to Slane on the N2. Follow the Battle of the Boyne marked route.

It does not take a great effort of the imagination to picture the field of battle in 1690, when the armies of William of Orange and James II met in a conflict that was significant for Ireland, Britain and Europe. The Battle of the Boyne Visitor Centre at Oldbridge is located by the main battle site, while helpful signs along the way show where the opposing armies camped, where battle was joined and where the river was crossed. The route passes along the Boyne Navigation Canal, once a link in Ireland's waterways system.

Take the N51 back to Drogheda.

12th-century St. Kevin's Church is one of the surviving features of the monastery founded at Glendalough

Dun Laoghaire

This is a place to promenade along the extensive harbor piers, amble past the villas on the seafront or wander through the parks. Savor the Victorian features of the place that was called Kingstown from the visit of George IV in 1821 until the establishment of the Irish Free State. When the granite piers were completed in 1859, the harbor was the biggest artificial haven in the world. Ships and ferries to England use the port and it is home to several yacht clubs, of which the Royal St. George and the Royal Irish are the oldest. The town also boasts Ireland's National Maritime Museum, housed in the Mariners' Church.

Built during the Napoleonic Wars in the early 19th century, the Martello Tower, which was home briefly in 1904 for James Joyce and Oliver St. John Gogarty, is now a museum displaying Joyce's personal letters, manuscripts, books, photographs, walking stick, waistcoat and other personal possessions. Lectures and poetry readings are held here, and there are marvelous sea views from the parapet. The Martello Tower and the nearby

"Forty-foot" gentlemen's bathing place are vividly described in James Joyce's novel *Ulysses*.

➕ C3

Tourist information ✉ Ferry Building, Dun Laoghaire (walk-in office only) 🕐 Mon.–Fri. 9:30–5:30 **James Joyce Tower and Museum** ✉ Sandycove ☎ 01 214 3964; www.mariner.ie 🕐 Tue.–Sun. 11–5 and bank holidays 🚆 DART Sandycove Station 💷 $$$

Glendalough

Glendalough, the glen of two loughs, is the loveliest and most historic of all its County Wicklow rivals. Two beautiful loughs lie deep in a valley of granite escarpments and rocky outcrops. On its green slopes are the gentle contours of native trees, on its ridges the jagged outline of pines. Add to this picturesque scene a soaring round tower and ruined stone churches in the valley, and you have a combination that makes Glendalough one of the most beautiful and historic places in Ireland. St. Kevin found solitude and spiritual peace in this place of exquisite natural beauty, and he lived a hermit's existence here for many years. Farther up the valley is St. Kevin's Bed, a precarious rocky ledge high on a cliff-face (only safely accessible by boat) where the saint used to sleep. When he died at an advanced age in 617, he left as his legacy the great school that had grown up around his teachings, and had gained much respect throughout the Western world as an important institution of higher learning.

Throughout this mystical glen, ruins trace the history of his time here and the turbulent centuries since. The main group of ruins are just east of the Lower Lake. Among the most interesting are the *Tempall na Skellig* (Church of the Rock) and St. Kevin's Bed (a tiny hollowed-out hole) to the east of the oratory and about 30 feet above the lake. There are several stone churches, numerous crosses and a round tower. All in all, this is a place to linger, with an excellent choice of routes for avid walkers.

✠ C2

Glendalough Visitor Centre ✉ 7 miles east of Wicklow town ☎ 0404 45352; www.glendalough.ie ⏱ Daily 9:30–6, mid-Mar. to mid-Oct.; 9:30–5, rest of year (last admission 45 minutes before closing) ☐ St. Kevin's bus service from Dublin twice daily (check with website for times of departure ☎ 01 281 8119; www.glendaloughbus.com) 🎟 $$$

Howth

The pretty village of Howth sits at the northern end of Dublin Bay's curve, and Howth Castle crowns a steep hill with splendid views of the bay and village. While the castle is not usually open to the public, visitors are welcome to walk the pathways of its renowned 30-acre garden, which is open all year. In May and June more than 2,000 varieties of rhododendron burst into bloom. The Transport Museum on the castle grounds holds a small collection of horse-drawn trams and buses, as well as other public and military forms of transportation. A growing suburb of Dublin, this fishing village still has a busy harbor.

✠ C3

Howth Castle Gardens and Transport Museum
☎ 01 832 0427; www.nationaltransportmuseum.org ⏱ Castle gardens: Mon.–Sat. dawn–dusk; museum: Mon.–Sat. 10–5, Jun.–Aug.; Sat.–Sun. 2–5, rest of year ☐ 31, DART Howth Station 🎟 Museum $

Kilkenny

Kilkenny's narrow, winding streets and well-preserved structures make it a perfect example of a medieval town in Ireland today. Its Irish name is Cill

Yachts in Howth Harbour, less than 10 miles from Dublin city center

Kilkenny Castle, overlooking the Nore, has towers and sections of curtain wall dating from the 12th century

Chainnigh (St. Canice's Church). A little monastery was established here by the saint in the sixth century on the grounds of the present St. Canice's Cathedral, whose round tower dates back to the original settlement. But it was the Normans and later the Anglo-Normans who built up the town as a trading center, which was protected by royalty until the mid-14th century.

It was in 1366 that the infamous Statutes of Kilkenny forbade any mingling of Anglo-Normans with the native Irish. By the time Englishman Oliver Cromwell arrived in 1650, the city's population was demoralized, making it easy for him to seize the town, slaughter many residents and banish others to Connacht and confiscate their property.

Both Kilkenny Castle and the lovely 13th-century St. Canice's Cathedral were badly treated by the occupiers. Now beautifully restored, the cathedral is a repository for many fine medieval monuments, including 13th-century carvings and colorful stained-glass windows. In good weather you can climb its ninth-century tower for views over the town.

The impressive Kilkenny Castle, seat of the Butler family, was also restored and continued to be used as a residence until 1935. In 1967 the Marquess and Earl of Ormonde sold the dilapidated castle for a nominal £50 to the people of Kilkenny, who passed it on to the state. Rich in artworks and elegant furnishings, it is open for tours led by guides well-versed in stories of past inhabitants. Ask about

"Black Tom," and get set to hear some far-fetched tales.

Taking a leisurely stroll around the streets of Kilkenny is a delight. Opposite the castle is Kilkenny Design Centre. Established in the 1960s, it is the spearhead of a crafts revival, showcasing carefully chosen pieces from more than 200 studios and workshops countrywide. Also be sure to visit the Rothe House on Parliament Street, a typical Tudor home, and the Tholsel, Kilkenny's arcaded city hall, which was erected in 1761 as a tollhouse and market. Note its curious octagonal copper clock tower.

Dunmore Cave, 7 miles from Kilkenny, is chronicled as the site of a Viking massacre in 928. Once feared as a gate of hell, it is now well lit and fun to explore. ✚ B2

Tourist information ✉ Shee Alms House, Rose Inn Street ☎ 056 77 51500; www.kilkennytourism.ie ⏰ Mon.–Sat. 9:15–5 (Good Friday 10–2)

St. Canice's Cathedral ✉ Irishtown ☎ 056 77 64971; www.stcanicescathedral.com ⏰ Mon.–Sat. 9–6, Sun. 1–6, Jun.–Aug.; Mon.–Sat. 10–1 and 2–5, Sun. 2–5, Apr.–May and Sep.; Mon.–Sat. 10–1 and 2–4, Sun. 2–4, Oct.–Mar. 🖐 $$

Kilkenny Castle ✉ The Parade ☎ 056 770 4100 ⏰ Daily 9:30–5, Mar., 9:30–5:30, Apr.–May and Sep., 9–5:30, Jun.–Aug., 9:30–4:30, Oct.–Feb. 🖐 $$

Kilkenny Design Centre ✉ Castle Yard ☎ 056 77 22118; www.kilkennydesign.com ⏰ Mon.–Sat. 10–7, Sun. 11–7, Apr.–Dec.; Mon.–Sat. 10–6, rest of year

Dunmore Cave ✉ Ballyfoyle, 7 miles from Kilkenny ☎ 056 77 67726 ⏰ Daily 9:30–6:30, mid-Jun. to mid-Sep.; 9:30–5, Mar. to mid-Jun. and mid-Sep. to Oct.; Wed.–Sun. 9:30–5, Nov.–Feb. 🍴 Tearooms 🖐 $

Drive
Castles and Ecclesial Gems

Duration: 1–2 days

Norman castles, ecclesial ruins and tales of medieval witches haunt Kilkenny, the starting point for this 201-mile drive. Kildare's horse country appeals to followers of the sport of kings, and beautiful gardens near Portlaoise have universal appeal. Celtic kings and St. Patrick draw you on to Cashel.

From the tourist office in Kilkenny, take the R700 southeast for 11 miles to Thomastown. This prosperous little market town on the banks of the River Nore is named after Thomas FitzAnthony Walsh,

seneschal of Leinster, who built a castle and walled the town in the early 13th century. Among its interesting and ancient ruins are the remains of the 13th-century church, where there are fragments of a high cross and some badly weathered effigies. Three miles away, the Kilfane church ruins have an impressive medieval stone effigy of a crusader in full armor. Grennan Castle, 1.5 miles to the southwest, is now in ruins. The most impressive remains of ancient buildings in the town are those of a large church dating to the 13th century.

  Jerpoint Cistercian Abbey, 2 miles southwest of Thomastown on the N9, is one of Ireland's finest monastic ruins. Founded in the 12th century, it was dissolved and its lands given to James Butler, Earl of Ormond, in 1541. The extensive remains are awe-inspiring, with the original Romanesque pillars, a fine chancel and the most decorative

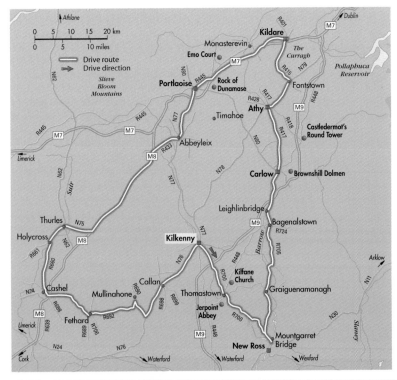

cloister arcade of any Irish church. The detailed secular and religious carved figures are an accurate portrayal of the armor and clothing of 15th- and 16th-century Ireland. A small visitor center provides information on the abbey's long history, and has picnic grounds. Jerpoint Abbey dates back to 1158, and the riverside ruins of the Benedictine and later Cistercian monastery contain many monuments and sculptures of saints and knights from medieval times. Here you'll find a 15th-century tower and cloister.

Mount Juliet (follow the signs from the town center), was once one of Ireland's largest private estates, covering 1,411 acres of woodlands, pastures and landscaped lawns. Now a luxury hotel, the grounds provide an exceptionally beautiful drive off the main roads, and its public rooms are open to everyone. **Take the R700 southeast for 14 miles to Mountgarret Bridge, where it joins the N30 for the short drive to New Ross.** There is much evidence of medieval origins in the narrow streets of New Ross, which was built on a steep hill overlooking the River Barrow.

The town invites exploration on foot, as many of the streets are stepped and inaccessible to vehicles. The long bridge in the town center connects County Wexford to County Kilkenny. The original bridge was built around 1200 and the town was soon walled. In 1643, New Ross held off a siege by the Duke of Ormonde, but fell to Englishman Oliver Cromwell just six years later. It was captured and then lost by insurgents in 1798, leaving the town in flames and many of its inhabitants slain.

The Tholsel (Town Hall) had to be rebuilt in 1806 when the original 18th-century structure fell victim to subsidence. It has a fine clock tower and holds the maces of kings Edward III and Charles II and ancient volumes of the minutes of the old town corporation. The 1798 memorial at the Tholsel

depicts a "croppy boy," typical of the insurgents who assaulted the town. **Head north on the N30, turn left on the R700, then right after a short distance on the R705 for 23 miles to join the M9 at Leighlinbridge for the 7-mile drive into Carlow.**

The village of Graiguenamanagh (the Granary of the Monks), between New Ross and Carlow, was once a place of great ecclesiastical importance. Occupying the site was the Abbey of Duiske, built between 1207 and 1240. It was suppressed in 1536, but determined monks stayed on for many years afterward before abandoning the extensive settlement. By 1774 it stood in ruins and the tower collapsed. A large part of the church was roofed in 1813 and Catholic services were resumed. In the 1970s, a group of dedicated locals undertook a major restoration, and today the completely restored abbey serves as the parish church.

The county town of Ireland's second smallest county, Carlow was an Anglo-Norman stronghold, strategically placed on the border of the English "Pale," a protected area around Dublin and its environs. The 640 insurgents who fell here during their 1798 attack on the town are remembered by a fine Celtic cross.

The west wall and the two flanking towers of 13th-century Carlow Castle can be seen near the bridge across the Barrow. This Norman castle was destroyed not by Cromwell, who captured it in 1650, but by one Dr. Middleton in 1814. In his zeal to convert it into an asylum, he tried to reduce the thickness of the walls with explosives, rendering it no more than a dangerous shell, most of which had to be demolished. The ruins of the castle, a stronghold of the earls of Thomond, are near the Barrow Bridge.

The Cathedral of the Assumption on Tullow Street is a fine Gothic-style building erected between 1828 and 1833. Of special interest are its 151-foot lantern tower and the marble monument of the 19th-century political writer Bishop Doyle by the renowned sculptor John Hogan.

Two miles east of Carlow on the L7, Brownshill Dolmen is thought to be the largest of these structures in Europe, topped by a 100-ton capstone. Its exact purpose is a matter of speculation, but many believe the megalithic structure marks the burial place of an ancient local king.

Follow the R417 north to Athy. Turn northeast on the N78 toward Kilcullen, then northwest on the R415 going under the M7 expressway, west to Kildare.
En route to Kildare, stop in Athy to view the strikingly modern Dominican church. Inside are George Campbell's outstanding Stations of the Cross. To the southeast of Athy, Castledermot's ecclesiastical ruins are a round tower, two high crosses and the remains of a Franciscan friary church.

In the heart of Ireland's horse-breeding and training country, the market town of Kildare sits on the edge of the vast Curragh plain, and the National Stud, Ireland's most famous breeding ground, is nearby. Stroll around here and you'll understand why Irish horses are so prized around the world. You can visit the stalls and watch horses being groomed and exercised. The history of the horse from prehistoric times to the present day is represented in the Horse Museum. The Japanese garden, whose design symbolizes the lifespan of man, took four years to lay out (1906–10) and today is considered Europe's finest Oriental garden (see page 108).

East of town, horse racing has reigned supreme for centuries at The Curragh, where all the Irish Classics are run. The Curragh Camp, handed over to the Irish army in 1922, has been an important military station for a century. Here you can see the famous 1920 armored car "Slievenamon" in which Michael Collins was traveling when the fatal ambush of 1922 took place.

The Hill of Allen, legendary home of Irish folk hero Finn MacCool (see page 199) and the site of three royal residences in ancient Leinster, is northeast of town and is crowned by a 19th-century battlemented stone tower.
Take the M7 southeast to Portlaoise.
Set at the intersection of the Dublin-to-Limerick and Dublin-to-Cork main roads, Portlaoise is also the site of Ireland's national prison. Four miles east of town, the Rock of Dunamase rises 200 feet above the plain, with the ruined 12th-century castle of Dermot MacMurrough, one-time king of Leinster.

Emo Court, 8 miles northeast of Portlaoise off the N7, is probably the premier attraction of County Laois. "Magnificent" is the only word for this neoclassical mansion designed in 1790 by the celebrated architect James Gandon, designer of the Custom House and several other Dublin landmark buildings. The grand house is open to the public by guided tour only. The formal gardens and extensive parkland are famous for their statuary, an avenue of giant sequoia trees and sweeping lawns dotted with neatly clipped yew trees, all providing a perfect foil for this fascinating mansion. If you enjoy walking, the superb lake and woodland areas are a real treat.

To the west of town, the many roads crossing the Slieve Bloom Mountains offer scenic drives.
Take the N77 for 9 miles south to Abbeyleix.
This attractive town has tree-lined streets, neat town houses and a fountain in the square. It is noted for the de Vesci Demesne, known as Abbeyleix House. The great house, which dates to 1773, is not open to the public, but the splendid grounds are. They include formal terrace gardens to the west of the house, a "wild garden" called the Paradise Garden, which is carpeted with bluebells in spring, and an American garden with magnolia trees. There is also a magnificent avenue of lime trees. The

Heritage House in Abbeyleix is a fine example of Gothic architecture built in 1884 and designed to be a focus for visitors to this historic town. Interactive multimedia displays tell the story of Abbeyleix and the surrounding area.
Take the R433, then the M8 southwest to the N75 turnoff to Thurles.
In ancient times, the O'Fogartys fortified this site on the River Suir, and although the Norman Strongbow's army was soundly defeated here in 1174, Anglo-Normans returned later to build a castle that would protect the crossing. Today it is a busy, well-laid-out marketing center for the surrounding agricultural area. It is also the cathedral town of the archdiocese of Cashel and Emly.
Take the R660 south for 13 miles to reach Cashel.
Cashel is a prosperous town best known for the Rock of Cashel (see page 129). Look above the second floor of the store opposite city hall to see the battlements and gargoyles of what was 15th-century Quirke's Castle, named for a family who lived there in the 19th century. At the southwest end of Main Street, the ornamental fountain is in memory of Dean Kinane and his efforts to bring a much-needed extension of the railway to Cashel in 1904.
Take the R692 southeast to Fethard.
Fethard was an important Anglo-Norman settlement in medieval times. Remnants of the old town walls and their towers can still be seen. In the town center there are keeps of three 15th-century castles, including that of Fethard Castle. Well-preserved remains of a 14th-century Augustinian priory contain several 16th- and 17th-century tombs. More than 1,000 exhibits depicting rural life in this part of Ireland are on display at the Folk, Farm and Transport Museum.
Take the R692 northeast to Mullinahone. Turn right for Callan, then turn north on the N76 for the 11-mile drive back to Kilkenny.

Jerpoint Abbey ✉ Thomastown, Co. Kilkenny ☎ 056 772 4623; www.heritageireland.ie ◷ Daily 9–5:30, early Mar.–Sep.; 9–5, Oct.; 9:30–4, Nov.–early Dec.; pre-booked tours only, early Dec.–early Mar.; closed Christmas period ❚❚ Tearooms 💷 $$
The National Stud ✉ Tully, Kildare, Co. Kildare (off Dublin to Limerick road, N7) ☎ 045 521 617; www.irishnationalstud.ie ◷ Daily 9:30–5, mid-Feb. to Dec. ❚❚ Restaurant 💷 $$$
Emo Court ✉ Emo, Co. Laois (6 miles northeast of Portlaoise) ☎ 05786 26573; www.heritageireland.ie ◷ Daily 10–6, Easter–Sep.; gardens: daily dawn–dusk 💷 $
The Heritage House ✉ Abbeyleix, Co. Laois ☎ 057 873 1653; www.heritagehousemuseum.com ◷ Mon.–Fri. 9–5, Sat.–Sun. 1–5, May–Sep.; Mon.–Fri. 1–5, rest of year 💷 $
Fethard Folk Farm and Transport Museum ✉ Cashel Road, Fethard ☎ 052 31516 ◷ Sun. 11–4:30 💷 $

The mysterious Brownshill Dolmen

Malahide

The speed at which Malahide is growing as a favored residential suburb of Dublin has not robbed it of its old-fashioned seaside atmosphere, and its popularity is enhanced by many quality restaurants. There is a good beach to the east of the town, and an even better one farther along the coast at Portmarnock. There are two historic buildings on the way to Portmarnock – a martello tower, built in the early 1800s as a provision against Napoleonic invasion, and Robswall's Castle, a tower house to which a Victorian house has been added.

Malahide's most famous relic of history is its castle, one of the major showpieces of the Dublin area. Its core is medieval and, in spite of considerable changes from the intervening centuries, it still appears from the outside as a product of the Middle Ages. Malahide Castle is the stately residence that was occupied until 1973 by the descendants of Lord Talbot de Malahide, its founder in 1185. One of the many historic happenings within its walls occurred in 1690 when some 14 Talbot cousins sat down to breakfast together one morning before leaving to fight for King James II in the Battle of the Boyne, a battle in which all met their deaths.

Set on 268 acres, its formal gardens alone are worth a visit, and the castle still retains traces of the original moat. Inside there is magnificent oak paneling

and plasterwork, fine Irish period furniture and many paintings.

The castle reopened in summer 2012 following renovations and now offers a revitalized visitor experience, with a castle tour, interpretative center, exhibition of Irish and local history, a secret garden, café and shop.

A separate building holds the Fry Model Railway Museum, the first of its kind in Ireland, with more than 300 handmade model trains, trams and railroad artifacts left by the late Cyril Fry, an enthusiastic railway engineer.

North of Malahide is Newbridge House, another magnificent mansion on 350 acres. Dating from 1737, it has one of the finest Georgian interiors in the country. The great red drawing room is just as it was when the Cobbe family lived here, giving you a perfect picture of how wealthy families entertained. To see how the house staff and the estate-workers kept the wheels turning, visit the kitchen and laundry, as well as the coach house, dairy, carpenter's shop and blacksmith's forge, all equipped with 19th-century implements. Within the grounds there's a 29-acre traditional farm, complete with farm animals, which is always a hit with little ones.

✚ C3

Tourist information ✉ Dublin Tourism, Suffolk Street ☎ 01 605 7700 🕐 Mon.–Sat. 9–7, Sun. 10:30–5, Jun.– Aug.; Mon.–Sat. 9–5:30, Sun. 10:30–3, rest of year

Malahide Castle and Fry Model Railway Museum
✉ Malahide ☎ 01 846 2184, www.malahidecastle. com 🕐 Castle: daily 10–5, Apr.–Sep.; Mon.–Sat. 10–5, Sun. 11–5, rest of year; museum: Tue.–Sat. 10–1, 2–5; 1–5, Apr.–Sep. 🍴 Restaurant 🚌 42 (from Beresford Place), DART Connolly Station to Malahide 💶 $$$ combined ticket

Newbridge House and Traditional Farm ✉ Donabate (12 miles north of Dublin on Belfast road) ☎ 01 843 6534; www.newbridgehouseandfarm.com
🕐 Mon.–Sat. 10–5, Sun. and public hols 11–6, Apr.– Sep.; Tue.–Sun. and public hols 11–3:30, rest of year
🍴 Coffee shop 💶 House $$$; farm $

Russborough House

This, one of the most imposing of Ireland's Great Houses, was designed by architect Richard Castle for Joseph Leeson, later the Earl of Milltown. It was built from granite and in the Palladian style between 1741 and 1751, and its striking interior features fine stucco ceilings and sumptuous displays of silver, bronze and porcelain. The rhododendron garden is open in spring by appointment only.

✚ C3

✉ Blessington, Co. Wicklow (about 2 miles south of Blessington) ☎ 045 865 239; www.russborough.ie
🕐 Daily 10–6 (last tour at 5), May–Sep. 🍴 Tearoom
🚌 65 from Dublin 💶 $$$

Malahide Castle dates largely from the 14th century

Wexford

As the safest haven close to the southeastern point of Ireland, Wexford has always been a natural landing place for travelers from Wales, Cornwall in England, and France, and it was the first Irish settlement to fall to the invading Normans in 1169. They did not have the distinction of being the first invaders however – the Vikings settled here in the ninth or 10th century and gave the town its name.

Wexford exudes an air of the past, its central streets still adhering to the medieval plan, and the quays reflecting a long maritime heritage. Fragments of the medieval town walls survive. At the northern edge of town, near the train and bus station, the Westgate Tower is the only surviving gateway of five that once punctuated the old town walls. It is fairly well preserved.

Nearby Selskar Abbey is the site of the signing of the first Anglo-Irish treaty. It stands on the site of an ancient pagan temple dedicated to Odin, and later a Viking church. King Henry II came here in 1172 to do penance for the murder of the devout Thomas à Becket.

Go by the wide intersection known as the Bull Ring at the north end of Wexford's Main Street and spend a few minutes reflecting on the bravery of the pikemen who are portrayed by the bronze statue there. Until Oliver Cromwell visited his wrath on the town in 1649, a great high cross stood here; when Cromwell destroyed it, he massacred some 300 people who knelt in prayer before it. While bull-baiting was once the main attraction here, there is now an open-air market every Friday.

On Wexford's Crescent Quay, take a look at the Commodore John Barry (1745–1803) statue, and if you pass through Ballysampson, Tagoat (10 miles from Wexford), tip your hat to his birthplace – this seafaring Irishman is credited with founding the U.S. Navy after being appointed by George Washington in 1797.

Take a drive down the scenic Hook peninsula through historic and quaint old villages. The ruins of the Knights Templar's foundation still stand at Templetown; Hook lighthouse, built more than seven centuries ago, is the oldest in Europe. Near Fethard-on-Sea,

Hook Head Lighthouse, built with local limestone, is one of the oldest operational lighthouses in the world

the Normans first landed in Ireland. At Ballyhack, catch the car-ferry over to Passage East on the County Waterford side for 10 minutes on the water to see these shores as they were seen by Viking and Norman invaders.

Just three miles west of Wexford, overlooking the River Slaney, the Irish National Heritage Park is a marvelous 35-acre park holding reconstructions of historic buildings from Ireland's past. These include a campsite, farmstead and portal dolmen (tomb) from the Stone Age (7000–2000 BC) and a cist burial and stone circle from the Bronze Age (2000–500 BC). You can also view an ogham (alphabet) stone, ringfort and souterrain (an early Christian monastery), corn-drying kiln, horizontal water mill, Viking boathouse and an artificial island habitat known as a crannog, all from the Celtic and early Christian ages (500 BC to AD 1169). Also here are a Norman motte-and-bailey fortification and a round tower from the early Norman period (1169–1280). There's also a nature walk of real beauty, and an excellent craft and book shop.

In 1858, when Patrick Kennedy left Dunganstown (near New Ross, see drive page 101) for America, it was to escape the ravages of a famine. He left behind a thatched home set among stone farm buildings. A little more than a century later, his great-grandson, John Fitzgerald Kennedy, held the office of president of the United States and returned to visit his ancestral home. The John F. Kennedy Park and Arboretum is the tribute paid to the president by the Irish government and United States citizens of Irish origin. It was officially opened by President Eamon de Valera in 1968 and covers 623 acres, of which more than 300 are set aside as the arboretum. Already there are 4,500 species of trees and shrubs, and the number is expected to reach 6,000 in a few years.

In the Forest Garden, there are trees from all five continents, and shaded walks throughout the park, with shelters and resting spots. Follow the signposts to the top of Slieve Coillte and you'll be rewarded with a panoramic view of south Wexford and the splendid estuary of the Barrow, Nore and Suir rivers. Be sure to stop by the visitor center where you can see the unusual explanatory display fashioned in beaten copper.

Bird watchers should visit the reserve adjacent to Wexford Harbour, where more than 240 species of birds and more than a third of the world's Greenland white-fronted geese winter. There is an informative visitor center and observation tower.

✛ B1

Tourist information ✉ Crescent Quay
☎ 05391 23111; www.visitwexford.ie 🕐 Mon.–Fri. 9–7, Sat. 10–6, Sun. 11–5, Jul.–Aug.; Mon.–Sat. 9–6, May–Jun. and Sep.; Mon.–Fri. 9:15, Oct.–Apr.

Irish National Heritage Park ✉ Ferrycarrig (3 miles outside town) ☎ 05391 20733; www.inhp.com
🕐 Daily 9:30–6:30, May–Aug.; 9:30–5:30, rest of year
🍴 Restaurant 💰 $$$

John F. Kennedy Park and Arboretum
✉ New Ross, Co. Wexford ☎ 051 388 171 🕐 Daily 10–8, May–Aug.; 10–6:30, Apr. and Sep.; 10–5, Oct.–Mar. 🍴 Tearoom 💰 $

Wexford Wildfowl Reserve ✉ North Slob (3 miles east of Wexford town) ☎ 05391 23129; www. wexfordwildfowlreserve.ie 🕐 Daily 9–5 💰 Free

A Long Tradition of Gardens

Leinster is one of Ireland's most fertile regions, with County Wicklow billed as "The Garden of Ireland."

Fernhill Gardens
Overlooking Dublin Bay, Fernhill includes some 40 acres of parkland, woodland, rockery and water garden, with an unusually wide range of native plants and animals. Many of the trees date back over 200 years and were planted by Willliam Darley. The Kitchen Garden is enclosed within clipped beech hedges divided into four quadrants with a now rarely seen potager-style layout. A long track, the Broadwalk, leads the visitor into a lovely light woodland full of beeches, oak and larches.

Japanese Gardens and St. Fiachra's Garden
On the grounds of the Irish National Stud (see page 102), the breathtakingly beautiful Japanese Gardens' underlying theme of the "Life of Man" depicts human progression from the cradle to the grave and beyond. Japanese lanterns, small brooks crossed by Japanese-style bridges and other Oriental touches make this garden unique in Ireland.
To celebrate the millennium, St. Fiachra's Garden was planted in 1999 around a natural setting of wetland, woodland, rocks, lakes and islands.

Mount Usher Gardens
Mount Usher Gardens' 20 acres of flowers, trees, shrubs and lawns lie in the sheltered Vartry river valley and its plants come from many parts of the globe. Spindle trees from China, North American sweet gum and swamp cypress, the New Zealand ti tree, African broom and Burmese juniper are among those represented.

National Botanic Gardens
Since 1795 the National Botanic Gardens have fostered the native Irish affinity for all growing things. Their 50 acres hold a variety of garden groupings, from decorative plantings to vegetable, herbal, scientific and medicinal plants and economic plants and exotic species from around the globe. There are tropical greenhouses and a small orchid room. Dedicated

18th-century Powerscourt Gardens and mansion in Enniskerry

gardeners will delight, and even those who have never had dirt under their fingernails will find this a place of beauty and tranquility.

Powerscourt Gardens

Powerscourt Gardens were designed and laid out between 1745 and 1767. Perched on high ground with a view of Great Sugar Loaf Mountain, magnificent Japanese and Italian gardens slope downward and are dotted with statuary and ornamental lakes. The 1,000-acre estate holds rare shrubs, massive rhododendrons and a deer park.

St. Anne's Park and Rose Garden

The pretty St. Anne's Park and Rose Garden has climbers, floribunda, hybrid tea and old garden roses aplenty. In spring, daffodils are in bloom.

Tullynally Castle Gardens

The 30-acre grounds on the massive Gothic Tullynally Castle estate date from the early 1800s. In addition to ornamental lakes and a grotto, there's a Chinese garden and a Tibetan garden of streams and waterfalls. An avenue of 200-year-old yew trees leads to the walled gardens.

Fernhill Gardens ✉ Sandyford, Co. Dublin ☎ 087 264 6053 🕔 Tue.–Sat. 11–5, Sun. 2–5, Mar.–Oct. 🚌 44 🍴 $$
Japanese Gardens and St. Fiachra's Garden ✉ Tully, Co. Kildare ☎ 045 521 617; www.irishnationalstud.ie 🕔 Daily 9:30–6, mid-Feb. to Nov. 🍴 $$$
Mount Usher Gardens ✉ Ashford, Co. Wicklow ☎ 0404 40205; www.mountushergardens.ie 🕔 Daily 10:30–6, Mar.–Nov. 🍴 $$$
National Botanic Gardens ✉ Glasnevin Hill Road, Glasnevin, Dublin ☎ 01 804 0300; www.botanicgardens.ie 🕔 Mon.–Fri. 9–5, Sat.–Sun. and public hols 10–6, Mar.–Oct.; Mon.–Fri. 9–4:30, Sat.–Sun. and public hols 10–4:30, rest of year 🚌 13A, 19 🍴 Free; charge for parking
Powerscourt Gardens ✉ Enniskerry, Co. Wicklow ☎ 01 204 6000; www.powerscourt.ie/gardens 🕔 Daily 9:30–5:30; varies in winter months 🍴 $$$
St. Anne's Park and Rose Garden ✉ Mount Prospect Avenue, Clontarf, Dublin ☎ 01 833 1859 🕔 Open all the time 🚌 130 🍴 Free
Tullynally Castle Gardens ✉ Castlepollard, Co. Westmeath ☎ 04496 61159; www.tullynallycastle.com 🕔 Gardens: Thu.–Sun. 1–6, May–Sep. 🍴 Tearoom 🍴 $$

Munster

Introduction and Map 112

Cork 114

Introduction and Map 114

Sights 117

Walk: Cork's Mercantile Past 120

Drive: Island City, Magic Stone 122

Feature: Cork's Cultural Scene 125

Regional Sights 126

Drive: Ring of Kerry 138

Feature: Medieval Castle Banquets
and Traditional *Céilí* 144

Feature: Kerry's Festivals 147

Opposite: Blarney Castle and grounds in the Fall

Munster

Munster's six counties – Clare, Cork, Kerry, Limerick, Tipperary and Waterford – straddle the southern part of Ireland, which is a sort of mini version of the country in itself. Outstanding examples of the scenic, archeological, historical and cultural charms that make this country so special are liberally scattered across the face of Munster, a virtual grab-bag of sightseeing riches. Here you'll find the world-famous lakes of Killarney, Blarney's magical stone and Waterford's exquisite crystal. You'll also find the country's sunniest and driest climate in east Munster, the wettest in the west.

The dramatic coastline changes from wide, sandy beaches to steep, surf-fringed cliffs that soar above secluded coves and small fishing village harbors to deep-water commercial ports and craggy peninsulas. Mizen Head is Ireland's southernmost mainland point, crowned by a lighthouse whose summit perch overlooks striking cliffscapes. The bustling port cities of Cork, Limerick and Waterford encircle the coast, with reminders of their legends and history happily rubbing elbows with the sounds and sights of an astonishingly progressive present.

Inland mountain chains march across Munster, vibrant in spring with deep hues of rhododendrons, softened in the fall by more subtle shades of heather. To the east, the Knockmealdown and Comeragh ranges give way to the midland Galtees, Slieve Felims and Silvermines. Some of the earliest traces of the Stone Age inhabitants are found in Blackwater Valley. Ireland's highest peak, 3,406-foot-high Carrauntoohil, is the star of Kerry's Macgillycuddy's Reeks, while the gentler slopes of the

Tiny St. Finbarr's Hermitage sits beside the lake in the forest park of Gougane Barra, Cork

Slieve Mish range form the backbone of the Dingle Peninsula (Corca Dhuibhne), "the last parish before America." Ireland's famed "forty shades of green" create a glorious patchwork quilt of Tipperary's Golden Vale plain and fertile stone-walled fields. Sprinkled in this rural scene are small market towns.

Amid all these scenic splendors, ancient ringforts, dolmens, cairns and other archeological relics bring to life the ghosts of a prehistoric landscape. Monasteries, massive castles and round towers trace Christian, Viking and Norman invasions over long centuries.

If cultural and artistic activities are high on your priority list, traditional Irish music is featured in many pubs. You may find your most memorable evenings happen when that same music spontaneously breaks out in the most unlikely rural settings. Munster's cities arrange year-round programs of opera, first-rate jazz and musical and theatrical productions. Its art galleries rank with the best in Europe.

The Irish have an inborn flair for drama, and several local drama groups present surprisingly professional productions. Count yourself lucky if you run across a night of theater featuring an amateur troupe – when the last curtain falls, the cast often adjourns to the nearest pub along with members of the audience. It's great fun.

It's also great fun to show up for at least one day's racing at the three-day "meets" held at racetracks in Clonmel, Tramore, Mallow, Killarney and Limerick, where the atmosphere is not unlike that of old-time county fairs in the United States. For more energetic outdoor enthusiasts, excellent facilities for almost every sport, from golf to river (freshwater) and deep-sea fishing are never far away.

County Kerry's Dingle Peninsula and Ring of Kerry in County Waterford are important *Gaeltacht* (pronounced "gwale-tuct") areas, where Irish is still spoken every day, the language preserved and thriving.

In short, Munster is a shining example of modern Ireland building and flourishing on the enduring foundation of its past.

Cork

Cork's charter dates to 1185, by which time the city already had a rather rich and colorful past, beginning when St. Finbarr arrived in the early seventh century to found a monastery on a small swampy island cradled by hills to the north and south and called it Corcaigh (Marshy Place). Since then, Cork has seen Vikings come storming in search of plunder in the ninth century, only to settle as permanent residents, followed by the Normans in the 12th century, who stayed on to build fortifications, great churches and abbeys. It was Englishman Oliver Cromwell who broke the pattern when he captured the city in 1649 and proceeded to impose a harsh, repressive regime. Inevitably, resistance to such measures spawned a fierce sense of independence that even today underlies the Cork spirit.

Cork's status as a European Capital of Culture in 2005 resulted in a major facelift. These days, the cosmopolitan city is an important industrial and financial center, with a commercial harbor that comes right into the heart of the city. A busy ferryport 10 miles to the southeast at Ringaskiddy provides a convenient passenger service to France.

The People

The citizens of Cork are a lively, cultural bunch, among Ireland's most able traders and merchants. "Sure, it's only an accident of geography that Dublin is the capital of Ireland" is a sentiment readily expressed by Cork natives.

The people of Cork love nothing more than to show off their city, and they are quick to welcome strangers in their unique, lilting accent (delivered at breakneck speed), which may take a little getting used to. They have also retained in their speech many words and phrases that have been long disused elsewhere. If you overhear a woman described as "mauzy," you'll know that, heavy of hips, she's really "a fine lump of a woman." Friendly they most certainly are, and perhaps because of their

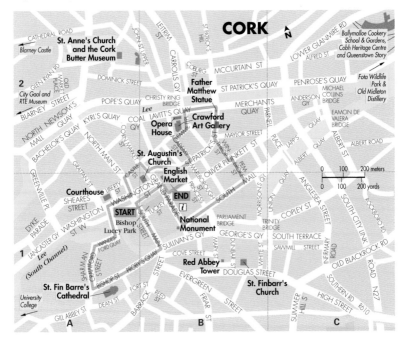

Pedestrians cross the bridge over the Lee from Sullivan's Quay to the Grand Parade

mercantile bent, that friendliness often expresses itself in practical terms.

Cork Cuisine

A leading Irish food critic based in Dublin wrote, "There are considerably more good restaurants per head of population in Cork than we can even dream of in the capital." While this might be stretching the truth, you can find almost any ethnic cuisine offered in at least one of those eateries. Menus vary from traditional boiled bacon and cabbage to gourmet European dishes. Unique to this city is drisheen, not unlike the black pudding you'll encounter throughout the country.

Cork is also home to the Beamish and Crawford brewery, now producing many varieties of beer as well as stout and tasty bitter. Irish Distillers Ltd., formerly Cork Distillers Company, gave the world Cork Dry Gin, and at Midleton, east of the city, Jameson's whiskey is made and visitors are welcomed to the Jameson Experience visitor center.

Finding Your Way Around

Cork's compact city center sits on an island ringed by the two-pronged Lee River, crossed by no fewer than 16 bridges – a bit confusing when you suddenly encounter another channel of the river you thought you had just left behind.

Vessels actually sailed up Patrick Street as late as 1760 (it was paved over in 1791), and in 1780 there was a canal down the center of the Grand Parade. The river cuts across the city from east to west and the city is bounded by hills on the north and south.

Munster

The major points of reference in the city center are St. Patrick's Street (just call it Patrick Street) and the Grand Parade. Other main arteries are Washington Street (which becomes Western Road as it runs past University College and heads out toward Killarney); South Mall, from which you turn onto Mary Street to reach Douglas Road en route to the airport; and MacCurtain Street, a busy one-way thoroughfare just across St. Patrick's Bridge that leads to both the main Cobh, Youghal and Waterford road and the Cork to Dublin highway. St. Patrick's Hill, at the foot of Patrick Street, is breathtakingly steep, its stepped sidewalk leading to a sweeping view of the city and harbor from the Montenotte section.

Essential Information

Tourist Information
Cork Kerry Regional Tourism Authority
✉ Aras Fáilte (Tourist House), Grand Parade
☎ 021 425 5100;
www.discoverireland.com/cork
🕐 Mon.–Sat. 9–6, Sun. 9:30–4:30, Jun.–Sep.;
Mon.–Sat. 9:15–5, rest of year
There is also a toll-free information service in the arrivals terminal of Cork Airport.

Urban Transportation
Double-deck buses cover the city, with 20 routes running north to south. Hours are 7 a.m. to 11 p.m. Monday through Saturday, less frequently on Sunday. Most buses can be boarded on Patrick Street. A short walk from Patrick Street, the Parnell Place Bus Station (☎ 021 450 8188) offers a frequent service to the airport and such nearby points as Blarney, Cobh, Kinsale and Crosshaven as well as major destinations around the country.

March through October, an open-air double-deck bus will get you to such Cork highlights as Cork City Gaol, City Library, St. Fin Barre's Cathedral, Crawford Municipal Art Gallery, Triskel Arts Centre, English Market, Cork Opera House, Custom House and the Courthouse. Stay on the bus for the entire 75 minutes or opt to get off at an attraction and rejoin the tour on the next bus. You can buy a ticket for the whole day at the tourist office or from the driver on the tour bus at one of its stops (Cronin's Coaches ☎ 021 430 9090; www.croninscoaches.com). Cork is well served by taxis, with major stands along Patrick Street, the South Mall and many hotels. For taxi pickup elsewhere, call Cork Taxi Co-op ☎ 021 427 2222; www.corktaxi.ie.

Cork Railway Station, Lower Glanmire Road (☎ 021 455 7277), about a five-minute walk from the city center, provides service to Cobh, Dublin, Mallow, Milstreet, Killarney and Tralee.

Airport Information
Located only 4 miles from the city center, Cork Airport (☎ 021 431 3131; www.corkairport.com) is reached via the Kinsale road and provides services to national and international destinations. There is a Skylink Express bus service every 30 minutes from the main airport entrance to Cork city bus station. It takes 15 minutes and the fare is €5 (return €8). If you're heavily loaded or in a hurry, the trip by taxi will take less time and costs around €15.

Climate – average highs and lows for the month

Jan.	Feb.	Mar.	Apr.	May	Jun.	Jul.	Aug.	Sep.	Oct.	Nov.	Dec.
8°C	8°C	9°C	12°C	14°C	16°C	16°C	18°C	16°C	13°C	10°C	8°C
46°F	46°F	48°F	54°F	57°F	61°F	61°F	64°F	64°F	55°F	50°F	46°F
4°C	4°C	4°C	5°C	8°C	10°C	12°C	12°C	11°C	8°C	5°C	4°C
39°F	39°F	39°F	41°F	46°F	50°F	54°F	54°F	52°F	46°F	41°F	39°F

Cork Sights

Ballymaloe Cookery School and Gardens

Food expert Darina Allen has brought international fame to the very best of Irish cuisine by fostering the proper use of seasonal local products in an exciting variety of cooking courses. The outstanding herb garden holds the largest collection of culinary and medicinal plants in Ireland, alongside fruit and vegetable gardens. Just for fun, wander through the Celtic maze. The restaurant practices what the school preaches in its lunch and dinner menus, and the adjoining shop stocks quality cookware.

⊞ Off map at C2 ✉ Shanagarry, East Cork, on N25 at Castlemartyr, between Youghal and Cork ☎ 021 464 6785; www.cookingisfun.ie ⊘ Gardens and shop: daily 11–5:30, May–Sep., guided tours by appointment ⓦ Gardens $$

Blarney Castle

There's a sense of tranquility about the grounds and ruins of this historic castle – and a sense of magic about its stone that, legend says, bestows the gift of eloquence on anyone who climbs the 120 steep steps to lean backward from the battlements and bestow a kiss on it.

The legend arose from Queen Elizabeth I's frustration in dealing with Irish chieftain Cormac MacCarthy, Lord of Blarney, and his smiling flattery that veiled wiliness with eloquence. Her declaration, "This is nothing but blarney – what he says, he never means!" added a new word to the English language and may have given rise to the legend of the "gift of eloquence" associated with the stone. But it was Father Prout who, in the 1830s, may have also bestowed magic on the stone when he wrote, "There is a stone there That whoever kisses Oh! He never misses To grow eloquent." However, by the time you've gone through all that exertion, you'll have earned a silver tongue! The Rock Close in the castle gardens is said to have been much favored by ancient Druids.

Take a short stroll from the castle and you'll find Blarney Woollen Mills, one of

Blarney Castle, home to the famous Blarney Stone

Ireland's oldest mills, turning out fine wools and cloths since 1741. These days, the large premises hold a vast collection of different Irish crafts to see and buy, and there's a lovely, traditional-style pub.

🕂 Off map at A2 ✉ Blarney (4 miles northwest of Cork city on N617, signposted from Patrick Street Bridge) ☎ 021 438 5252; www.blarneycastle.ie 🕐 Mon.–Sat. 9:30–6, May; 9–7, Jun.–Aug.; 9–6:30, Sep.; 9–sundown Oct.–Apr.; Sun. 9–5:30, May–Sep. 🚌 Buses and coach tours from Parnell Street Bus Station, Cork 💷 $$$ **Blarney Woollen Mills (retail shop)** ✉ Blarney ☎ 021 451 6111; www.blarney.com 🕐 Mon.–Sat. 9:30–6, Sun. 10–6

City Gaol and Radio Telefís Éireann Museum

This infamous building housed many a patriotic rebel in the late 1800s and early 1900s. Their grim prison existence is re-created vividly by fascinating exhibits and the cells in which they lived.

   On a happier note, in the former governor's house, the Radio Telefís Éireann Museum collection is well worth a visit. RTE operates Ireland's state-sponsored television and radio. Located in the original studio of 1927, exhibits cover the early days of radio. Allow two hours.

🕂 Off map at A2 ✉ Sunday's Well ☎ 021 430 5022; www.corkcitygaol.com 🕐 Daily 9:30–5, Mar.–Oct.; 10–4, rest of year 🚌 No bus service – short walk from city center 💷 Gaol $; museum $$$ (less expensive to buy a combined ticket)

Cobh Heritage Centre – The Queenstown Story

There is a heart-wrenching pull for thousands of Americans descended from Irish families who left in their hordes from Queenstown, now named Cobh, as they fled the famine in search of a better life across the ocean. Sadly, many never reached America because of the terrible conditions in the overcrowded "coffin ships." The Queenstown Story in Cobh's Victorian station tells their tale in detail through a moving multimedia exhibition and startlingly lifelike figures of emigrant families.

While in Cobh, take time to visit the Gothic-revival St. Colman's Cathedral, with its 47-bell carillon, rose window above the main doorway, mosaic flooring and richly colored windows.

🕂 Off map at C2 ✉ Cobh Heritage Centre, Cobh, 15 miles east of Cork city, via Waterford Road (N25) to signposted turnoff for R632 ☎ 021 481 3591; www. cobhheritage.com 🕐 Mon.–Sat. 9:30–6, Sun. 11–6 (last admission 1 hour before closing) 🍴 Restaurant 🚆 Frequent rail service from Cork city 💷 $$$

English Market (City Market)

This cavernous market, in a 1786 building, carries on a Cork tradition that dates from the 1600s. Wall-to-wall stalls offer meats, vegetables, pastries and just about anything else that shows up on Cork tables. It's ideal for eavesdropping and an opportunity to mingle with Cork residents going about their daily lives.

🕂 B1 ✉ Entrances from Grand Parade, Patrick Street, Oliver Plunkett Street, and Princes Street ☎ 021 492 4258; www.corkenglishmarket.ie 🕐 Mon.–Sat. 8–6 💷 Free

Fota Wildlife Park and Fota House

More than 90 species of exotic animals, including giraffes, ostriches, zebras, red pandas, oryx, kangaroos and lemurs, roam the 40 acres of open enclosures. More than just a zoo, the park is also heavily involved in conservation and rehabilitation of threatened species. The adjoining Fota Arboretum features trees and shrubs from China, Japan, Australia, the Himalayas and other countries.

   Fota House, the former home of the Smith Barry family, has beeen restored to its former glory by the Irish Heritage Trust and is also open to the public.

🕂 Off map at C2 ✉ Fota Island, Carrigtwohill, 10 miles east of Cork city on the Cobh road ☎ 021 481 2678; www.fotawildlife.ie 🕐 Mon.–Sat. 10–6, Sun. 10:30–6 (last admission 5); closed Christmas Day and Dec. 26 🍴 Oasis or Savannah Café 🚆 Frequent rail and bus service from Cork city 💷 $$$ **Fota House** ✉ Next to Fota Wildlife Park ☎ 021 481 5543; www.fotahouse.com 🕐 Daily 9–5 (house only from Apr.–Oct.)

Old Midleton Distillery
The Jameson Experience

This marvelous old distillery traces the history of Irish whiskey since it was perfected by Irish monks in the 16th century, when they called it *uisce beatha*, "the water of life." The informative guided tour ends with a complimentary glass of Jameson whiskey.

➕ Off map at C2 ✉ Midleton, Co. Cork, 12 miles east of Cork ☎ 021 461 3594; www.jamesonwhiskey.com ◉ Daily 10–4:30 (tours on demand), Apr.–Oct.; tours daily 11:30, 1, 2:30 and 4, Nov.–Mar. 🍴 Restaurant 🚌 From Cork and Waterford 💷 $$$

St. Fin Barre's Cathedral

The site of Cork city's birthplace, this magnificent Church of Ireland, 1870 French Gothic cathedral descends from a seventh-century monastery that grew into a seat of learning of international renown. A later, 18th-century cathedral was demolished to make way for the current building, chosen after a competition for which there were 63 entries. Its ornate interior is a real draw, with unique mosaics and an impressive great west window.

➕ A1 ✉ Dean Street ☎ 021 496 3387; www.cathedral.cork.anglican.org ◉ Mon.–Sat. 9:30–5:30, Sun. 12:30–5, Apr.–Oct.; 10–12:45 and 2–5, rest of year 💷 Free (donations welcome)

Shandon – St. Anne's Church and the Cork Butter Museum

St. Anne's is distinguished by its red-and-white "pepper pot" steeple, which houses its famous bells and a "four-faced liar" clock that never shows the same time on its four faces. Climb the winding belfry stairs and your reward is to follow numbers on the bell strings that send *The Bells of St. Mary's* ringing out over the city. Nearby is the interesting old Butter Exchange, which houses the Cork Butter Museum. An unusual subject for a museum, but well worth a visit.

➕ A2

St. Anne's Church ✉ Church Street ☎ 021 450 5906 ◉ Mon.–Sat. 10–5, Sun. 11:30–4:30, Jun.–Sep.; Mon.–Sat. 10–4, Sun. 11:30–3:30, Mar.–May and Oct.; Mon.–Sat. 11–3, Nov.–Feb. 🚌 3 from city center 💷 $$

Cork Butter Museum ✉ O'Connell Square ☎ 021 430 0600; www.corkbutter.museum ◉ Daily 10–6, Jul.–Aug.; 10–5, Mar.–Jun. and Sep.–Oct. 🚌 3 from city center 💷 $$

University College Cork

The University College Cork campus is one of the jewels in Cork's crown, with its Gothic revival architecture, gardens, stones with ancient Irish ogham inscriptions and Crawford Observatory. Of special interest is the Honan Chapel, which features Harry Clarke stained-glass windows. The Glucksman Gallery creates one of the most significant spaces for visual art in Ireland. The gallery shop and Café Glucksman offer views of the grounds.

➕ Off map at A1 ✉ Western Road ☎ 021 490 3000; www.ucc.ie. Gallery: 021 490 1844; www.glucksman. org ◉ Tue.–Sat. 10–5, Sun. 2–5 🚌 5, 8 💷 Free

Bottles of Jameson Irish whiskey, part of Ireland's heritage since 1780

Walk
Cork's Mercantile Past

Refer to route marked on city map on page 114

Walking is free from urban pressure and is without a doubt the best way to get around the city if you want to capture its true flavor and mingle with the people who give it life. Cork constantly challenges Dublin's supremacy, refusing to play second fiddle. Allow 90 minutes minimum.

Begin at Bishop Lucey Park, across the Grand Parade from the tourist office.
Also known as City Park and named for a much-loved bishop of Cork, Bishop Lucey Park contains a section of the medieval city walls. The eight bronze swans adorning a sculptured fountain celebrate the 800th anniversary of Cork's 1185 charter.
Walk right to reach the intersection of Grand Parade and South Mall, and turn left onto South Mall.
That impressive statue at the intersection of the two streets commemorates Irish rebels in the 1798 and 1867 uprisings. Irishmen who perished in the two World Wars are honored by the War Memorial alongside the river, and the uncarved granite stone nearby is the Hiroshima Memorial. South Mall is a wide, tree-lined street that was once an open channel bringing ships right up to waterside cellars to unload merchandise.
Turn left onto Pembroke Street, then left onto Oliver Plunkett Street.
The General Post Office on your left as you walk east on Oliver Plunkett Street was built on the site of the late 18th-century Theatre Royal, complete with busy coachyard facilities.
Turn immediately right down Winthrop

Street and right again onto St. Patrick's Street (known simply as Patrick Street).
The statue in the center of the street at the foot of Patrick Bridge depicts Father Matthew, the "Apostle of Temperance" fondly remembered in these parts for his lifelong fight against Irish alcoholism in the 1800s.
Turn left across Patrick Street into Lavitts Quay, then left at the Opera House into Emmet Place.
This modern, glass-fronted opera house might not be to everyone's taste, but the 1960s building regularly presents ballet, opera and dramas (see page 125). By contrast, its next-door neighbor is an imposing building that houses the Crawford Art Gallery. It was built in 1724, when ships could unload onto what is now the sidewalk, as the Custom House. Irish and international artists are represented in its fine collections, which include classical casts from the Vatican Galleries presented to Cork in 1818. The museum houses a collection of local landscape painting.
Turn left on Academy Street, then right on Patrick Street and look to your right for the three tiny streets described below.
The tiny lanes of French Church Street, Carey's Lane and Sts. Peter and Paul's Street became a safe haven for a colony of Huguenots who fled France in the 18th century to escape religious persecution and settled first on French Church Street. A few steps farther on, Carey's Lane was the site of a chapel in 1776, when Catholics were forbidden by law to have churches on main streets. The Huguenot graveyard is just behind the old wall on the right of the lane. Pause at the next small street on your right to feast your eyes on the elaborate stonework of the Church of Sts. Peter and Paul, which blossomed from the original chapel in the lane and opened in 1868.
Follow Patrick Street to where it curves to the left onto the Grand Parade and turn right to the intersection of Cornmarket and Castle streets.

St. Fin Barre's Cathedral was consecrated in 1870 on the site of two earlier places of worship

Once a lively and thriving open-air flea market, the Coal Quay (Cornmarket Street) was a vibrant part of the city's life for at least a century. It's lined with stalls presided over by shrewd, witty Irish countrywomen hawking odds and ends of every description. These days you're more likely to find secondhand clothing and furniture.

From Castle Street, turn left at South Main Street, then right on Washington Street and left onto Hanover Place; cross Clarke's Bridge, then turn right onto Wandesford Quay to Sharman Crawford Street and on to Bishop Street.

Built in French Gothic style and designed by William Burges, the majestic limestone St. Fin Barre's Cathedral boasts three splendid spires and a magnificent interior with angels gazing down from a starry apse. It's a true "must see" (see page 119).

Turn right along French Quay and cross the bridge to South Main Street; just before Washington Street, take the small right turn on Tobin Street.

At first glance, this narrow little street seems an unlikely setting for the arts, but the newly renovated Triskel Arts Centre (Tue.–Sat. 10–5) is alive with contemporary arts and crafts exhibitions and a variety of theatrical productions and some cutting-edge movies.

Continue down Tobin Street to Grand Parade and cross over to the entrance of the colorful English Market.

Also known as the City Market (see page 118), the English Market is an ideal place for a cup of tea or light meal in the restaurant as you end your walk.

Drive
Island City,
Magic Stone

Duration: 1–2 days

This 159-mile drive from the center of Cork heads to Blarney to kiss the famous stone and northwest through historic towns before turning east and south for the spectacular drive across the Vee.

Start at Tourist House, Grand Parade, in Cork. Cross Patrick Street Bridge and turn left for the marked 6-mile drive to Blarney, traveling northwest on the N20 for around 5 miles before turning left onto the R617.
The well-preserved ruins of Blarney Castle, built in 1446, draw visitors not just for their history, but also for the magical powers attributed to the famous stone embedded in its parapet wall. Kissing the stone involves lying on your back and hanging over an open space (see page 117). Close to the castle is the

superb Scottish baronial mansion, Blarney Castle House, set amid lovely 18th-century gardens.
Leave Blarney on the R617. In a few miles turn northwest on the R579 to Kanturk.
One mile south of town, unfinished Kanturk Castle was begun in 1609 by Irish chieftain MacDonagh MacCarthy, who planned the building as the largest mansion in Ireland, with a large quadrangle and four-story towers at each corner. Alarmed at its size and strength, the English Privy Council ordered work to cease, declaring that it was "much too large for a subject." The roofless, stout walls and towers have survived in remarkably good condition.
Drive southeast on the R576 to its intersection with the N72, then turn east for 9 miles to reach Mallow.
Set on the River Blackwater, Mallow was a popular spa town during the 18th and early 19th centuries; its lively social life prompted the traditional song "The Rakes of Mallow." The fortified 16th-century house replacing 12th-century Mallow Castle, which was burned in 1689 on the orders of King James II, now stands in near ruins in its

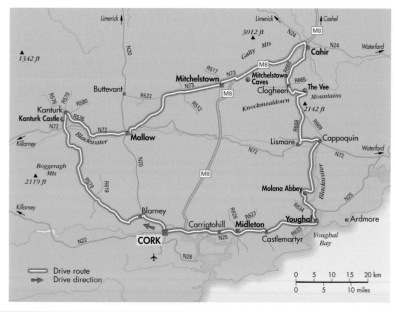

Drive route
Drive direction

0   5   10   15   20 km

0   5   10 miles

own park by the river crossing. From the tourist office in Cork or Youghal, ask for the Blackwater drive map and chart that shows a wealth of historic relics.

About 9 miles north of Mallow via the N20, the little town of Buttevant saw the world's first steeplechase in 1752, run between its church steeple and the one in Doneraile. Buttevant was the model for "Mole" in Edmund Spenser's *The Faerie Queene*.

Take the N73 northeast for 21 miles to Mitchelstown.

Ten miles northeast of this tidy, attractive 19th-century town via the M8, the Mitchelstown Caves are an underground wonderland of passages and high-ceiling limestone chambers, including the biggest chamber in the British Isles. The Old Caves were used as a refuge for a 16th-century Earl of Desmond, who had a price on his head. There are escorted tours through 2 miles of the fantastic netherworld.

Follow the M8 for 18 miles to Cahir.

Occupying a small islet in the River Suir, Cahir Castle was built in the 13th century by the de Berminghams and was held by the Anglo-Norman Butlers until 1599, when the Earl of Essex captured it after a three-day siege. Englishman Oliver Cromwell made a fierce show of force before the walls in 1650 and sent in surrender terms. Historians differ as to whether the garrison accepted the terms immediately or held out until they saw the heavy ordnance ranged against them. They did, however, surrender before another attack and the castle thus remained in sound condition. It has been restored and there is an excellent audiovisual show.

Head south on the R668 through Clogheen to begin the Vee mountain pass road en route to Lismore.

The scenic overlooks along this drive through a gap in the beautiful Knockmealdown Mountains provide spectacular panoramic views of some of the area's famous landscapes:

A 19th-century lighthouse stands guard in Youghal

Killballyboy Wood, Boernagore Wood, the Galtee Mountains, the Golden Vale of Tipperary, Bay Lough and the Comeragh mountain range.

Continue south on the R668 for 8 miles to Lismore.

This historic little town, site of an ancient monastic center, is beautifully located on the Blackwater River. Its most outstanding attractions are Lismore Castle, whose seven acres of historic gardens are open to the public, the Protestant St. Carthage's Cathedral, which features grave slabs from the ninth and eleventh centuries, and the modern Romanesque-style Catholic church. A program in the Heritage Centre depicts the town's history.

Take the N72 east for 4 miles to the bridge on the outskirts of Cappoquin and turn right on the R571 to an intersection. Turn right on the road to Youghal that follows the Blackwater River south to the sea, then turn right on the N25 south for Youghal.

Youghal (pronounced "yawl" meaning yew wood) is filled with mementos of its past. The picturesque harborside town was once the home of Sir Walter Raleigh, who brought tobacco and the potato to Ireland, and the setting for the 1954 movie *Moby Dick*. At the tourist office on the harbor, ask for the Tourist Trail booklet for information about the town's history and major sights, including the impressive 1776 clock tower, which now holds a museum featuring Walter Raleigh memorabilia, remnants of the old town walls, and Myrtle Grove, the home of Sir Walter Raleigh. Harbor cruises are sometimes available, and deep-sea fishing charters can be booked at the tourist office.

Eight miles east of Youghal, via a well-marked turnoff from the N25, is the pretty seaside village of Ardmore (see page 126). Its fine group of ecclesiastical remains includes one of the best preserved round towers in Ireland. There are also bracing cliff walks along the sea's edge. **Follow the N25 west for 28 miles to return to Cork.**

Tourist information ✉ Heritage Centre, Market House, Market Square, Youghal ☎ 024 92447 🕐 Daily 9:30–5:30, Apr.–Sep.; 10–2, rest of year

The 12th-century round tower and St. Declan's Oratory, Ardmore

Cork's Cultural Scene

Cork city is packed with cultural activities, both traditional and contemporary. No matter what time of year you visit, you can count on attending a cultural event, and in most cases costs are moderate. The city was designated a City of Culture for 2005.

Music and the Arts

Cork's opera house presents plays and musical stage shows of the highest caliber, concerts by leading orchestras and musical stars, and ballet and other dance performances.

The Everyman Palace Theatre is housed in the venerable gilt-and-gingerbread Old Palace Theatre, a venue steeped in the city's theatrical history. It hosts high-quality performances of its resident company, as well as visiting troupes from around the country, Great Britain and America. There's coffee service during intermission, and audiences often mingle with actors who relax in the agreeable Theatre Bar.

Cork is the perfect place to enjoy traditional Irish music at its best, and the best of the best can be found in many of the city's numerous pubs. The Corner House, a cheerful traditional venue, has a great array of musicians performing Irish music plus Cajun and occasional Bluegrass Sunday and Monday. There is a big traditional session every first Friday of the month. Bagpipes, *bodhráns*, fiddles and guitars hold forth every Wednesday and Sunday night at The Gables Bar. Both pubs sometimes present contemporary music. Check local newspapers for other pubs featuring music, traditional and contemporary. Check also for weekend discos or clubs, which change times and places frequently.

Festival Time

Cork holds so many special events and festivals that it sometimes seems its citizens stand ready to throw a party at the drop of a hat.

The Cork International Choral Festival has been a world-class competition and concert showcase since 1954 and is held in early May. The popular Cork International Folk Dance Festival is in late July and in September/October the Cork Folk Festival keeps alive the deep-rooted music that is so much a part of Irish culture.

Considered by many to be the star of Cork's festivals, the Cork Guinness Jazz Festival in October attracts greats of the jazz world, making the city ring with lively music. It is ranked among the top three jazz festivals in the world. The equally famed Cork Film Festival in October/November is one of Ireland's oldest and biggest movie events, giving independent movie-makers a showcase for their work. Established in 1956, the festival brings the best of international cinema to the Irish audience – and the visitors. It also gives Corkonians a chance to don their best bib and tucker for the many gala evenings that are so much a part of the festivities.

Corner House ✉ 7 Coburg Street ☎ 021 450 0655

Cork's Opera House ✉ Emmet Place ☎ 021 427 0022; www.corkoperahouse.ie

The Everyman Palace Theatre ✉ 15 MacCurtain Street ☎ 021 450 1673; www.everymanpalace.com

The Gables Bar ✉ 32 Douglas Street ☎ 021 431 3076

Regional Sights

Ardmore

One of the most perfectly preserved round towers in Ireland rises some 98 feet above the attractive little seaside village of Ardmore. St. Declan came from Wales to found a monastic settlement here in the fifth century, and the tower is just one of several remarkably intact remains still on display. Look for the incredibly tiny St. Declan's Oratory – legend says that the grave in one corner is that of St. Declan himself. Traces of architectural styles of the 10th to 14th centuries are visible in the ruins of the cathedral, and of special interest are a set of panels on its west gable, which present sculptured biblical scenes such as the Adoration of the Magi, the Weighing of Souls and the Judgment of Solomon. This pretty village invites a leisurely stroll along the sandy beach.

➕ C1

Tourist information ✉ Seafront parking lot, Ardmore ☎ 024 94444 🕐 Seasonal opening

Bantry and the Beara Peninsula

Named for an ancient Celtic chieftan, the little town of Bantry sits at the head of 21-mile-long Bantry Bay, surrounded by hills. Twice (in 1689 and 1796) the French attempted naval invasions of Ireland from this inlet, only to be defeated by great storms and faulty communications. Between Bantry and Glengarriff, you can still see a sign marking the "Artist's Studio" of award-winning Welsh-born artist Raymond Klee. Unfortunately, ill health has meant the veteran artist can no longer paint, but look for his Irish landscape paintings in regional galleries.

Bantry House sits on the southern outskirts of town in a magnificent estate, where landscaped lawns and gardens look out over the bay. The 1750 Georgian mansion is the ancestral home of the earls of Bantry, and has an impressive collection of European antiques, paintings, sculptures, tapestries and other precious items.

Many of these artifacts were brought back to the house by Viscount Berehaven, son of the 1st Earl, Richard. Berehaven traveled extensively in Europe, collecting the many precious pieces as he went. The house was subsequently used as a hospital in 1922 during the Irish Civil War, and in World War II both the house and the stables were occupied by the Second Cyclist Squadron of the Irish Army. The house was opened to the public in 1946. The beautiful gardens, laid out from plans gleaned from the 2nd Earl and his wife's visits to the Continent, fell into disrepair but were brought back to their present glory in 1997.

Interesting statues stand in Bantry House Gardens

Imposing 18th-century Bantry House has views of Bantry Bay

The 30-mile Beara Peninsula is a narrow, mountainous finger of land stretching out to sea between Bantry Bay and the Kenmare River. Its northwest corner falls within County Kerry, marked by the Cork–Kerry border that runs along the Caha mountain range. Glengarriff sits at its head, and a drive through the wild, sparsely populated landscape of the peninsula is a pleasant three- or four-hour diversion when you're traveling from Glengarriff to Kenmare or Killarney.

About a mile offshore from Glengarriff, in a sheltered inlet of Bantry Bay and reached from Glengarriff by ferry, is lovely little Garinish Island. Its elaborately landscaped Italianate garden boasts plants and flowers from around the world, interspersed with classical pavilions and meandering pathways. Playwright George Bernard Shaw loved the place, and parts of *St. Joan* were written here.

Ireland's first national park, Gougane Barra's densely wooded mountains have over the centuries been a natural refuge for those desperately seeking religious freedom. St. Finbarr chose an island in the lake at its center as the setting for his first Christian monastery in the sixth century. During the time of the Penal Laws, when they were forbidden to celebrate Mass, Irish worshipers held services in this secluded setting. The woods are laced with lovely walkways, making this a delightful stop.

Mizen Head is Ireland's most southwesterly mainland point, and its signal station sits high above the wild Atlantic water. A breathtaking 172-foot suspension bridge soars 150 feet above crashing waves at the cliff base. Views of the coasts are magnificent. The visitor center is located in the keeper's house and engine room, with audiovisuals, archives, maps and a bird and sea lookout – keep an eye out for dolphins, whales and basking sharks.

🞢 A1

Tourist information ✉ The Courthouse, The Square, Bantry ☎ 027 50229 🕐 Daily 9:15–6, Jun.–Aug.; Mon.–Sat. 9:15–5, Apr.–May and Sep.–Oct.

Bantry House ✉ Bantry (east side of town) ☎ 027 50047; www.bantryhouse.com 🕐 Daily 10–6, mid-Mar. to Oct. 🎟 House and gardens $$$; Armada Exhibition Centre and gardens $$

Garinish Island ✉ Glengarriff ☎ 027 63040; www.garnishisland.com 🕐 Mon.–Sat. 10–6:30, Sun. 1–5, Apr.–Sep.; Mon.–Sat. 10–4:30, Sun. 1–5, Mar. and Oct. 🎟 Boat to island $$$; island $$

Gougane Barra National Forest Park ✉ 15 miles northeast of Bantry off R584, signposted on Macroom–Glengarriff road ☎ www.gouganebarra.com 🎟 Free; $$ parking fee Jul.–Aug. and weekends Apr.–Oct.

Mizen Head Signal Station Visitor Centre
✉ Mizen Head, 6 miles west of Goleen ☎ 028 35115/35225; www.mizenhead.net 🕐 Daily 10–6, Jun.–Sep.; 10:30–5, mid-Mar. to May and Oct.; 11–4, Nov. to mid-Mar. 🎟 $$

High waters surround the 13th-century Norman castle in Cahir, Co. Tipperary

Cahir

Cahir, a rocky islet in the River Suir, has been the natural site of fortifications as far back as the third century. It was one of Brian Ború's homes during his reign as high king of Ireland. The present castle was built by the 13th-century Normans and held by the Anglo-Norman Butlers until Queen Elizabeth I's favorite, the Earl of Essex, captured it in 1599. Articles ending the Cromwellian wars were signed here in 1652. The state took over in 1964 after the death of the last Butler descendant, restored the castle to near-original condition, and refurnished the residential living quarters with accurate reproductions that bring alive its centuries-old history. Guided tours of the castle are available on request. Don't miss the excellent audiovisual show, "Partly Hidden and Partly Revealed."

The town of Cahir is something of a time warp and some of its shops and houses appear little changed from decades ago. Unusually for towns in the Irish Republic, there is a war memorial in the main square dedicated to the local men who joined Irish regiments and fell in World War I.

The other curiosity here is the quaint Swiss Cottage that stands in woodland gardens by the river just outside the town. Its thatched, corkscrew-timbered building with "eyebrow windows" looks like something out of *Hansel and Gretel* rather than the Swiss Alps. Designed in 1810 by British architect John Nash for the Butler family, it was rescued from dereliction in 1985–89 by enthusiastic conservationists and restored. The original hand-painted French wallpapers and fabrics have been copied, and it is now furnished with many period pieces.

✠ C2

Tourist information ✉ Castle parking lot, Cahir ☎ 052 41453 ⊙ Mon.–Sat. 9:15–6, Jun.–Aug.; 9:15–5:30, Apr.–May and Sep.–Oct.

Cahir Castle ✉ Castle Street, Cahir (on the east side

It seems likely that Anne Boleyn, daughter of the Earl of Ormond and mother of Queen Elizabeth I, was born here. Today the town is proud of a more recent hero, Sean Kelly, a racing cyclist world champion. Carrick rejoiced when Kelly won the 1988 Tour de France, and a square in the town is named for him. ✚ C2

Ormond Castle ✉ Castle Park (off Castle Street), Carrick-on-Suir ☎ 051 640787; www.heritageireland. ie ⏰ Daily 10–6 (last admission 5), mid-May to Sep. 👋 Free 🛈 Access by guided tour only

Cashel

Undoubtedly Ireland's most majestic historical landmark, the lofty Rock of Cashel soars 300 feet above the town of Cashel and its surrounding plains. After you watch the audiovisual "Strongholds of the Faith," wander among the ancient stones and ruins, climb to the top of the cathedral tower to view Tipperary's Golden Vale plains, and gaze at the stone Cross of Cashel, standing on a base that may have been a pre-Christian sacrificial altar. Ancient Celts worshiped here, and Irish kings built their palace on the sacred site. St. Patrick came here in 450 to preach to Aengus, king of Munster, using the shamrock as a symbol of the Trinity. Aengus and his family accepted baptism.

Murtough O'Brien gifted the Cashel of the Kings to the church in 1101, and in 1127 Cormac MacCarthaigh built the little Romanesque chapel that bears his name. The architectural features and decoration of the chapel are highy prized, so the construction of a roof is under way to help preserve them. Work is expected to take another two years, during which there is limited access to Cormac's Chapel by guided tour only. There's also no access to the tomb of Miler McGrath, Archbishop of Cashel from 1571 to 1622.

No visit to the Rock of Cashel is complete without a look at the Brú Ború Heritage Centre next door. The Brú Ború traditional musicians and dancers

of the town) ☎ 052 744 1011; www.heritageireland.ie ⏰ Daily 9:30–6:30, mid-Jun. to Aug.; 9:30–5:30, Sep. to mid-Oct.; 9:30–4:30, mid-Oct. to mid-Jun. 🍴 Crock of Gold tearoom, across the road 👋 $

Swiss Cottage ✉ Ardfinnan Road ☎ 052 744 1144; www.heritageireland.ie ⏰ Daily 10–6 (last admission 5:15), Apr.–Oct. 👋 $

Carrick-on-Suir

The town of Carrick is noteworthy for its beautiful Tudor mansion – rare amid Ireland's hundreds of fortresses and abbeys. Despite its name, Ormond Castle is unfortified: The 15th-century castle fell into ruins centuries ago. Not so the adjoining manor house, built by the 10th Earl of Ormond ("Black Tom") to entice Queen Elizabeth I to visit. The grand edifice never did succeed in that effort, but it did survive the centuries to stand as Ireland's best example of that period. Two of the 15th-century towers are consolidated into the manor house, and the fine decorative plasterwork is among the best in the country.

perform most days during the summer, and facilities include a subterranean exhibition and an information center, craft center and folk theater.

Although the town tends to be overshadowed by the Rock, as one of Ireland's designated Heritage Towns it is well worth a visit in its own right. A good place to start is the town hall's Folk Village, an attractive reconstruction of local village lifestyles. Wandering from one thatched village shop to another is a step back in time. In the informal setting, shops are interspersed with other facets of daily life, including a forge and the Penal Chapel. Cashel's ecclesiastical prominence predates the arrival of St. Patrick, as changing exhibitions at the Heritage Centre portray. On permanent display is a large-scale model of the town in the 1640s, and the "Royal Heirlooms and Relics of the House of McCarthy Múr" exhibit provides a little glimpse into the lifestyles of ancient Gaelic royalty.

From June to September, the quaint old Cashel heritage tram departs the center to tour the historic sites in the town. Adjoining the Georgian St. John the Baptist Cathedral and nearby 14th-century town walls, the Bolton Library holds fascinating manuscript collections, some of which date to the 12th century. The complete works of Machiavelli are here, as is the Nuremberg Chronicle of 1493, works by Dante and a host of other larger-than-life figures, including part of Chaucer's *Book of Fame*, printed by Caxton.

✚ C2

Tourist information ✉ Town Hall, Main Street ☎ 062 61333; www.cashel.ie ◷ Daily 9:30–5:30, Mar.–Oct.; Mon.–Fri. 9:30–5:30, rest of year

The Rock of Cashel ✉ Cashel ☎ 062 61437 ◷ Daily 9–5:30, early Sep. to mid-Oct. and mid-Mar. to May; 9–7, Jun.; 9–4:30, rest of year; tours of Cormac's Chapel May–Sep. only 🎟 $$

Brú Ború Heritage Centre ✉ Cashel ☎ 062 61122; www.bruboru.ie ◷ Daily 9 a.m.–11:30 p.m., mid-Jun. to mid-Sep.; Mon.–Fri. 9–1 and 2–5, rest of year 🍴 Restaurant 🎟 Center free; exhibition $$; show $$$ ⓘ Ask about banquet and show evenings in summer

Cashel Folk Village ✉ Dominick Street (near the Rock of Cashel) ☎ 062 63601; www.cashelfolkvillage. ie ◷ Daily 9:30–7:30, May–Oct.; 10–5:30, Mar.–Apr. 🎟 $

The lofty Rock of Cashel ruins look over the town from the west

Cashel Heritage Centre and Tram Tour ✉ Town Hall
☎ 062 62511; www.cashel.ie 🕐 Daily 9:30–5:30,
mid-Mar. to Nov.; Mon.–Fri. 9:30–5:30, rest of year
💷 $
St. John the Baptist Cathedral and GPA Bolton Library
✉ John Street ☎ 062 61944 🕐 Mon.–Wed. 10–3,
Thu. 10–2:30 💷 $

Dingle Peninsula (Corca Dhuibhne) and the Blasket Islands (Na Blascaodai)

The Dingle Peninsula is the most westerly point of land in Europe, its offshore Blasket Islands the "last parish before America." Its beginnings are shrouded in the mists of prehistory, which left its marks scattered over the face of the Slieve Mish mountains, along its coves and rocky cliffs, and in the legends that remain.

West of town, Ventry (Ceann Trá) Harbour was, according to legend, the scene of a fierce and bloody battle between "King of the World" Daire Doon and Fianna warrior leader Fionn MacCumhaill (see page 199). Still farther west, Dunbeg Fort perches on a high promontory, one side surrounded by earthen trenches, and its 22-foot-thick wall riddled with an elaborate souterrain (inner passage).

From the high cliffs of Slea Head (Ceann Sléibhe) is a sweeping view of the sheltered coves below and across the water to the remote Blasket Islands. The last of their tiny population was moved to the mainland in 1953, when the fishing industry failed to provide a living wage and the government gave land grants for small farm holdings on the peninsula. Visitors from Springfield, Massachusetts may feel a special bond to the people of the Blaskets, since many islanders emigrated to that city.

Boats go out from Dunquin (Dún Chaoin) Harbour during the summer months. There are very good potteries on the peninsula: Louis Mulcahy operates a pottery studio and workshop at Clogher Beach, Ballyferriter (Baile an Fheirtéaraigh) where he trains local

Boats tethered at busy Dingle harbor

potters in the production of many unusual items. Ballyferriter is also the focal point for a summer-school program that brings students to study Gaelic and live with families who use the language in their everyday lives. Stop at the town-center old schoolhouse, now the Oidhreacht Chorca Dhuibhne (Corca Dhuibhne Regional Museum). Dingle's history is illustrated by more than 200 artifacts, photographs and text, and you'll leave acquainted with the region's beehive huts, standing stones, mysterious graves, ring forts and relics.

One of the peninsula's most astonishing remains is Gallarus Oratory between Dunquin and Ballyferriter, a marvelous specimen of early Christian architecture. Built in an inverted-boat shape, it has remained completely watertight for more than a thousand years, its stones perfectly fitted without benefit of any kind of mortar.

Look also for the Alphabet and Ogham Stones in the churchyard of the ancient ruined Kilmalkedar church. One is carved with the Roman alphabet and the other with ogham strokes.

In a low, sprawling building, the Blasket Centre (Ionad an Bhlascaoid Mhóir) presents the story of the Blasket Islanders in innovative displays and productions that bring to vivid life the harshness of their daily lives and the richness of their literary works. Every image inside is enhanced by the clear view of the islands through a seaward-looking wall of glass.

Dingle (its ancient Irish name is An Daingean, The Fortress) is a busy market town that sits at the head of the Dingle Peninsula. Both town and peninsula have become a mecca for some of Ireland's most talented crafts people, and you may want to pick up at least one Irish treasure here. Most of the crafts shops cluster along Green Street, including Celtic jeweler John Weldon (www.johnweldonjewellers.com) and Kathleen McAuliffe Millinery (www. kathleenmcauliffe.com). Here you will also find silversmith Brian de Staic, who fashions unique necklaces with your name inscribed in strokes of the ancient ogham language.

In 1984, Fungi the dolphin moved in to Dingle Bay (Bá na Daingin), promptly becoming the beloved pet of locals and visitors alike. Though the original Fungi has passed away, there's still a dolphin there and it's fun to watch as he cavorts through the water, following the small boats that bring visitors out for a closer look (daily year round) and perhaps a swim with the playful dolphin.

To reach the northern shores of the peninsula, take the Connor Pass road from Dingle town to Castlegregory. The views from the narrow pass and up along the coastal road stretching from Castlegregory into Tralee are spectacular.

➕ A2

Tourist information ✉ The Quay, Dingle ☎ 066 915 1188 ⏰ Mon.–Sat. 9–6, Apr.–Oct; Sun. 10–5, May–Sep. ℹ You can make reservations on one of the many boats that visit the dolphin daily during summer months

Louis Mulcahy ✉ Ballyferriter ☎ 066 915 6229; www.louismulcahy.com ⏰ Daily 9–7, (from 10 Sat.–Sun.) Jun.–Aug.; 10–5:30, rest of year 🍴 Café

Corca Dhuibhne Regional Museum ✉ Ballyferriter ☎ 066 915 6155; www.oidreacht.ie ⏰ Daily 10–6, Apr.–Oct.; by appointment rest of year 🍴 Coffee shop 💰 $

The Blasket Centre ✉ Dunquin ☎ 066 915 6444 ⏰ Daily 10–6, Easter–Oct. 🍴 Café 💰 $

The Wood ✉ Ceardlann Na Coille, less than a mile west of Dingle on the coast road

Dunbeg Fort ✉ Fahan on the R559 west of Ventry ☎ 066 915 9070; www.dunbegfort.com 🍴 Café 💰 $

Doolin

This tiny village has an international reputation for Irish music, and musicians from around the world flock here to play in O'Connor's Pub. The audiences are as diverse as the musicians and even in winter you'll find a lively night of music and *craic* here.

Ballyferriter Bay on the Dingle Peninsula seen from Clougher Head

Don't be put off by Doolin's sprawl as it is an excellent base for exploring The Burren and has a good choice of cafés and restaurants. Because it is so popular it's advisable to book hotels ahead during summer months.

Doolin is the closest mainland point to the Aran Islands (Oileáin Árann, see page 38), and boats leave the pier daily for the 30-minute voyage to Inishmore (Inis Móir) and Inisheer (Inis Óirr) islands. There are also boat trips to see the Cliffs of Moher (see page 134).

In 2006 Doolin Cave opened to the public. It contains the longest stalactite in the northern hemisphere (the largest in the world that you can actually visit). Measuring 20 feet, it hangs from a cathedral-like cavern. The one-hour tour (maximum 20 people) starts with 120 steps down to the mouth of the cave. Visitors are fitted out with a hard hat and flashlight for an exciting underground experience.

✚ B3

Tourist information ✉ The Cliffs of Moher, Liscannor ☎ 065 708 1171; www.doolin-tourism.com 🕓 Daily 10–5, mid-Mar. to May; 10–6, Jun.–Sep.

O'Connor's Pub ✉ Doolin ☎ 065 707 4168; www.gusoconnorsdoolin.com

Doolin Cave ✉ Doolin (pick up by bus) at Bruach na Haille restaurant) ☎ 065 707 5761; www.doolincave.ie 🕓 Tours daily 10–4, mid-Feb. to Easter; 10–5, Easter–Aug. (tours every half hour, Jul.–Aug.); Mon.–Fri. 10–4, Sat.–Sun. 11–4, Sep. to mid-Oct.; Sat.–Sun. only until end Dec.; by appointment only, rest of year

Ennis and County Clare

In the region of Shannon, Ennis is a bustling market town with historical buildings and tiny, winding streets. Of special note is the 13th-century Franciscan friary on Abbey Street. The carved image of St. Francis displaying the stigmata and carvings of the Virgin and Child on the corbels supporting the south arch are particularly impressive. For exploration of the town, stop by the tourist office for *Ennis – A Walking Trail*, an excellent guide for a 90-minute tour. County Clare's incredible history is captured in displays at the County Clare Museum, located in a former convent.

The Craggaunowen (pronounced "crag-an-owen") Project brings a sense of reality to everyday Irish life during the Bronze Age and early Christian era. The small castle has interesting medieval art objects. In the lake a short walk away is a fascinating recreation of a crannog (a Bronze Age lake dwelling). There's a cooking site of the Iron Age, and the earthen ring fort on the grounds holds a reconstructed farm home of some 15 centuries ago. Of special interest is the glass shelter that has been built to house the tiny leather *curragh* built by Tim Severin for his daring voyage across the Atlantic in 1976 to retrace St. Brendan's legendary route of AD 700.

There's an eerie moonscape look to much of the 100-square-mile limestone area of The Burren. Its sense of remoteness belies the rich plant life at first glance. Make your first stop The Burren Centre, whose exhibits explain what you'll see. Nearby in Carron, the Burren Perfumery has an organic herb garden and demonstrations of essential oil extraction.

Walking part of the 76-mile Burren Way is the best way to discover the relics of ancient civilizations and the astonishing flora thriving in such an unlikely setting. Nearby, a local farmer discovered Aillwee Cave about 50 years ago. Its awesome stalactites, stalagmites, waterfall and relics of brown bears who

eons ago hollowed out snug pits have made it one of the most popular visitor attractions in the area. This region has many ancient buildings, often restored to achieve full tourist potential. Besides Bunratty (see page 144), there are tower houses like Knappogue Castle, which was built in 1479 and has since played host to rebels, Roundheads, and even Clare County Council. Its restoration has unveiled its original character.

If you've been looking for a mate, Lisdoonvarna, 7 miles north of Ennistymon on road N67, is the place to be in September. That's when Europe's largest matchmaking festival imbues this little North Clare town with song, dance, storytelling and matchmaking. The tourist office in Ennis has exact dates. Lisdoonvarna is also known for its Victorian Spa Complex and Health Centre, where you can drink or bathe in the mineral waters which have been dispensed here since the 18th century.

If you have any County Clare ancestors, it is quite likely you can trace them among the thousands of family records at the Clare Heritage and Genealogical Centre (write for a Genealogical Research Form). The "Ireland West 1800–60" exhibition is fascinating as it takes you through the famine and emigration years.

The five-mile stretch of the Cliffs of Moher that rise to as high as 754 feet can only be described as breathtaking. They are best seen from O'Brien's Tower, built on the highest cliff to afford a good vantage point for early 19th-century tourists. Mountains as far apart as Kerry and Connemara and the Aran Islands (Oileáin Árann) are clearly visible in good weather. Clifftop walks are tempting, but be cautious, as there is a danger that the ground may give way.

The Visitor Experience at the Cliffs of Moher, incorporating the Atlantic Edge interpretive center, is in a cavernous underground building and has interactive exhibits and displays about the ocean, local geology and plantlife, as well as stories from folklore and real life.

🔢 B3

Tourist information ✉ Arthur's Row, Ennis ☎ 065 682 8366; www.visitennis.ie 🕐 Daily 9:30–5:30, Jun.–Oct.; Mon.–Sat. 9:30–5:30, May and Oct.–Jan.; Mon.–Fri. 9:30–5:30, Feb.–Apr.

Ennis Friary ✉ Abbey Street, Ennis ☎ 065 682 9100; www.heritageireland.ie 🕐 Check website

County Clare Museum ✉ Arthur's Row, Ennis ☎ 065 682 3382; www.clarelibrary.ie/eolas/claremuseum 🕐 Tue.–Sat. 9:30–1 and 2–5:30 👋 Free

Craggaunowen Project ✉ Quin, Co. Clare, 10 miles from Ennis, signposted from Quin, north on R469 ☎ 061 711 200; www.shannonheritage.com 🕐 Daily 10–5, Easter–Aug. (last admission 4) 🍴 Tearoom 👋 $$$

The Burren Centre ✉ Kilfenora, 8 miles northwest from Ennis on the Lahinch Road ☎ 065 708 8030; www.theburrencentre.ie 🕐 Daily 9:30–5:30, Jun.–Aug.; 10–5, Mar.–May and Sep. 🍴 Tea shop; Vaughan's Pub in Kilfenora 👋 $$

Burren Perfumery ✉ Carron ☎ 065 708 9102; www.burrenperfumery.com 🕐 Daily 9–7, Jul.–Aug.; 10–6, May–Jun. and Sep.; 10–5, Oct.–Apr. 🍴 Tearooms 👋 Free

Aillwee Cave ✉ Ballyvaughan, Ennistymon (28 miles from Ennis) ☎ 065 707 7036; www.aillweecave.ie 🕐 Daily 10–6:30, Jul.–Aug.; 9:30–5:30, Mar.–Jun. and Sep.–Oct.; 10–5, rest of year 🍴 Café 👋 $$$

Knappogue Castle ✉ Quin (9 miles from Ennis, south on R469) ☎ 061 360 788; www.shannonheritage.com 🕐 Daily 10–5 (last admission at 4:15), Apr.–Sep. 👋 $$$

Clare Heritage and Genealogical Centre ✉ Church Street, Corofin, 6 miles northwest from Ennis ☎ 065 683 7955; www.clareroots.com 🕐 Genealogical Centre: Mon.–Fri. 9–5; museum: daily 9–5:30 👋 $$

Visitor Experience at the Cliffs of Moher ✉ Cliffs of Moher ☎ 065 708 6141; www.cliffsofmoher.ie 🕐 Daily 9–9, Jul. to mid-Aug.; 9–8, mid- to end Aug.; 9–7:30, Jun. and Sep.; 9–7, May; 9–6:30, Apr.; 9–6, Mar. and Oct.; 9:15–5:30, Feb.; 9:15–5, Jan., Nov. and Dec. 🍴 Restaurant and café 🚌 From Ennis bus station 👋 $$

Poulnabrone Dolmen, an ancient burial site in a landscape of gray karstic limestone rock in The Burren

Cattle graze in fields near Killarney, with the Aghadoe Hills rising beyond

Killarney

The friendly, ebullient residents of Killarney more than offset what is a popular perception of the town as more commercial than any other town in Ireland. "Commercial," in Killarney's case, simply translates into an abundance of good accommodations, eateries and entertainment.

Killarney's wealth of natural beauty can be a bit overwhelming. Not to worry – the "jarveys" (drivers of open horse-drawn vehicles), boat operators and bus-tour people have it all worked out. Their routes will take you to the high points, and although it is perfectly possible to wander around on your own, do go along for at least one of the organized tours, whether by car, boat or coach. It's great fun. The guides know and love the scenery and embellish every spot with the folklore that will make the experience even more memorable. If you're ready for a break from driving, Bus Eireann runs several good day trips to nearby locations, such as the Ring of Kerry and the Dingle Peninsula (page 131).

For a lasting memento of your visit, stop in the Frank Lewis Gallery (www.franklewisgallery.com), which specializes in landscapes of the area, portraits and sculptures by local artists.

A broad valley holds the three main lakes, with Lough Leane (the Lower Lake) closest to Killarney and separated from the Middle Lake by Muckross peninsula. It was on one of its 30 islands that dedicated monks faithfully recorded Irish history from the 11th to the 13th century in the *Annals of Innisfallen*. The Middle Lake covers 600 acres, has four islands, and is connected to the small, narrow Upper Lake and its eight islands by a broad river called the Long Range. The lakes and streams are connected to the Atlantic by the River Laune. Their waters catch the shimmering reflections of birch, mountain ash and arbutus, while hovering over all are the peaks of some of Ireland's finest mountains: Macgillycuddy's Reeks, including Carrauntoohil, the country's highest mountain; the Tomies; the Mangerton range; and Torc. As a Killarney jarvey was once thought to have said, "Sure, 'tis a grand sight, one of God's blessings."

Killarney's boat operators are legendary for their skillful navigation of the lakes and their store of wondrous tales. Boats depart in summer from the Ross Castle pier for two-and-a-half-hour tours, which include the Gap of Dunloe, Ross Castle, Muckross House, Gardens and Traditional Farms, and Torc Waterfall. Check at the tourist office for times and reservations. These sights are on the Ring of Kerry Drive (see pages 138–140).

Set on 11,500 acres of parkland and surrounded by marvelously landscaped gardens, the Victorian mansion Muckross House was built in 1843, bought by Americans in 1911, and presented as a gift to the Irish people in 1932. The first two floors are furnished in the manner of the great houses of Ireland, while its upper floors hold fascinating exhibits of maps, prints and other documents, as well as a small wildlife and bird collection. A folk museum and crafts shop bring to vivid life the Kerry country lifestyle of a time long past.

Step back in time at the Muckross Traditional Farms, where Irish farm life of years gone by continues in living exhibits – crops are sown and harvested, homemakers go about their chores, and carpenter, blacksmith and wheelwright carry on their trades. Both adults and children will delight in the authentic barnyard with its animal occupants.

The tower house and two rounded towers that join remnants of a curtain wall are all that remain of Ross Castle, a late 15th-century O'Donoghue Ross stronghold on the shores of the Lower Lake, about 2 miles from town. You can imagine it as an Irish chieftain's home. Late 16th- and early 17th-century furnishings are on display, and the view from the top is superb.

Near Cahersiveen, Valentia Island is joined to the mainland by a small road bridge. Silhouetted against the horizon,

10 miles offshore, the sharply pointed Skellig Islands are home to thousands of puffins, gannets and other seabirds. It was not always a sanctuary for just birds, however; it was on Skellig Michael (An Sceilg Mhicil), a massive rocky hulk that rises steeply 700 feet above the sea, that a colony of sixth-century monks did the seemingly impossible when they built a retreat of *clocháns* (stone beehive huts). For six centuries it was an impenetrable monastic refuge, abandoned in the 12th century.

Today the Skellig Islands are a UNESCO World Heritage Site. In good weather there is a boat trip at 10 a.m. taking 45 minutes. Once on the island you'll have to climb 640 steps to reach the ruins. Your rewards are the magnificent views and a sense of wonder at the *clocháns*, which have survived all these centuries without mortar, two oratories and a church.

Begin or end your visit to the Skelligs with a stop in the Skellig Heritage Centre on Valentia Island. The stone building, framed by grassy mounds, seems to grow out of the landscape. Here you can see programs and displays on the area's history. Pick up a guide book from the crafts shop, and ask for ferry service information.

✠ A2

Tourist information ✉ Beech Road ☎ 064 663 1633 🕐 Daily 9:15–5:15, Jul.–Sep.; Mon.–Sat. 9:15–5:15, rest of year

Muckross House ✉ Kenmare Road (N71) ☎ 064 667 0144; www.muckross-house.ie 🕐 Daily 9–5:30 (until 7, Jul.–Aug.); farms: daily 10–6, Jun.–Aug.; 1–6, May; Sat.–Sun. 1–6, Mar.–Apr. and Sep.–Oct. 🍴 The Garden Restaurant 🚌 From Killarney 🎟 House and farm $$$; house and gardens $$

Ross Castle ✉ Ross Road, off Muckross Road (N71) ☎ 064 663 5851; www.heritageireland.ie 🕐 Daily 9–5:45, Apr.–Sep.; 9:30–5:45, mid–end Mar. and Oct. 🎟 $$

The Skellig Experience ✉ Skellig Heritage Centre, Valentia Island, off the Ring of Kerry on R765 ☎ 066 947 6306; www.skelligexperience.com 🕐 Daily 10–7, Jul.–Aug.; 10–5, Mar.–Apr. and Sep.–Nov. (can vary) 🍴 Restaurant 🎟 $$; with cruise $$$

Red *Crocosmia*, or coppertips, flower on Valentia Island, off the Iveragh Peninsula in Co. Kerry

Drive
Ring of Kerry

Duration: 1–2 days

The 112-mile Ring of Kerry takes top billing on this tour as you travel from one scenic wonder to the next. The route skirts the edges of the Iveragh Peninsula to Kenmare, then circles back over the mountains via Moll's Gap and Ladies' View to Killarney. Mountains, lakes, sandy beaches and offshore islands form a superb panorama, and Killarney town has its own fair share of lakes and legends.

Starting at the tourist office on Beech Road in Killarney, take the N72 northwest for 13 miles to Killorglin.
Perched on hills above the River Laune, Killorglin is an ideal starting point for this drive. In mid-August, this quiet town is abuzz with the three-day Puck Fair dating from 1613 (see page 147). Pubs stay open around the clock, and every sort of street entertainment goes on nonstop. This is also a traditional gathering place for the country's traveling people, who come to engage in some hard-driving horse trading.
Turn southwest on the N70 to Glenbeigh.
On the main street of this village, look for the bog village adjoining the Red Fox

Inn (www.kerrybogvillage.ie). Bogs have always played an important role in Ireland, and this recreation is an authentic depiction of the lives of the peatbog communities.
Follow the N70 southwest to Cahersiveen.
The drive along the southern banks of Dingle Bay (Bá na Daingin) from Glenbeigh to this small town at the foot of the Bentee Mountain is one of craggy coastal scenery and fields studded with prehistoric stone ring-fort ruins, with clear views of the Dingle Peninsula (Corca Dhuibhne) across the water. At Cahersiveen, Valentia Island comes into view (see page 137). There is a ferry service from Portmagee and another from Reenard Point to Knightstown. The island is noted for its superb scenery of cliffs, mountains, seascapes and vivid subtropical flowers.
Drive 10 miles south on the N70 to Waterville (An Coireán).
Set on a strip of land that separates Ballinskelligs Bay (Bá na Scealg) from the island-sprinkled Lough Currane (Loch Luíoch), this popular resort and fishing center is also known for its superb golf course. Mountains rise from the lake's shores, and on Church Island there are ruins of a 12th-century church that was dedicated to a sixth-century holy man, St. Fionan.
Continue south, then east on the N70 for 22 miles toward Sneem.
Just beyond Coomakista Pass on the N70, and a mile before Caherdaniel

(Cathair Dónall), is Derrynane House. Set in the wooded National Historic Park, this was the birthplace of Daniel O'Connell in 1775. The house is maintained as a museum containing memorabilia on Ireland's beloved "Liberator." Most of O'Connell's political life was spent here; Cahersiveen's Old Barrack's Heritage Centre includes displays on his life.

On the drive east on the N70 from Waterville to Sneem, just east of Caherdaniel, is Castlecove, where, about 1.5 miles north of the road, you will see Staigue Fort, one of the country's best-preserved Iron-Age stone forts. The circular stone walls, 13 feet wide and 18 feet high, have held over the centuries without the benefit of mortar. Along their interior are several flights of stairs in near perfect condition.

Derrynane National Historic Park covers 320 acres and incorporates semitropical plants and coastal trees and shrubs, as well as fine coastal scenery. There is a well-marked nature trail, and swimming is accessible to visitors. The pretty town of Sneem, situated where the Ardsheelaun estuary joins the Kenmare River, is popular for brown trout and salmon fishing, and its fine sandy beaches provide safe swimming. George Bernard Shaw wrote part of *St. Joan* here. Sneem is also the last resting place of Father Michael Walsh, who was a parish priest in the area for 38 years in the 1800s and was immortalized as "Father O'Flynn" in a well-known Irish ballad. Two miles to the south in Parknasilla, the elegant Parknasilla Resort is famed for its rock gardens and colorful subtropical blooms.

Continue east on the N70 for 17 miles to Kenmare.

The drive from Sneem along the banks of the Kenmare River has lovely views of the Caha and Slieve Miskish mountains on the opposite shore. Kenmare faces the broad Kenmare River estuary, with impressive mountains at its back.

Known as *Ceann Mara* (Head of the Sea) by the ancients, today it is a lively heritage town, noted for its sea fishing, safe swimming, walks and climbs, homespun woolen industry and lace. Kenmare is one of Ireland's planned estate towns, dating from 1670. The Heritage Centre details its history, as

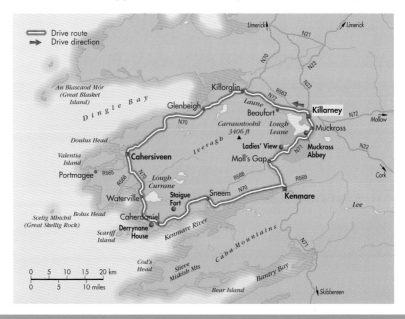

well as covering such intriguing exhibits as the Nun of Kenmare, the Landlords of Kenmare, the Effects of the Famine, and Kenmare Lace Exhibition. A Heritage Trail map focusing on historical sites within walking distance from the center is provided at no charge.

Turn north on the N71 to reach Moll's Gap.
The drive north to Moll's Gap is one of rugged mountains and stone-strewn valleys. The viewing point here affords sweeping views of Macgillycuddy's Reeks and of Ireland's highest mountain, 3,406-foot Carrauntoohil. The Avoca restaurant and craft shop make this a good refreshment stop.

Follow the N71 northeast for 3 miles to Ladies' View.
This excellent mountainside scenic overlook allows far-reaching views over the broad valley of the Killarney lakes. Queen Victoria and her ladies-in-waiting were so enthralled by this view that it was promptly named in their honor.

Some 9 miles north on the return to Killarney are the well-preserved ruins of Muckross Abbey. The abbey dates from 1448 and was built on the site of an earlier religious establishment. Elizabethan-style Muckross House is surrounded by landscaped gardens that slope down to the lake (see page 137).

On the upper floors of the house you will find a small wildlife and bird collection, plus displays of maps and prints. The basement houses a folk museum, weavers' workshop, an audiovisual display about nature and an exhibition about Killarney's copper mines and oak woods. The Muckross Craft Centre consists of craft workshops, a restaurant and gift shop. Muckross Traditional Farms is a working museum that farms the land with the methods used in the 1930s (see page 137).

About a mile before Muckross House, a signpost on the N71 directs you to a scenic footpath that leads to the 60-foot Torc Waterfall. Continue to the top for splendid views or a picnic, or on to the teashop at Muckross House.

Continue for 11 miles northeast on the N71 to Killarney.

Old Barracks Heritage Centre ✉ Bridge Street, Cahersiveen ☎ 066 947 2777; www.theoldbarracks. com 🕐 Mon.–Fri. 10–4:30, Sat. 11:30–4:30, Sun. 1–5, Apr.–Oct.; call to confirm winter hours 🖐 $$
Derrynane House ✉ Caherdaniel ☎ 066 947 5113; www.heritageireland.ie 🕐 Daily 10:30–6, late Apr.–Sep.; Wed.–Sun. 10:30–5, rest of year 🖐 $
Kenmare Heritage Centre ✉ The Square ☎ 064 664 1233 🕐 Daily 9:15–7, Jul.–Aug.; 9:15–6, Jun. and Sep.; 9:15–5, Apr.–May; Mon.–Fri. 9:15–5, Oct. 🖐 Free

Picturesque hillsides – and plenty of shades of green – around Killarney, Co. Kerry

Working fishing boats moor in the waters of Kinsale harbor, overlooked by pretty Kinsale town houses

Kinsale

A picturesque fishing and boating town, Kinsale (18 miles south of Cork city via N71) is a gateway to a meandering coastline drive through west Cork. From its beginnings in 1333, it has witnessed – and participated in – the ebb and flow of Irish history. This is traced through exhibits and photos housed in Kinsale's Regional Museum (weekends only) in the Old Courthouse, built in 1600.

Today Kinsale is a popular yachting center, and home to several top-rated gourmet restaurants. Its narrow, winding streets make for great strolls through the town. The Earl of Desmond built Desmond Castle in the 1500s as a custom house, but over its long history it has served as a prison, wine storage depot and a workhouse during the famine years. These days it has an International Museum of Wine, illustrating Ireland's contribution to the wine trade.

South of town at Castlepark, you can visit the remains of James Fort, which dates back to 1602. The Old Head of Kinsale is a narrow promontory with a ruined 12th-century castle on a high cliff. It overlooks the spot where in 1915 the *Lusitania* was sent to a watery grave by a German submarine, with the loss of 1,198 souls.

In Summer Cove on the eastern side of the estuary stands the still intact Charles Fort. Built in 1683 and in constant use until 1922, the fort was designed in the classic star-shaped style. It sits high on a clifftop, with spectacular views of Kinsale harbor.

Built in the middle of the 13th century, Timoleague Abbey, 10 miles southwest of Kinsale, is one of Ireland's best-preserved Franciscan friaries. Nearby, the Castle Gardens have been maintained by the same family for the past 150 years.

✚ B1

Tourist information ✉ Pier Road ☎ 021 477 2234; www.kinsale.ie 🕐 Daily 9:15–1 and 2:15–5:30
International Museum of Wine ✉ Desmond Castle, Cork Street, Kinsale ☎ 021 477 4855 🕐 Daily 10–6, Easter–Oct. 🖐 $
Desmond Castle ✉ Cork Street ☎ 021 477 4855; www.heritageireland.ie 🕐 Daily 10–6, mid-Apr. to Sep. 🍴 Many restaurants and cafés in Kinsale 🖐 $
Charles Fort ✉ Summer Cove ☎ 021 477 2263; www.heritageireland.ie 🕐 Daily 10–6, mid-Mar. to Oct.; Sat.–Sun. 10–5, rest of year (last admission 1 hour before closing); closed Dec. 25 🍴 Man Friday (see page 209) 🖐 $ ℹ Wear suitable shoes for the uneven terrain; parking nearby

Lough Gur is popular with bird watchers

Limerick

Limerick, the Republic of Ireland's third largest city, gets its name from the Irish *Luimneach* (Bare Spot). Centuries ago, that's just what was here – a barren, hilly bit of land on an island, and because the island sat at the lowest ford of the Shannon, it is believed early Celts built an earthen fort at its highest point. Then came the Danes in 831 to build a base from which to launch their plundering. More than a century later, Brian Ború sent them packing and installed the O'Briens as rulers. St. Mary's Cathedral, built in this period on the site of a Viking meeting place in the oldest part of the city, has a fine view from its bell tower and has intriguing antiquities.

Next came the Normans, building stout city walls and castles. Portions of their walls remain to this day, as does King John's Castle, whose impressive fortification on the banks of the Shannon has guarded Limerick since the early 1200s. The imaginative admissions building sits atop excavated remains of ancient city walls and homes of pre-Norman residents. The massive gate house, corner towers, curtain walls and battlements reflect the authority of royalty, while in the courtyard medieval war machines usually seen only in period movies beguile the imagination. Don't rush through this one – it is a definite "don't miss."

The marvelously restored 15th-century Bunratty Castle was built for the O'Briens, earls of Thomond, and its restoration includes furnishings that look as though they've been here since the days of those first residents. Enter across a drawbridge into the vaulted Great Hall, the center of castle life where elaborate feasts are served up nightly just as they were in days of yore (see page 144). Reconstructions in the Folk Park include a blacksmith shop, post office, draper, tearoom and a tiny pub.

In the 18th century, the city spread beyond the boundaries of the early Irish Town and English Town thanks to Edward Sexton Pery. He spearheaded the building of Georgian townhouses in an area that became known as Newtown Pery, which encompasses much of today's city center.

With 800 years of turbulent history behind it, Limerick has transformed itself from a town with a slightly grubby image to one of progressive modernity built around its cherished monuments from the past. Modern places of interest include the worthwhile Hunt Museum, one of the finest art museums in the country outside the National Gallery in Dublin (see page 81). It contains works by Picasso, Renoir and Henry Moore. Along with medieval statues in stone, bronze and wood, there are Egyptian, Greek and Roman artifacts, Neolithic flints and other Irish relics.

If flying is your passion, you'll know that the first commercial direct flight between the United States and Europe was flown by Pan Am's luxury flying boat *Yankee Clipper*, which landed at Foynes on the broad estuary of the Shannon. Now restored and preserved, the Foynes Flying Boat Museum translates nostalgia for that era into exhibits, an audiovisual show and the radio and weather room with original navigation equipment.

At Lough Gur, in addition to the lake dwelling that dates between AD 500 and 1000, there's a wedge tomb from 2500 BC, one of Ireland's largest stone circles and replicas of weapons, tools and pottery found in this area. The remains of animals no longer seen in Ireland (giant Irish deer and bear) have been unearthed in nearby caves. The area is good for bird watching.

✚ B2

Tourist information ✉ Arthurs Quay ☎ 061 317 522 🕐 Mon.–Sat. 9–6, Sun. noon–5, mid-May to Sep.; Mon.–Sat. 9–5, rest of year

St. Mary's Cathedral ✉ Bridge Street ☎ 061 310 293; www.cathedral.limerick.anglican.org 🕐 Daily 9:30–5 💲 Donation $

King John's Castle ✉ Nicholas Street ☎ 061 360 788; www.shannonheritage.com 🕐 Daily 10–5 (last admission 4) 💰 $$$

Bunratty Castle and Folk Park ✉ Shannon Airport Road (N18) ☎ 061 360 788; www.shannonheritage. com 🕐 Mon.–Fri. 9–5:30, Sat.–Sun. 9–6, Jun.–Aug.; daily 9–5:30, rest of year (last admission 1 hour before closing) 🍴 Tearoom in folk park 🚌 Limerick and Shannon Airport bus 💰 $$$

Hunt Museum ✉ The Custom House, Rutland Street ☎ 061 312 833; www.huntmuseum.com 🕐 Mon.–Sat. 10–5, Sun. 2–5 🍴 Restaurant 💰 $$$

Foynes Flying Boat Musuem ✉ Foynes, 23 miles west of Limerick ☎ 069 65416; www.flyingboatmuseum. com 🕐 Daily 10–5, Mar.–Nov; prebook, rest of year 🍴 Café 💰 $$$

Lough Gur Stone Age Centre ✉ Lough Gur, 16 miles from Limerick ☎ 061 385 186; www.loughgur.com 🕐 Daily 10:30–5 (last admission at 4:30), May–Sep. 🚣 Access to lake free; center $$ ℹ️ Walking tours in Jul. and Aug.

Lismore

Among the several scenic drives around the Cappoquin and Lismore area, the most spectacular is the one that passes through a gap in the Knockmealdown Mountains, known as the Vee. From the outskirts of Lismore, it climbs through larch and rhododendron, and heather-covered mountainsides, to the V-shaped pass. The views from numerous stopping points overlook Tipperary's Golden Vale, before descending to the little town of Clogheen in County Tipperary. High on one mountain slope

stands a most curious grave, that of Samuel Grubb, one-time owner of Castle Grace, who decreed he should be buried upright overlooking his lands. There's a small pathway leading up to the stone cairn that is his final resting place.

✚ C2

Tourist information ✉ Lismore ☎ 058 54975 🕐 Seasonal

Listowel

There is a decidedly literary bent to this north Kerry town, 17 miles northeast of Tralee. It has nurtured several of Ireland's leading writers, including John B. Keane and Bryan McMahon. The tradition lives on during Writer's Week in late May or early June, when lectures and workshops are designed to encourage new writers. Theater thrives with performances by Irish and international troupes in St. John's Arts and Heritage Centre on the square. If you're visiting in September, pay a visit to the Listowel Races.

✚ A2

Tourist information ✉ St. John's Church, The Square ☎ 068 22590 🕐 Mon.–Sat. 10–6, Jun.–Sep.

St. John's Arts and Heritage Centre ✉ The Square, Listowel ☎ 068 22566; www.stjohnstheatrelistowel. com 🕐 Mon.–Sat. 10–1 and 2–6, and evening events (times may vary)

Bunratty Castle, County Clare

Medieval Castle Banquets and Traditional *Céilí*

The medieval banquets at Bunratty and Knappogue castles and the traditional *céilí* at Bunratty Folk Park are a unique experience and appeal to all age groups. No matter which you choose, you'll not regret it – at least one should go on your "don't miss" list. You stand a good chance of being disappointed though if you fail to make reservations through a travel agent or the Shannon Heritage website before you leave home. If you arrive without a reservation, any tourist office in Ireland will try to make one for you (with as much advance notice as you can give them). There is free parking, and tourist offices in Ennis or Limerick can furnish information about bus transportation.

Any lord and lady of the castle spirit you might anticipate for the medieval banquet at Bunratty Castle quickly dissolves into one of great fun and hilarity, and even the stuffiest of types will want to join in as story follows story and song follows song. The internationally famed Bunratty Singers serve up enchanting melodies, and the golden notes of an Irish harp melt the stoniest heart.

Somewhat harder to reach than Bunratty (it's 19 miles from Limerick and 9 miles from Ennis, signposted from Quin, south on R469 and there's no public transportation), Knappogue Castle's medieval banquet is slightly more sedate, but far from stuffy.

Alternatively there's an Irish Night held at Bunratty Folk Park. This evening is smaller and more intimate, and the colorful entertainment focuses on mythical and real women of Ireland – queens, saints and sinners from a Celtic past. The traditional music of pipes, fiddle, *bodhrán* and accordion is what the people of Ireland have made their own and handed down through the centuries. This is the most informal of the three feasts, where audience and performers join together in song and dance. The menu here features spare ribs with honey and whiskey sauce, chicken with apple and Bunratty mead, and fresh homegrown garden produce.

Shannon castle banquets ✉ Town center, Shannon (office) ☎ 061 360 788; www.shannonheritage. com ⓖ Bunratty Castle banquets: twice nightly 5:30 and 8:45; Knappogue Castle's banquet: 6:30, Apr.–Oct.; traditional Irish night *(céilí)* at Bunratty Folk Park: daily 7 p.m., Apr.–Oct. subject to demand

Breathtaking Bunratty Castle in the west of Ireland

Thurles

A large market town on the River Suir, Thurles (pronounced "thur-less") has two castles and a splendid Italianate cathedral, based on the one at Pisa in Italy. The town's Semple Stadium is a major venue for all Gaelic games, and it was in the 18th-century Hayes Hotel that the Gaelic Athletics Association was founded in 1884 to codify and encourage Irish sports.

On the west bank of the River Suir 4 miles south of Thurles, Holycross Abbey was founded in 1168 and was ever after a revered place of pilgrimage. Among its treasures was a particle of the True Cross preserved in a golden shrine dating from 1110, now in the Ursuline Convent in Blackrock, Cork. Restored in 1971, the abbey still contains many religiously significant ruins, and Sunday pilgrimages continue to take place from May through September.

✚ C2

Tourist information ✉ Slievenamon Road, Thurles ☎ 050 422 702 🕓 Daily 9:30–5:30, Mar.–Oct.; Mon.–Fri. 9:30–5:30, rest of year

Tralee

The county town of Kerry, and the northeast gateway to the Dingle Peninsula (Corca Dhuibhne), Tralee grew around the 13th-century Desmond Castle, of which a tiny portion can be seen where Denny Street meets the broad Mall. Kerry County Museum in the Ashe Hall provides a fascinating guide to the archaeological riches and heritage of the "Kingdom" from the Stone Age to the present day. Priceless treasures are displayed in the Museum Gallery, while the Medieval Experience reveals the streets of Tralee as they were in 1450, with all the sights, sounds and smells of a bustling community. You can see what people wore, what they ate, where they lived, and discover why the earls of Desmond, who founded the town, also destroyed it. A trek through the award-winning Tom Crean Room will show you what drove Kerry's

famous explorer, Tom Crean, to risk his life repeatedly in Antarctica with Scott and Shackleton. Touring the narrow, winding streets of the town, you'll see the Gothic-style Holy Cross Church designed by British architect Edward Pugin, with splendid stained glass by Michael Healy. St. John's Church includes a statue of a notable Kerry saint – Brendan the Navigator.

Located two miles out of town along an old ship canal is the 65-foot-high windmill at Blennerville. Built in 1800, it worked continuously until 1850, and was restored to full working order in the 1990s. The exhibition center tells the story of 19th-century emigration from Blennerville port. Train buffs will not want to miss the scenic, narrated two-mile ride from Tralee to Blennerville on the beautifully restored narrow-gauge steam train. Trains leave Tralee on the hour, Blennerville on the half-hour.

For entertainment, don't miss the superb Siamsa Tíre (pronounced "sheem-sa tee-ra" – it means merrymaking), Ireland's National Folk Theatre troupe, which regularly performs in Tralee. This is Irish theater

The windmill at Blennerville, outside Tralee

with a difference – a depiction of rural life in the past through music, song, dance and mime. Performances are in the Irish language, but don't let that put you off – the meaning of every stage action is made clear. Another popular event is the summer Rose of Tralee Festival, when young women with Irish roots come from around the world and compete to become the "Rose" (see pages 19 and 147).

Ballybunion, lying 21 miles northwest of Tralee, has some of Kerry's most glorious beaches, overlooked by soaring cliffs and 14 Celtic promontory forts. For panoramic views, take the cliff walk to the summit of Knockanore. Ballybunion is also home to a seaside golf course that challenged President Clinton during his visit in 1998. The lively Ballybunion Busking (street entertainment) Festival is held every year in August.

✚ A2

Tourist information ✉ Ashe Memorial Hall, Denny Street ☎ 066 712 1288 🕐 Mon.–Sat. 9–7, Sun. 9–6, Jul.–Aug.; Mon.–Sat. 9–6, May–Jun. and Sep.; Mon.–Sat. 9:15–5, Oct.–Apr.

Kerry County Museum ✉ Ashe Memorial Hall, Denny Street ☎ 066 712 7777; www.kerrymuseum.ie

🕐 Daily 9:30–5:30, May–Oct.; Tue.–Sat. 9:30–5, rest of year 🍴 Café 🎫 $$$ ℹ Tralee tourist office on site

Blennerville Windmill and Steam Train ✉ Windmill: on R559, 3 miles west of Tralee; steam train: Ballyard, Tralee ☎ 066 712 1064 🕐 Windmill: daily 9:30–5, Apr.–May and Sep.–Oct.; 9–6, Jun.–Aug.; steam train: daily 11–5, May–Aug. 🍴 Coffee shop 🎫 $$$, joint ticket

Siamsa Tíre ✉ National Folk Theatre, Town Park ☎ 066 712 3055; www.siamsatire.com 🕐 Box office: daily 9–6, call for performances 🎫 $$$ (varies)

Tramore

Tramore's three-mile sand beach and 50-acre amusement park are ideal for families. Kids will love the beach and Splashworld, an enclosed swimming complex. The Tramore Golf Club is nearby and welcomes visitors to its 18-hole course. That giant statue looking down from Great Newtown Head is known locally as "Metal Man," and although the statue was erected to protect mariners, legend has it that any unmarried female who hops three times on one foot around its base will then hop down the aisle within the next year.

✚ C2

Crashing surf along the rugged Tramore coastline

Kerry's Festivals

For five days and nights in August, international beauties with Irish ancestry gather in Tralee to decide who best fits the time-honored description "...lovely and fair as the rose of the summer." The Rose of Tralee International Festival, however, is a far cry from other such competitions. This festival is one of light-hearted fun and frolic that entails parades, pipe bands, street entertainment and the crowning of the "Rose." It's a grand time to be in County Kerry so try and fit it into your visit.

If you'd like to be part of the fun, there are several package deals that cover transportation and accommodations available from local tourist offices. Be sure to make arrangements well in advance, whether you plan to stay in Tralee or in Killarney, 20 miles to the south.

Lighthearted also best describes Killarney's St. Patrick's Weekend Dancing Festival in March. Alongside the lively St. Patrick's Day Parade and parties, the dancing festival sees country music fans descend on the town. There might be a lot of people in fancy dress, but you'll notice a lot of them in cowboy hats and western clothing all ready for a hoedown. There's live music at the Gleneagle Hotel throughout the three-day event.

In mid-August, the hillside market town of Killorglin lets its hair down in three days of what many Irish call sheer madness disguised under the name of the Puck Fair. This bacchanalian event has been held every year since 1613, originally to celebrate the beginning of the harvest. Things get off to a rowdy start when a tremendous male (or puck) goat is hauled up to a high platform in the square and crowned as "King of the Fair." What follows is a free-for-all carnival and country fair, with most pubs staying open around the clock. There is all sorts of street entertainment, and over on the green, you can witness some pretty serious horse and cattle trading.

Just how all this began is a matter of dispute: Some say a goat bleated to alert a shepherd boy of approaching enemy forces and he then alerted the town. This is traditionally a gathering place for the country's traveling people, who come to drive hard bargains in the horse-swapping business, catch up with tinker gossip and indulge in nonstop revelry.

Rose of Tralee Festival Office ☎ 066 712 1322; www.roseoftralee.ie ✉ Ashe Memorial Hall, Denny Street, Tralee

Irish beauties compete at the Rose of Tralee Festival

Waterford

Waterford, Ireland's fifth-largest city with a population of around 50,000, reflects virtually every phase of Irish history. Its fine harbor, the southeast's main seaport, is as alive with freighters along the broad River Suir as it was when Viking longships plied its waters.

Prehistoric dolmens, promontory forts and passage graves speak of the earliest settlers. Legends of valor and incredibly beautiful Iron Age metalwork mirror the two sides of the flamboyant, battle-loving and artistic Celtic clan of the Deise.

The city's walls are among the most extensive Viking remains in the country, and are reminders of those sea-raiders who came in 853 looking for a safe haven from which to launch their plundering forays. They settled here as traders for more than 300 years, and built Waterford City in AD 914. After a bloody battle in 1170, Anglo-Normans took the city and began their own period of dominance and construction.

Reginald's Tower was built in the 13th century on the site of a previous Viking

A new visitor center showcases Waterford Crystal

defensive structure, and has stood sentinel at the end of the quay ever since. Originally, the River Suir lapped at its 12-foot-thick walls, and entry was from inside the city walls only. The strongest fortification on the river, it resisted attacks from a variety of forces, including those of Oliver Cromwell. Now a museum, its fascinating collection of historical and archaeological artifacts cover the city's history from the Viking invasions to the arrival of the Normans in the 12th century. Some of the rebels involved in the 1798 Rebellion were hanged from its beams.

The town has long been associated with Waterford Crystal, its modern factory which produced age-old crystal glass. Sadly the company went into receivership in March 2009 with many job losses. The Waterford brand was bought by an American private equity firm and the glassware is produced in Germany and the Czech Republic. A visitor center, House of Waterford Crystal, opened in 2010 showcasing the best of its products and processes, so visitors can also buy Waterford Crystal made in Ireland and tour the factory.

In the 1980s, Waterford underwent extensive excavations that unearthed fascinating details of the lives of its ancient inhabitants. The former Waterford Museum of Treasures has now closed, but has been replaced by two new attractions. A Medieval Museum planned for early 2013, situated in two medieval undercrofts (a 13th-century chorister's hall and 15th-century wine cellar) will cover the period after the Normans up until the Battle of the Boyne in 1690, with highlights including such medieval manuscripts as the 13-foot-long illuminated Charter Roll featuring some of the earliest depictions of English kings ever seen.

Meanwhile, the restored Bishop's Palace on The Mall covers the more modern history and culture of Waterford from the 18th century to the arrival of the Irish Free State in the early 20th century. Legacies from this period include Waterford's 18th-century architecture, silverware and glassware, particularly Waterford Crystal, and the gardens surrounding the Bishop's Palace.

In the heart of Waterford city on Barronstrand Street, Holy Trinity Cathedral is Ireland's oldest Roman Catholic cathedral, designed and built by John Roberts in 1793. The interior is adorned with extravagant decorations and Waterford crystal chandeliers.

The magnificent 1770s Christ Church Cathedral sits on the site of an 11th-century cathedral. Its Renaissance-style architecture was designed by John Roberts, a noted Waterford architect. A 45-minute audiovisual presentation each Monday and Friday evening at 8 during July and August tells the story of the city from its beginnings to the present.

The people of Waterford are especially welcoming to visitors. One-hour walking tours led by knowledgable and entertaining storytellers are scheduled daily at 11:45 and 1:45 from the massive

riverside stone Granary and depart from the Granville Hotel on the quay at noon and 2. The Green Plaque Trail is a self-guided walking tour outlined in a helpful booklet and map available at the tourist office.

✛ C2 (regional map on page 112)

Tourist information ✛ B2 ✉ The Granary, The Quay ☎ 051 875 823 ◷ Daily 9–6, May–Sep.; Mon.–Fri. 9–6, Sat. 10–6, Sun. 11–5, rest of year ⊓ Restaurant

Reginald's Tower ✛ C1 ✉ The Mall ☎ 051 304 220 ◷ Daily 10–6, Easter to mid-Sep.; 10–5, rest of year ▣ $

House of Waterford Crystal ✛ C1 ✉ The Mall ☎ 051 317 000; www.waterfordvisitorcentre.com ◷ Tours: Mon.–Sat. 9–4:15, Sun. 9:30–4:15, Apr.–Oct.; until 3:15, rest of year. Shop: Mon.–Sat. 9–6, Sun. 9:30–6, Apr.–Oct.; 9:30–5, rest of year

Bishop's Palace ✛ C1 ✉ The Mall ☎ 051 849 650; www.waterfordtreasures.com ◷ Daily 9–6

Holy Trinity Cathedral ✛ B1 ✉ Barronstrand Street ☎ 051 874757; www.waterford-cathedral.com

Christ Church Cathedral ✛ C1 ✉ Cathedral Square ☎ 051 858 958; www.christchurchwaterford.com ◷ Mon.–Fri. 9–6; Sat. 10–4, Jun.–Sep.; Mon.–Fri. 10–5, Sat. 10–4, rest of year ▣ Guided tours $$; donations welcome

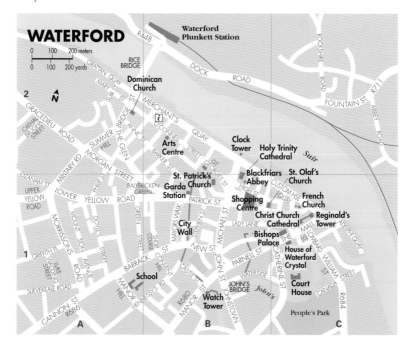

Ulster and Northern Ireland

Introduction and Map 152

Belfast 155

Introduction and Map 155

Sights 160

Walk: Between Old and New 167

Drive: Strangford Lough 169

Regional Sights 172

Feature: American Connection 176

Feature: In St. Patrick's Footsteps 182

Drive: Fermanagh Lakeland 186

Feature: Fionn MacCumhaill 199

Opposite: The Ring of Gullion in County Armagh

Ulster and Northern Ireland

Since 1921, the ancient province of Ulster has consisted of the six counties of Northern Ireland – Antrim, Armagh, Down, Fermanagh, Londonderry and Tyrone – and the three Republic of Ireland border counties of Cavan, Donegal and Monaghan.

Border Counties

At the very top of Ireland, County Donegal is awash with scenic beauty, its jagged coastline bordered by wide strands backed by steep cliffs, inland mountains cut by deep valleys and a countryside filled with antiquities and legends. In the rhythmic patterns of Donegal speech can be heard the distinctive cadence of Ulster, and the Irish language thrives in *Gaeltacht* (Gaelic speaking) areas. From Donegal cottages come some of the world's most beautiful hand-woven tweeds, prized the world over.

The great Irish poet Patrick Kavanagh was born in County Monaghan, and wrote of his home county, "O stoney grey soil of Monaghan, You burgled my bank of youth." Although early on he managed to "escape" to make Dublin his home for 30 years, his poetry is sprinkled with references to and influences from the nearly flat, faintly rolling land that seems to nurture creative talent, from literature to exquisite handmade lace. In the end, he was brought back home to Inishkeen and laid to rest in his native county.

Cuilcagh Mountain, at the Northern Ireland border just south of Enniskillen, rises to 2,188 feet, the highest point in County Cavan's gently undulating landscape of water-splashed rolling hills. The Shannon, Ireland's longest river, rises on its southern slopes, and the Erne flows northward from Lough Gowna through the center of the county into the Upper Erne river, spreading its waters into myriad lakes along the way.

Fishing and water sports draw modern-day residents and visitors alike to the more than 365 lakes in the county.

Northern Ireland

Like the Republic to the south, Northern Ireland is a veritable cornucopia of travel treasures and experiences. Its green fields, cliff-studded and cove-indented coastline, forest-clad mountains and, above all, its hospitable inhabitants invite a visit to this unique part of Ireland.

Highlights include the gentle shoreline of County Down, with its romantic Mountains of Mourne that sweep down to the sea and its firm claim on a good part of St. Patrick's sojourn. Quiet little villages on the Antrim Coast look across to Scotland (clearly visible in many places) whilst the countryside is dotted with Norman castles. Visit County Fermanagh's Lough Erne and its 300 square miles of exquisite scenery, the fabulous Marble Arch Cave, Devenish Island or Armagh's two cathedrals – one Protestant, one Catholic, both named for St. Patrick. Not to be missed are the Sperrin Mountains of County Tyrone, the unique Ulster American Folk Park, which depicts the rural lives of Irish immigrants on both sides of the Atlantic, and Derry/Londonderry's massive old city walls.

Glenariff, "the ploughman's glen" or "Queen of the Glens," is the best known of the nine Glens of Antrim

The Ulster Way provides excellent walking along some 560 miles of interconnected and well-marked footpaths that crisscross the land.

Northern Ireland spreads before the visitor a wealth of other scenic splendors throughout all six counties. Because the province is small (about the size of Connecticut), in the space of one week it is possible to comfortably visit most of the major attractions.

Myths

It was in this part of Ireland that the champion Cuchulainn singlehandedly guarded the border against the onslaught of Connacht Queen Maeve when she set out to capture the Brown Bull of Cooley. This was home territory for Fionn MacCumhaill (see page 199) and his faithful Fianna warriors, and it was within the borders of Ulster that the beautiful Deirdre o' the Sorrows played out her life's tragedy.

The People

The accents of the north fall on the ear with the soft burr of Scotland, mingled with the lilting Irish brogue of the Republic. It's an enchanting mix, and don't be at all surprised if you find yourself ending sentences with the distinctive lift that characterizes so much of what you hear.

Along with their speech, the people of the north have inherited a mix of influences, with Celtic history overlaid with cultural elements brought by English and Scottish planters. You'll see squash and cricket played more often north of the border and hear music tinged with both traditional Irish and Scottish melodies. Belfast's magnificent Opera House is as likely to present an English pantomime as homegrown Irish theater.

Although one-third of Northern Ireland's population is concentrated in Belfast, due to their largely rural heritage Northern Ireland's inhabitants tend to be outdoor people who make the most of the plentiful natural resources lavished on them by nature.

With the British Isles' largest lake (Lough Neagh), 50 miles of tranquil cruising waters on Lough Erne and rivers teeming with fish, water sports rank high in leisure activities – from fishing, both freshwater and coastal, to deep-water sea angling, to boating and water skiing. Golf, hiking and cycling follow closely behind.

Politics

For many years tensions rose in Northern Ireland at particular times of the year, when different communities celebrated events important to them. The marching season marked by the Unionist community was particularly volatile, tensions rising to a peak around July 12 with annual marches or "demonstrations" for King Billy's victory in 1690 at the Battle of the Boyne. The main issue arose around marching through Republican or Catholic areas, but these have dissipated and little policing is necessary these days. Likewise, the St. Patrick's Day celebrations are more family events, discouraging all flags except the cross of St. Patrick to maintain neutrality. Despite intermittent dissident activity, the Troubles are now very much muted and political parties are working together to maintain peace.

With the ending of the hostilities, the economy of Northern Ireland began to thrive again, with new industries starting up and a lot of city regeneration in evidence – although, like the rest of Europe, the province suffered a setback in the recession that hit in late 2008.

One thing is certain: Both traditions welcome visitors warmly and are equally proud of the natural beauty and historical monuments of their homeland. Perhaps because of their turbulent recent history, Northern Ireland natives are also especially anxious that visitors return home with positive memories.

Belfast

Belfast's name in Irish, Béal Feirste, means Mouth of the Sandy Ford, originally a crossing over the River Farset. It flowed along what today is known as Castle Street, which, in turn, takes its name from the castle built here by Norman John de Courcy in the 12th century. Nothing remains of this castle now, but the city grew up all around this point, its population boosted by English and Scottish Protestants who came here during the Plantation of Ulster in the 17th century. The city continued to grow and develop over the following years, thanks in large part to a thriving linen industry.

In 1791 Wolfe Tone founded the Society of United Irishmen in Belfast to bring together Protestants and Catholics who chafed under the repressive Penal Laws. In 1798 their efforts led to an uprising, one that was quickly subdued by English forces.

The shipyard, that was to become one of the largest shipyards in the world and contribute so much to the city's growth, was opened in 1791. By the time the Industrial Revolution was in full bloom during the 19th century, both ship-building (the *Titanic* was built here) and the linen trade had welcomed newer, more modern operating methods. Both industries prospered, and Belfast's population grew rapidly.

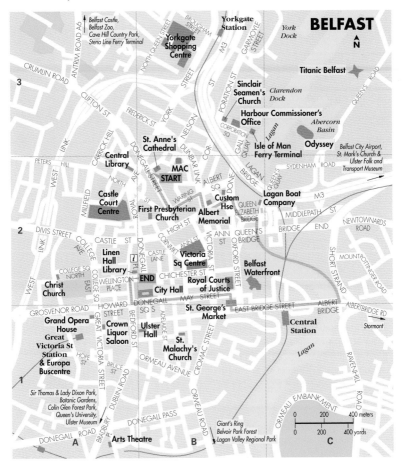

Queen's Bridge across the River Lagan, Belfast, with the *Beacon of Hope* sculpture on the right

The city today is a bustling, energetic center of industry. Belfast's unique character has developed through the combination of economic and political struggle, hard work and a special brand of Irish humor.

For the visitor it is easy to get around, and has many points of interest. The most prominent landmark – City Hall – must be credited to Queen Victoria, whose statue adorns Donegall Square and whose era of architectural style is in evidence around the city. Belfast's ambience today, however, is far from Victorian. Both the city center, the riverfront and the Titanic Quarter are taking on new faces, incorporating pedestrian areas dotted with benches and street entertainers. The Titanic Quarter is undergoing the most radical

changes. It began with the millennium enertainment center, "Odyssey," and has been spreading through the quarter (see page 164). The latest addition is the Titanic Belfast project, a six-floor building that looks like a cross between an iceberg and the RMS *Titanic* itself.

Belfast is a leading tourist destination within Europe with more than 400 places to eat and drink. The city center is a first-rate shopping destination, with many of Britain's leading stores, as well as shops selling local crafts.

Belfast city center is fairly compact and most of the important sights are within easy walking distance. To explore the city on foot, take it neighborhood by neighborhood and use local buses to get you from one to another. The Shankill Road area (Protestant, loyalist) is northwest of the center; the Falls Road area (Catholic, nationalist) is to the

The Parliament Buildings at Stormont – the seat of the Northern Ireland Assembly

west; Malone and Ballynafeigh areas are to the south; and the Sydenham, Bloomfield, Belmont and Ballymacarrett areas are to the east.

The City Hall marks Donegall Square as the hub of Belfast city center. From the square, Donegall Place leads north to the important shopping area along Royal Avenue, while to the south, Bedford Street leads into Dublin Road and the Queens University area.

With the easing of political tensions, a vibrant cultural scene has emerged in this relatively young city. It caters to all tastes, from classical music and theater to the latest in popular music led by Van Morrison, who began his career with a Belfast rhythm-and-blues group.

Venues are as varied as the choice of performances. The Waterfront Hall on the River Lagan presents a variety of entertainment, as does the Grand Opera

Tracing Your Roots

If tracking down your Northern Ireland ancestors is a top priority, collect as much information about your forebears as possible before leaving home. It is also a good idea to contact Northern Ireland genealogical organizations well in advance of your arrival. They will reply to every letter, but they ask that you enclose three international reply coupons with your query to help with the cost of mailing to you.

The Public Record Office is the main source for genealogical research in Ulster. While they do not conduct individual genealogical research, members of the public are welcome to search the records themselves.

The General Register Office has records of births and deaths from 1864 and marriage registrations since 1922. For a small fee, the Registrar General will arrange searches of any births, marriages or deaths in Northern Ireland prior to 1922.

You can, of course, employ a professional to do your research. For a list of members and the services they offer, write to: Association of Ulster Genealogists and Record Agents (AUGRA), Glen Cottage, Glenmachan Road, Belfast BT4 2NP. Or visit their website: www.augra.com.

Belfast City Council now has an online search facility for burial records since 1869 at Belfast City, Roselawn and Dundonald Cemeteries; www.belfastcity.gov.uk.

Public Record Office (PRONI)

✉ 2 Titanic Boulevard, Belfast BT3 9HQ
☎ 028 9053 4800; www.proni.gov.uk
🕐 Mon.–Fri. 9–4:45, Thu. until 8:45

The General Register Office

✉ Oxford House, 49–55 Chichester Street, Belfast BT1 4HL
☎ 028 9025 2000; www.groni.gov.uk
🕐 Mon.–Fri. 9:30–4

House on Great Victoria Street (see page 163). Ulster Orchestra concerts are scheduled in Ulster Hall, now restored to its original Victorian splendor, on Bedford Street, and Waterfront Hall on the River Lagan, while the international superstar concerts are likely to be in the Odyssey, Ulster Hall or Kings Hall. Traditional, folk, jazz, blues and rock music are found in such pubs as McHughs (Queen's Square), the Fibber Magees (Blackstaff Square) and Ronnie Drew's (May Street), formerly

Magennis's Bar. If you want to sample the famous Irish *craic*, head for the Empire Bar on Botanic Avenue where there are lively themed nights, live music, cover bands and plenty of relaxed fun on most nights of the week.

Irish and international plays are staged in the Lyric Theatre on Ridgeway Street and visual and performing arts are featured at the Old Museum Arts Centre on College Square North. The MAC (Metropolitan Arts Centre) is Belfast's new performing arts venue.

Essential Information

Tourist Information
Belfast Welcome Centre ✉ 47 Donegall Place ☎ 028 9024 6609; www.gotobelfast. com 🕐 Mon.–Sat. 9–7, Sun. 11–4, Jun.–Sep.; Mon.–Sat. 9–5:30, Sun. 11–4, rest of year

Urban Transportation
In Belfast, Metro operates a network to all parts of the city, with departures from Donegall Square East, West and North, Upper Queen Street, Wellington Place, Chichester Street and Castle Street. Information on which buses go where is posted at Donegall Square West, and routes are listed on the Belfast city map available from the tourist office.

For bus service details (both Metro and Ulsterbus), contact Translink Call Centre ☎ 028 9066 6630; www.translink.co.uk 🕐 Daily 7 a.m.–8 p.m. Translink also has information on Northern Ireland Railways.

City Sightseeing runs tours every 30 minutes 10–5 in summer, every hour 10–4 in winter; ☎ 02890 321321. Coiste Irish Political Tours are mostly led by former political prisoners and

visit the Falls Road Murals, Milltown Cemetery and places associated with the United Irishmen ☎ 028 9020 0770. Tickets are available from Belfast Welcome Centre.

Taxi stands are at main rail stations, ports and airports. Black cabs are metered and service stands are at Central Station, both bus stations and City Hall. If using a taxi without a meter, agree on a price before you get in.

Airport Information
Belfast International Airport is 17 miles northwest of the city in Crumlin. The George Best Belfast City Airport is 3 miles northeast, with UK and European flights. Most flights from the U.S. and Canada land at Belfast International. There are frequent Translink services to and from the city. From City Airport passengers can take the Translink bus into the city. ☎ Belfast International Airport: 028 9448 4848; Belfast City Airport: 028 9093 9093 ✋ Belfast City from City Airport £2 one way, £3 return. Taxi from £8; from Belfast International Airport Express 300 £7 one way, £10 return. Taxi from £25.

Climate – average highs and lows for the month

Jan.	Feb.	Mar.	Apr.	May	Jun.	Jul.	Aug.	Sep.	Oct.	Nov.	Dec.
8°C	9°C	11°C	13°C	16°C	18°C	19°C	19°C	17°C	14°C	11°C	8°C
46°F	48°F	52°F	55°F	61°F	64°F	66°F	66°F	63°F	57°F	52°F	46°F
3°C	3°C	4°C	6°C	8°C	10°C	13°C	13°C	11°C	8°C	6°C	4°C
37°F	37°F	39°F	43°F	46°F	50°F	55°F	55°F	52°F	46°F	43°F	39°F

Belfast Sights

Key to symbols

✚ map coordinates refer to the Belfast map on page 155 💷 admission charge: $$$ more than £6, $$ £3–£6, $ less than £3

See page 5 for complete key to symbols

Albert Memorial

The Albert Memorial Clock Tower, designed by W. J. Barre, looks loftily towards the River Lagan on High Street and pays tribute to Prince Albert, Queen Victoria's beloved consort. It is affectionately known as Belfast's "leaning tower" because it is slightly less than straight (more than a yard off true vertical). Unfortunately, you'll have to admire the lean from the outside as the tower is not open to the public.

✚ B2

Belfast Castle

From its perch on Cave Hill, 400 feet above sea level, Belfast Castle was built in the late 1800s as a family residence and was a gift to the city in 1934 from the Earl of Shaftesbury. Its Scottish baronial architecture features a six-story square tower. It is used primarily for private functions, but the Victorian arcade cellar has stores, a bar and cellar restaurant open daily. The visitor center has information on Cave Hill as well as the castle itself. There are also pleasant

Belfast Castle, on the slopes of Cave Hill, replaced a 12th-century Norman castle that burned down in 1708

Belfast

The Palm House conservatory at the Botanic Gardens is an early example of a curvilinear cast iron glasshouse

walkways in the castle's 200-acre estate, and an adventure playground.

✚ Off map at A3 ✉ Antrim Road (2.5 miles from city center, signposted from Antrim Road) ☎ 028 9077 6925; www.belfastcastle.co.uk 🕐 Mon.–Sat. 9 a.m.–10:30 p.m., Sun. 9–6 🍴 Cellar Restaurant 🖐 Free

Belfast Zoo

Belfast's Zoo, with its hillside location and views of the city, is a delight. The gorilla and chimp houses have won welfare awards, and some species roam free. Don't miss the penguin and sea lion enclosures. There are some 160 species of rare and endangered animals in total – keep a special lookout for the moloch gibbons and west lowland gorillas.

✚ Off map at A3 ✉ Antrim Road (4 miles north of city on Cave Hill) ☎ 028 9077 6277; www.belfastzoo.co.uk 🕐 Daily 10–7; last admission 5, Apr.–Sep.; 10–4, last admission 2:30, rest of year 🍴 Restaurants 🖐 $$$

Belvoir Park Forest

Located in South Belfast, this park comprises a mix of woodland and historical sites such as a Norman motte and bailey and a medieval graveyard. Take a trail map from the tourist office and navigate the paths to the arboretum, most striking in fall when the leaves are an array of reds and golden browns.

✚ Off map at B1 ☎ 028 9052 4480 🕐 Dawn–dusk 🖐 Free

Botanic Gardens

Established in 1827, these outstanding gardens are noted for the Victorian-style Palm House glass house and its rare plants, including banana, aloe, rubber, bamboo and Bird of Paradise flower. The Tropical Ravine, or Fernery, a profusion of tropical plants in a sunken glen, can be seen from the observation balcony. The outdoor gardens, first planted in 1927, feature colorful rose beds.

✚ Off map at A1 ✉ Stranmillis Road (signposted from the M1/M2, Balmoral exit) ☎ 028 9031 4762 🕐 Gardens: daily dawn–9 p.m., mid-Apr. to mid-Aug.; dawn–dusk, rest of year; Tropical Ravine and Palm House: daily 1–5, Apr.–Sep.; 1–4, rest of year 🚇 Metro 7 to College Park, 8 to Queen's University 🖐 Free

Cave Hill Country Park

Neolithic men carved the five caves that give this popular public park on the slopes of a 1,200-foot basalt cliff its name, and the caves have provided shelter for the generations that followed. From the top there are spectacular panoramic views of Belfast and the valley. Rebellion was on the minds of Wolfe Tone, Henry Joy McCracken and other United Irishmen when they met here for two days in 1795 to plot the 1798 uprising. There are more walks in the park (remember which color arrow you need to follow for your specific route) and for children there's an adventure playground.

➕ Off map at A3 ✉ 3 miles north of city, off Antrim Road. Numerous access points; parking at Castle or Zoo ☎ 028 9077 6925 🕐 Park: daily dawn–dusk; center: Mon.–Sat. 9 a.m.–10 p.m., Sun. 9–6 💷 Free

City Hall

This massive two-story Portland stone building crowned with a copper dome and set around a central courtyard took 10 years to build (begun in 1888). Inside Greek and Italian marble features alongside mosaic, stained glass, and wood paneling. Experienced guides lead free tours.

➕ B2 ✉ Donegall Square South ☎ 028 9027 0456 🕐 Mon.–Thu. 8:30–5, Fri 8:30–4.30; tours Mon.–Fri. 11, 2 and 3, Sat. 2 and 3 💷 Free

Colin Glen Forest Park

It is well worth a stop at the visitor center in this 200-acre park at the foot of Black Mountain to watch the audiovisual presentation and other displays in the visitor center before setting out on one of the nature trails.

➕ Off map at A1 ✉ Stewartstown Road (5 miles west of the city) ☎ 028 9061 4115; www.colinglentrust.org 🕐 Park: daily dawn–dusk; center: Mon.–Fri. 9–5, Sat. 11–3 💷 Free

Crown Liquor Saloon

Bend an elbow at least once or go for lunch at the Crown Liquor Saloon, which dates from 1849. This marvelous old pub has Corinthian pillars flanking the entrance and an elegant interior of carved woodwork, marble counters and painted ceramic tiles. The National Trust conservation organization rescued the building from over-zealous modernization and it is now back to its original state. The saloon is still lit by the original gas lamps.

➕ A1 ✉ 46 Great Victoria Street ☎ 028 9024 3187; www.crownbar.com 🕐 Mon.–Sat. 11:30 a.m.–midnight, Sun. 12:30–11 🍴 Restaurant

View from Cave Hill looking out over Belfast and Belfast Lough – on a clear day you can see Scotland

Giant's Ring

An impressive Bronze Age antiquity within easy reach of Belfast. The huge circular structure is more than 600 feet in diameter, and the enigmatic Druid's Altar dolmen inhabits its center. Its original purpose is a matter of speculation. Prehistoric rings were commonly thought to be the home of fairies, and consequently were treated with respect, but in the 18th century they were found to make terrific race courses. The earthen bank surrounding the ring, 20 feet wide and 12 feet high, is a natural grandstand.

✚ Off map at B1 ✉ Near Edenderry village, a mile south of Shaw's Bridge, off the B23 ✋ Free

Grand Opera House

Following a £10 million extension, this remains Northern Ireland's premier venue for cultural performance. The stunning late-Victorian masterpiece includes 24 gilt elephant heads separating boxes sporting canopies, Buddhas scattered about the draperies, and lots of gold and maroon.

✚ A1 ✉ 2–4 Great Victoria Street ☎ 028 9024 1919; www.goh.co.uk ⏰ Tours by appointment ✋ Tour $$; shows vary

Harbour Commissioner's Office

Built in 1854, this is probably the grandest building in Belfast. Exquisite mosaic floors inlaid with marble and beautiful stained-glass windows reflect Belfast's Victorian prosperity. In the barrel-roofed Barnet Room, maritime paintings adorn the walls and stained glass depicts the arms of colonial partners such as Canada and Australia.

✚ B3 ✉ Corporation Square ☎ 028 9055 4422 ⏰ Tours by appointment ✋ $$

Lagan Boat Company

Climb aboard the M.V. *Joyce Too* for a tour or a Titanic Special that takes in the Harland & Wolff shipyards with commentary about the ill-fated luxury liner. Passengers can embark or disembark outside the Odyssey center.

The Crown Liquor Saloon, Great Victoria Street

The company also runs a hop-on/hop-off water taxi, Harbour/Lough tours and a Carrickfergus day trip. Check for sailing times before turning up as schedules change frequently and the weather can also affect the trips.

✚ B2 ✉ Departures from Donegall Quay ☎ 028 9033 0844/07718 910423 (cell phone); www.laganboatcompany.com ⏰ Lagan tour: Sat.–Sun. 12:30, 2, 3:30, Jun.–Sep.; 12:30, 2, Oct.; Titanic Boat tour: Mon.–Fri. 12:30, Sat.–Sun. 12:30 and 2, Apr.–Oct. Harbour/Lough tour: Sun. 3:30, Jun.–Sep.; Carrickfergus: Thu. leaves 10, returns 2:30, Jul.–Sep. ✋ $$$

Lagan Valley Regional Park and Minnowburn Beeches

A walk along the 9 miles of paths on the banks of the River Lagan from Belfast to Lisburn takes you past old locks and lock houses from the late 1700s, when horses towed coal barges. If you are here in the fall, the blazing colors of the Minnowburn Beeches woodlands are wonderful. You can enjoy pleasant walks from the Beeches to Edenderry and the Giant's Ring (see page 163).

✚ Off map at B1 ✉ Towpath begins near Belfast Boat Club in Stranmillis and runs upstream from Moore's Bridge, Hillsborough Road in Lisburn. Minnowburn Beeches are 3.5 miles south of Belfast at Shaw's Bridge on Milton Road ☎ 028 9049 1922 ✋ Free

Linen Hall Library

Established in 1788, this is the oldest library in the city. It began life as a charitable project and is still supported by public subscription. Among its collections are books on heraldry, books by Robert Burns, documents of local history and an impressive array of press coverage during the "Troubles" that began in 1969. Thomas Russell, librarian here in 1803, was executed for his revolutionary activities.

🔲 A2 ✉ 17 Donegall Square North ☎ 028 9032 1707; www.linenhall.com ⏱ Mon.–Fri. 9:30–5:30, Sat. 9:30–4. Tours must be arranged in advance 🍴 Café 🎟 Free

Metropolitan Arts Centre (MAC)

The latest addition to Belfast's arts scene, the MAC opened in its new state-of-the-art, purpose-built home in the Cathedral Quarter in 2012. The focus here is on music, art and theater, as well as special family days like Super Saturday and Sunday. These are workshops aimed at getting families involved in a range of artistic activities such as sculpting and digital photography.

🔲 B2 ✉ Exchange Street ☎ 028 9023 5053; www.themaclive.com ⏱ Daily 10–7 (later on performance nights) 🍴 Canteen

Odyssey

Belfast's big millennium complex covers 23 acres of the riverfront. It includes W5, a science center with more than 100 interactive exhibits, an IMAX theater, a 12-screen multiplex movie theater and huge arena. The Pavilion next door contains restaurants, bars and shops.

🔲 C3 ✉ 2 Queen's Quay ☎ 028 9093 9074 (arena) or 028 9046 7700 (W5); www.odysseyarena.com; www.w5online.co.uk ⏱ W5 science center: Mon.–Sat. 10–5 (Fri. and Sat. to 6 on school holidays), Sun. noon–6. Call for times of other attractions 🚌 Metro 26 🎟 $$; Science Center $$$

Queen's University and Welcome Centre

Queen's University has a gallery and visitor center and is close to restaurants, accommodations and shops. The University District is a charming mixture of little mid-Victorian row houses (largely occupied by arts and law faculties), complete with front gardens, and the very formal Tudor-revival-style main building designed by Charles Lanyon in 1849. There's a strong emphasis on science studies, and the full-time student body numbers about 14,000, with another 10,000 part-time students. The visitor center features exhibitions and university memorabilia.

🔲 Off map at A1 ✉ University Road ☎ 028 9097 5252; www.queenseventus.com ⏱ Visitor center: Mon.–Sat. 9:30–4:30, Sun. 10–1. Campus tours Sat. noon 🎟 Tours $$

Sinclair Seamen's Church

Charles Lanyon, who designed so many Belfast buildings, was the architect for this unique 1857 church, whose interior is like a maritime museum. The pulpit is built like a ship's prow, and the nautical theme continues on the organ, with both port and starboard lighting.

🔲 B3 ✉ Corporation Square ☎ 028 9071 5997 ⏱ Wed. 2–5; Sun. services at 11 and 6:30

Sir Thomas and Lady Dixon Park

Named for Sir Thomas and Lady Dixon, the beautiful rose gardens in this park have won international acclaim and are widely acknowledged to be among the world's finest. The City of Belfast International Rose Garden is celebrated with Rose Week every July, drawing some 50,000 visitors. In addition to more than 20,000 rose bushes, there's an interesting Japanese garden and wooded areas and shrubberies on several levels plus a play area for the youngsters.

🔲 Off map at A1 ✉ Upper Malone Road ☎ 028 9032 0202 ⏱ Daily dawn–dusk 🍴 Coffee shop 🎟 Free

St. Anne's Cathedral

Belfast Cathedral (St. Anne's) was built between 1899 and 1904 and has a fine mosaic showing St. Patrick landing in Ireland at Saul in AD 432 above the entrance to the Chapel of the Holy

Belfast Cathedral on Donegall Street is dedicated to St. Anne

Spirit. Look for the large Celtic cross on the exterior and the stainless steel spire, added in 2007.

🕆 B2 ✉ Donegall Street ☎ 028 9032 8332; www.belfastcathedral.org 🕐 Mon.–Sat. 10–4, Sun. outside services; services Mon.–Sat. 1, Sun. 10, 11, 3:30

St. Malachy's Church
Its striking turrets overlooking the Upper Markets area, St. Malachy's Roman Catholic Church opened in 1844 and has a fine fan-vaulted ceiling.

🕆 B1 ✉ Alfred Street ☎ 028 9032 1713
🕐 Daily 8:30–5:45

Stormont
A mile-long avenue leads up to the huge white building that has been, since it opened in 1932, the seat of Northern Ireland self-governing parliaments. The Good Friday Agreement of 1998 was hammered out here, and it was the seat of the resultant executive committee of the Northern Ireland Assembly.

The statue standing in the middle of the avenue is of Sir Edward Carson, who was largely responsible for maintaining Northern Ireland's position as a part of the United Kingdom when he led the opposition of Irish home rule in 1912. The building itself is not open to the public, but the impressive grounds are open daily until 7:30 p.m.

✚ Off map at C2 ✉ Upper Newtownards Road
🚌 Metro 4

Exhibits at the Ulster Folk and Transport Museum

Titanic Belfast

Belfast's most exciting new attraction opened in 2012 with a festival commemorating the centenary of the sinking of the RMS *Titanic* in 1912. Spread over six floors, it has nine interactive galleries that take visitors on a journey through *Titanic*-era Belfast. There are temporary exhibition and performance spaces.

✚ C3 ✉ Queen's Road, Titanic Quarter ☎ 028 9076 6386; www.titanicbelfast.com ⏰ Timed tours: Mon.–Sat. 9–7, Sun. 10–5, Apr.–Sep.; daily 10–5, Oct.–Mar. 🍴 Restaurant

Ulster Folk and Transport Museum

The open-air Ulster Folk and Transport Museum, on 176 acres of beautiful parkland estate, feature a fascinating collection of rural and urban shops and other buildings, all furnished in 1900s style. Many were moved stone by stone from their original locations and rebuilt here. The result is a microcosm of Ulster life during the 18th and 19th centuries. Traditional Irish cottages, watermills, farms, a 1792 church, a pub, a flax-scutching mill, schools, printer's workshops and even a small town make this well worth a visit. Costumed interpreters and a schedule of craft demonstrations bring history to life.

The Transport Museum has a diverse range of exhibitions which include the largest locomotive (Old Maeve) built in Ireland, trams, buses, cars, and all sorts of motorized machines. Take in the popular "Titanica" exhibition on the "unsinkable" liner, and view the "Flight Experience," an interactive exhibition.

In addition to the various permanent exhibitions and buildings, the museum has lots of special events during the year such as horse-plowing, music days and spooky Halloween fun.

✚ Off map at C2 ✉ Bangor Road, Cultra Manor, Holywood, Co. Down (7 miles east of Belfast on the A2, the road to Bangor) ☎ 0845 608 000; www.uftm.org.uk ⏰ Tue.–Sun. 10–5, Mar.–Sep.; Tue.–Fri. 10–4, Sat.–Sun. 11–4, rest of year 🍴 Tearoom 🎫 Combined ticket $$$

Ulster Museum

In the lovely surroundings of the Botanic Gardens, the Ulster Museum has given remarkable insight into the life and history of the province. A £17.2 million project has redeveloped and extended the museum, and after three years and several delays, it finally relaunched in 2010. The museum has comprehensive collections of Irish art, history, natural sciences and archeology as well as sections devoted to world cultures, animal and plant life. Children can get hands-on in Discovery Centres.

Also of interest are the collections of fine and applied arts ranging from works by Gainsborough and Turner to pieces by contemporary Irish artists.

✚ Off map at A1 ✉ Stranmillis Road, next to Botanic Gardens ☎ 0845 608 000; www.ulstermuseum.org.uk ⏰ Tue.–Sun. 10–5 🍴 Café 🚌 Metro 7 to College Park, 8 to Queen's University 🎫 Free

The Big Fish by John Kindness, a printed ceramic mosaic sculpture containing a time capsule

Walk
Between Old and New

Refer to route marked on city map on page 155

This walk combines some of Belfast's major attractions with a portion of the exciting and ongoing rejuvenation of the city's waterfront, which is helping to make Belfast a popular European tourist destination. As you walk, notice the contrast between Belfast's distinctive Georgian, Victorian and Edwardian buildings and the newer structures along the river. Begin your tour at St. Anne's Cathedral. Allow about one and a half hours.

Located on Lower Donegall Street, the imposing Hiberno-Romanesque St. Anne's is sometimes called Belfast Cathedral. Take a look at the striking mosaic inside depicting the arrival of St. Patrick on his return to Northern Ireland (see page 182).

From the cathedral turn left and walk down Donegall Street, left onto Waring Street, right onto Skipper Street and left again onto High Street.

The poor old Albert Memorial Clock lists slightly to one side. This is due to the fine silty soil on which he stands, and because the River Farset (after which Belfast is named) runs underneath High Street into the Lagan. **From the Albert Memorial, walk straight ahead past Custom House Square and turn right to reach Donegall Quay.**

The Lagan Weir, beautifully spotlighted at night, is located close to the spot where Belfast began and maintains the river level close to the high-tide mark. The small conical building at the west end of the weir housed the former Lagan Lookout. Near here, you can take a boat tour of the shipyards where the *Titanic* was built (see page 163).

Leaving the Lagan Boat Company jetties by *The Big Fish* sculpture, cross the bridge and follow the marked Riverside Walk.

Notice the huge block of art nouveau apartments, quite a departure from Belfast's traditional architectural style.

At the beginning of a curve in the river, look across to the opposite bank for a view of the Waterfront Hall, the most strikingly modern resident of Belfast's riverfront. There's a bit of irony that its location is Lanyon Place, named for Sir Charles Lanyon, the architect largely responsible for the city center's Victorian buildings. A wonder of glass and metal, the badly needed concert and conference center seats 2,500 and hosts concerts, comedy and shows by renowned performing artists. Made of bronze, the auditorium exterior will eventually turn green and reflect the dome of the City Hall.

Next-door neighbors to the Waterfront Hall, the massive Hilton hotel and huge British Telecom Call Centre offices are tall, red-brick structures that could be called Belfast's skyscrapers.

Cross the river at Albert Bridge and walk along East Bridge Street to the intersection with Oxford Street.

One peek inside St. George's Market and it's a sure bet you'll linger to explore this 19th-century covered marketplace that has been a Belfast tradition for generations. Now renovated and revitalized, in Friday's Variety Market you'll find everything from fresh produce to secondhand books and antiques, while Saturday is the best day for foodies on Oxford Street. Sunday is a mix of the two.

Exit the market, turn left on May Street and continue forward to Donegall Square.

Built of white Portland stone in 1906, the Edwardian City Hall facade is 300 feet long, with a copper dome rising 173 feet. Equally impressive interior features are the marble grand staircase and main entrance (see page 162). The city council meets here, and in its custody is the Charter of Belfast granted by King James I in 1613.

Cross to Donegall Square North.

If you're interested in Irish politics or any phase of Northern Ireland culture, allow time to browse through the collections at Linen Hall Library, one of the oldest subscription libraries in the United Kingdom (see page 164).

End your tour here and walk north to Donegall Place for shopping, or head south on Bedford Street and Dublin Road to reach the Queen's University area.

The copper dome of the Waterfront Hall will turn green over time to match Belfast's Victorian buildings

Small boats are moored outside Portaferry, within sight of its brightly painted houses

Drive
Strangford Lough

Duration: 1 day

This 87-mile drive southeast of Belfast takes in Belfast and Strangford loughs, delves into the past at the Ulster Folk and Transport Museum and Downpatrick, explores picturesque villages such as Strangford and Portaferry and drops in on stately homes Mount Stewart and Castle Ward.

Take the A2, which leads east out of the city center, and then follow the signs to Bangor. After 7 miles (look for the brown sign at Cultra) turn left for the excellent and not-to-be-missed Ulster Folk and Transport Museum.

The Ulster Folk and Transport Museum, on the grounds of Cultra Manor, tells the story of the province's past through buildings that have been saved and meticulously reconstructed at this site. You can wander through a thatched cottage, a rectory and a terraced house, and watch demonstrations of traditional crafts. A church, schoolhouse, water-powered mills and other buildings give a vivid picture of the past.

The transport section spans the history of transportation, from creels used by a donkey carrying turf, through the grand ocean-going liners built in Belfast, to ultramodern aircraft from the Belfast

firm Short Brothers and Harland. This is undoubtedly one of the best museums in Ireland (see page 166).

Turn left and follow the A2 for 4 miles. Turn right onto the A21 following the sign for Newtownards, 3 miles farther on.

This thriving town lies among some of the richest arable land in Ulster. St. Finnian founded Movilla Abbey in AD 540, and the Dominican priory was established by the Normans in the 13th century. A hollow, octagonal, 17th-century market cross also served as the town watch and jail. The impressive town hall was built around 1770 by the Londonderry family who also built Scrabo Tower overlooking Strangford Lough.

Take the A20, following signs for Portaferry to Greyabbey.

Greyabbey, unsurprisingly, derives its name from its 12th-century Cistercian abbey. North of the village is Mount Stewart, a magnificent garden where exotic plants flourish in formal terraces and parterres or in natural settings. Lady Londonderry, the renowned hostess and leader of London society, created this unique garden after World War I. Each garden has a name, such as *Tir n'an Og* (the Land of Eternal Youth), the Mairi Garden, Peace Garden, the Dodo Terrace and the Italian Garden. The lake is particularly beautiful. The house, the early home of Lord Castlereagh, holds the 22 chairs used at the Congress of Vienna and a masterpiece by the painter Stubbs ranks among its treasures. Designed as a banquet house, the

Temple of the Winds is a superb piece of 18th-century landscape architecture.

Take the A20 for 4 miles to Kircubbin. Turn left on to the B173 for 3 miles, then turn left for Portavogie.

Up to 40 boats fill the attractive harbor of Portavogie when the fleet is in. Shellfish are plentiful and hotels also serve a good variety of fresh fish. Seals regularly follow the boats into the harbor to scavenge for food before the load is auctioned on the harborside.

Take the A2 south for 2 miles. At Cloghy turn left and follow the signs to Kearney. After a mile, turn left for Kearney and follow the signs at two left turns for Kearney, about 3 miles.

Kearney is a tiny village in the care of the National Trust conservation organization. Once a fishing village, it now offers fine walks along its rocky shoreline.

At Temple Cooey and St. Cooey's Wells on a remote and peaceful shore are a penance stone and holy well at a site founded in the seventh century and later used for worship in penal times. Mass is still celebrated here from time to time.

Turn left and left again to follow the road crossing the peninsula from Quintin Bay to Portaferry.

One of Ulster's most beautiful villages, Portaferry's attractive waterfront of colorful cottages, pubs and stores is framed by green meadows and wooded slopes. No fewer than five defensive tower houses guard the narrow neck of the lough. The Marine Biology Station, part of Queen's University in Belfast, is opposite the ferry jetty. Beside a pleasant park nearby is the Northern Ireland Aquarium, Exploris, which explains the unique nature of the marine life of Strangford Lough. More than 2,000 species of marine animals thrive in the waters of Strangford, including large colonies of corals and sponges in the fast-flowing tides of the Narrows, with sea anemones and brittle stars in the quieter waters. The lough is home to large fish, including tope and skate. A regular, five-minute car-ferry service to Strangford gives views of the lough.

Take the car ferry to Strangford. Boats leave at 30-minute intervals.

Strangford is a small village with two bays, pretty houses and a castle. Close by is Castle Ward, set in a fine park with

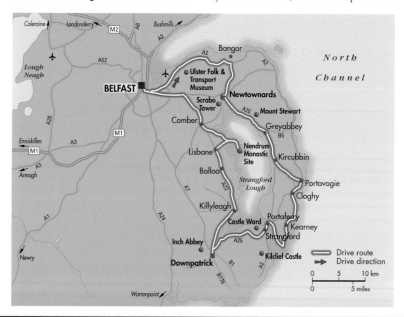

Scrabo Tower silhouetted against the sunset, on Strangford Lough

excellent views over the lough. This fascinating 18th-century mansion is an architectural hodgepodge – part pseudo-Gothic and part classical. Restored estate buildings show the busy organization that once supported a country house, including formal gardens, a Victorian laundry and theater in the stableyard, and a sawmill.

One mile south, on the A2 toward Ardglass, a stop-over to Cloghy Rocks is a great place for viewing seals when the tide is right. Farther south is Kilclief Castle and Killard Point at the narrowest point of the neck to the lough. This lovely grassland area with low cliffs and a small beach is rich in wildflowers.

Take the A25 to Downpatrick.
Down Cathedral stands on the hill above the town, while English Street, Irish Street and Scotch Street jostle together below (see page 183). Southwest is the popular Downpatrick race course and just outside the town (off the A7 Belfast Road) is the ruined Inch Abbey, founded by John de Courcy in the 1180. There are excellent views toward Downpatrick Cathedral across the lake here.

Follow the A22 to Killyleagh.
A fairy-tale castle with towers and battlements overlooks this quiet loughside village. The Hamilton family has lived here for 300 years, and although the original castle was built by the Normans, its present appearance owes more to the 19th century. Sir Hans Sloane, the physician and naturalist whose collection formed the nucleus of

the British Museum in London, was born in Killyleagh in 1660. It is said that the famous *Emigrant's Lament*: "I'm sitting on the stile, Mary," written by Lady Dufferin, a guest at the castle during the Famine, was inspired by the stile at Killowen Old Churchyard.

Follow the A22 for 8 miles to Lisbane, then turn right and continue for around 5 miles, following signs for Nendrum Monastic Site.
A place of great tranquility, Nendrum Monastic Site was established on one of the many islands along Strangford's calm middle waters; it is now reached by a causeway. The site is one of the most complete examples of an early monastery, and the ruins, in three concentric rings, are the stump of a round tower, monks' cells and a church.

Return across the causeway and join the A22 turning right to Comber, and on to Belfast.

Mount Stewart Gardens ✉ Portaferry Road (A20 from Newtownards towards Greyabbey) ☎ 028 4278 8387; www.nationaltrust.org.uk ⏰ House: daily noon–6, mid-Mar. to Oct.; Lakeside Gardens: daily 10–6; Formal Gardens: daily 10–6, mid-Mar. to Oct.; Temple of the Winds: Sun. 2–5, mid-Mar. to Oct. 🎟 $$

Exploris Aquarium ✉ The Ropewalk, Castle Street, Portaferry ☎ 028 4272 8062; www.exploris.org.uk ⏰ Mon.–Fri. 10–6, Sat. 11–6, Sun. noon–6, Apr.–Sep.; closes at 5, rest of year 🍴 Café 🎟 $$$

Castle Ward ✉ 1.5 miles west of Strangford Village on A25 ☎ 028 4488 1204, www.nationaltrust.org.uk ⏰ Mansion: daily noon–5, mid-Mar. to Oct. Park/ garden: daily 10–8, Apr.–Sep.; 10–5, Oct.; 10–4, rest of year 🍴 Tearoom 🎟 $$ (house only $)

Regional Sights

Key to symbols

➕ map coordinates refer to the region map on page 152 💷 admission charge: $$$ more than £6, $$ £3–£6, $ less than £3

See page 5 for complete key to symbols

Ards Peninsula

Some 23 miles of unspoiled countryside, the Ards Peninsula lies between Strangford Lough and the Irish Sea and runs from Bangor to Ballyquintin Point. Only about 5 miles wide, this long finger of land is dotted with picture-postcard villages, windmills and ancient ring forts. A bird sanctuary and wildlife reserve emphasize the peninsula's natural beauty. Of the two roads running down the peninsula, the lough road (A20) is more scenic than the coast road (A2).

Drive out to the little 19th-century village of Kearney for a taste of history. The car ferry that crosses from Portaferry to Strangford gives you a view straight out to sea, but look quickly because the entire crossing takes only four minutes.

➕ C2 ✉ 10 miles east of Belfast

Armagh

Your exploration of County Armagh's sightseeing treasures will be more meaningful if you make St. Patrick's Trian and Land of Lilliput your first stop. Inside, The Armagh Story brings alive stories of the Celts, St. Patrick and the Vikings through audiovisual exhibits and opportunities to dress up. The Land of Lilliput's giant reclining Gulliver surrounded by Lilliputians will delight the entire family.

Myths and legends of Queen Macha and the Red Branch knights surround Armagh, but historical fact outshines them all. At first glance, Navan Fort, a grassy 250-foot enclosure around a large mound, gives few clues to the fabulous kingdom that inhabited this site. You're better off visiting the Navan Centre below with a wealth of interactive exhibits and a short film, which help unfold the history of the area as well as the stories of Queen Macha's palace: Deirdre of the Sorrows, who first met her lover Naisi here; Cuchulainn, who polished his martial arts skills here; and the Red Branch knights. A 120-foot wide by 40-foot high Celtic temple once crowned its top.

Navan was the capital of the kings of Ulster from 600 BC to AD 332, and the burial in 1014 of the High King of Ireland, Brian Ború, is commemorated in the Church of Ireland Cathedral of St. Patrick. Standing on the site of a church founded in AD 445 by St. Patrick himself, this cathedral has been altered and added to over the centuries, whereas the Roman Catholic St. Patrick's Cathedral, built between 1838 and 1873, is a light Gothic-style building with a lavish interior.

The town's excellent county museum houses outstanding collections reflecting Northern Ireland life from prehistoric times to the present in an Ionic schoolhouse that dates from 1833. In addition to an extensive library, there are maps, photographs, and paintings by Armagh-born James Sleator and George Russell.

Armagh is without doubt Northern Ireland's most interesting cathedral town (St. Patrick called it "my sweet hill"), with imposing Catholic and Protestant edifices facing each other from their respective hilltops. Red hats of every cardinal archbishop of Armagh and medallions for each of Ireland's saints can be seen in the Catholic cathedral.

The city also has many beautiful buildings and some delightful old streets – Abbey Lane, lined with quaint shops, the Cathedral Close and Castle Street, which follows the contours of an ancient ring fortress. The tree-lined Mall, once a racecourse, is now one of Ireland's finest parks and is surrounded by Armagh's best Georgian buildings, including the

Intricate stone carvings adorn the facade of the Roman Catholic St. Patrick's Cathedral in Armagh

imposing Court House, the splendid Public Library and the Royal Irish Fusiliers Museum, where a large model of the Battle of Barossa in 1811 is only one of the exhibits that tell the story of the Royal Irish Fusiliers regiment from 1793 to 1968. At the entrance to the Palace Demesne is Ireland's longest friary, now in ruins. The 13th-century, 153-foot-long Franciscan friary was founded by Archbishop O'Scanail.

A 10-minute walk from town, off the Friary Road, will bring you to the grounds of Armagh Observatory, which although not open to the public does offer group tours on request. On the grounds is the Armagh Planetarium, which features Ireland's first 3D digital theater and, following an upgrade, the Digistar 4, the world's most advanced digital projection system.

Southeast of Armagh is Gosford Forest Park, where rare breeds of cattle and deer roam in open paddocks. It has marked nature trails and an arboretum.

✚ B2

Tourist information ✉ 40 English Street ☎ 028 3752 1800; www.armagh.co.uk ⏱ Mon.–Sat. 9–5:30, Sun. 2–5:30, Jun.–Sep.; Mon.–Sat. 9–5, Sun. 9–5, rest of year

St. Patrick's Trian and Land of Lilliput ✉ 40 English Street ☎ 028 3752 1801 ⏱ Mon.–Sat. 10–5, Sun. 2–5 🍴 Restaurant 💲 $$

Armagh County Museum ✉ The Mall East ☎ 028 3752 3070; www.armaghcountymuseum.co.uk ⏱ Mon.–Fri. 10–5, Sat. 10–1 and 2–5 💲 Free

Royal Irish Fusiliers Museum ✉ Sovereign's House, The Mall East ☎ 028 3752 2911; www.visitarmagh. co.uk ⏱ Mon.–Fri. 10–12:30 and 1:30–4 💲 Free

Palace Demesne ✉ Friary Road ☎ 028 3752 1801 ⏱ 24 hours 🍴 Restaurant 💲 $$

Armagh Friary ✉ At entrance to Palace Stables Heritage Centre 💲 Free

Armagh Planetarium ✉ College Hill ☎ 028 3752 3689; www.armaghplanet.com ⏱ Mon.–Fri. 1–5 (show 3 p.m.); Sat. 11:30–5 (shows noon, 1, 2, 3, 4) 💲 $$

Gosford Forest Park ✉ Markethill, off A28 ☎ 028 3755 1277; www.gosford.co.uk ⏱ Daily 10–dusk 🍴 Tearoom 💲 $$

Ballycastle and the Glens of Antrim

The seaside town of Ballycastle has a prized position on the North Antrim Coast, with a wide, sandy beach stretching to the east and the lush Glens of Antrim to the south. At the heart of the town is The Diamond (Market Square), packed with the stalls, entertainments and avid horse dealing of the famous Ould Lammas Fair at the end of August each year. For about a hundred years St. Patrick's Day has been celebrated with a horse show, and in June there is a festival of Irish music, dancing and games. Just outside the town are the ruins of Bonamargy Friary, founded by Rory MacQuillan around 1500 and burial place of the MacDonnell chiefs, including the notorious Scots-Irish chieftan Sorley Boy. The eastern range of cloister, gatehouse and church have remained virtually intact, lacking only the roof. Beyond Fair Head is the scenic Murlough Bay, which is now in the care of the National Trust conservation organization.

Ballycastle's museum illustrates the folk and social history of the Glens of Antrim. At the harbor is a memorial to Guglielmo Marconi, who carried out the first practical test on radio signals between White Lodge, on the clifftop at Ballycastle, and Rathlin Island in 1898. You can travel by boat to Rathlin, which is a mecca for divers and bird watchers.

Water of Life

Spelling apart, Irish whiskey is distinctively different from its Scottish sister. In Scotland, the malted barley is dried over an open peat fire, imparting its characteristic smoky flavor. Irish whiskey is distilled three times and dried in smoke-free kilns producing a clear, clean taste; most spirits are distilled twice. The art of distillation was introduced to Ireland by Christian missionaries around AD 600. The elixir was originally named *uisce beatha* (pronounced "ish'ke ba-ha," meaning water of life).

From the shore you can follow the B15 coastal route west to Ballintoy, then, turning right, follow the signs to Carrick-a-Rede. The mainland clifftops are connected to the small rocky island of Carrick-a-Rede by a swinging rope bridge strung across a deep 60-foot-wide chasm. The water here is too treacherous to cross in any other way. If you dare, cross over the wooden planks and grip the rope handrails, but be warned, this is not for the fainthearted. The bridge was put up each year by salmon fishermen who use Carrick-a-Rede, "the Rock in the Road," as a good place to net the fish. Today the bridge and the parkland around it are managed by the National Trust. The trust has made the bridge sturdier and safer but still it wobbles and is closed during bad weather. The rope bridge is approached from Larry Bane, where some quarry workings remain, and the quarry access to the magnificent seascape offers rewarding bird-watching. You can sit in your car and spot kittiwakes, cormorants, guillemots, fulmars and razorbills, though you might need binoculars to see the puffins on Sheep Island farther out to sea.

The nine green Glens of Antrim run through mountainous terrain between Cushendun and Larne before reaching the sea. All nine have individual names and virtually all have stories to tell: Glentaisie (Taisie's glen, named for a daughter of the king of Rathlin), Glenshesk (sedgy glen), Glendun (brown glen), Glencorp (glen of the dead), Glenaan (blue glen), Glenballyeamon (Eamonn's townland glen), Glenariff (ploughman's glen), Glencloy (glen of hedges) and Glenarm (glen of the army). "The Capital of the Glens," Cushendall sits on a pleasant, sandy bay below Glenballyeamon, Glenaan and Glencorp and in the curve of the Dall River. The rugged peak of Lurigethan broods over the village, while the softer Tieveragh Hill is supposed to be the capital of the fairies. Cushendall owes much to an

Glendun, one of the Glens of Antrim, was carved by giant glaciers during the Iron Age

East Indian nabob, Francis Turnley, who built the Curfew Tower in the center as a "place for the confinement of idlers and rioters."

Larne is the terminus for the shortest sea crossing between Ireland and mainland Britain. It also marks the start of the scenic Antrim Coast Road, constructed in the 1830s to link the remote Glens of Antrim to the rest of Ulster. To the north is Carnfunnock Park, which has a maze in the shape of Northern Ireland.

✚ C3

Ballycastle tourist information ✉ 7 Mary Street ☎ 028 2076 2024 ⏱ Mon.–Fri. 9–7, Sat. 10–6, Sun. 2–6, Jul.–Aug.; Mon.–Fri. 9:30–5, rest of year

Bonamargy Friary ✉ A2 (half a mile east of Ballycastle) 👆 Free

Ballycastle Museum ✉ 59 Castle Street ☎ 028 2076 2942 ⏱ Daily noon–6, Jul.–Aug. (or by arrangement) 👆 Free

Carrick-a-Rede rope bridge ✉ Larrybane, County Antrim (5 miles northwest of Ballycastle off A2) ☎ 028 2076 9839; www.ntni.org.uk ⏱ Daily 10–7, Jun.– Aug.; 10–6, Mar.–May and Sep.–Oct.; 10:30–3:30, Nov.–Feb. 🍴 Tearoom 💵 $$

Larne tourist information ✉ Narrow Gauge Road, Larne ☎ 028 2826 0088 ⏱ Mon.–Fri. 9–5, Sat. 10–4, Apr.–Sep.; Mon.–Fri. 9–5, rest of year

American Connection

America's military links to Northern Ireland date back as early as 1778, when John Paul Jones scored America's first naval victory when he sailed the USS *Ranger* up Belfast Lough and captured HMS *Drake* within sight of Carrickfergus Castle (see page 177). During those turbulent times, America's Declaration of Independence was printed by John Dunlap from Strabane, County Londonderry (who went on to found the *Philadelphia Gazette*, America's first daily newspaper). At least five of those who signed the Declaration of Independence were from Northern Ireland.

Among American presidents, Andrew Jackson's parents came from Carrickfergus; Andrew Johnson's grandfather was from Larne; Chester A. Arthur's father was born near Ballymena; Grover Cleveland's grandfather was a County Antrim merchant; William McKinley's great-great-grandfather emigrated from Conagher, near Ballymoney; and Theodore Roosevelt's maternal ancestors hailed from Larne. In 2011, President Barack Obama visited the small County Offaly village of Moneygall, the hometown of his great-great-great-grandfather. It is an impressive list.

Plenty of other American heroes had Northern Ireland roots, including Davy Crockett, Sam Houston, Mark Twain and Neil Armstrong. The founder of the American Presbyterian Church, Francis Makemie, sailed from Northern Ireland for America in 1682, and John Hughes, first Roman Catholic archbishop of New York, emigrated in 1817.

In June 1942 American troops arrived in Northern Ireland to begin intensive training in preparation for World War II battles.

All these connections take on even more meaning at the Ulster American Folk Park at Camphill just north of Omagh, County Tyrone (see page 196). The re-created cottages and working conditions of 250,000 18th-century emigrants give a real insight into their reasons for crossing the Atlantic, and the replicas of their log cabin settlements in America kindle a new appreciation of their contribution to U.S. history. Ask at tourist information centers for the Heritage Trail brochure that lists restored ancestral homes of U.S. presidents.

American hero with Irish roots: Neil Armstrong, the first man on the moon

Fishing boats moored in the harbor below Carrickfergus Castle

Carrickfergus

This small seaside and market town is dominated by a massive Norman castle. Dating from the late 12th and early 13th centuries and almost perfectly preserved, the imposing fortress was used as a garrison until 1928. In 1778, Commander John Paul Jones of the fledgling American Navy stood off shore just below Carrickfergus Castle in the USS *Ranger* and captured the much larger HMS *Drake*. A defensive stone wall was built around Carrickfergus (the only place in the north where English was spoken at the time) in 1611, and more than half of the wall is still intact.

Begin your exploration of the town at the Carrickfergus Museum and Civic Centre to learn about the town's history. Starting in AD 581, maritime, military and historical stories unfold before you during the monorail ride. There is an excellent exhibition of gas equipment and other machinery as well as an audiovisual presentation at "Flame – The Gasworks Museum of Ireland." Built in 1855 to light street lamps, these are the only Victorian coal-fired gasworks in Ireland and were in service until 1964.

The ancestral home of American President Andrew Jackson was just beyond the north end of Carrickfergus at Boneybefore, a site that is now marked by a plaque. Just a few yards away, the Andrew Jackson Centre, housed in a replica thatched cottage of the 1700s, gives an insight into the life of his forebears before they left for America in 1765, as well as his career, and other U.S. presidents with Ulster connections. On the grounds of the Jackson Centre, the U.S. Rangers Centre features an exhibition on the First Battalion U.S. Rangers (the U.S. Army's most decorated unit) and their strong connections with Carrickfergus in 1942. It also contains photographs and other memorabilia.

✚ C2

Tourist information ✉ 11 Antrim Street
☎ 028 9335 8049 🕓 Mon.–Sat. 10–6, Sun. 1–6, Apr.–Sep.; Mon.–Sat. 10–5, Sun. 1–5, rest of year

Carrickfergus Castle ✉ Marine Highway
☎ 028 9335 1273 🕓 Daily 10–6, Easter to Sep.; 10–4, rest of year 🍴 Café 💷 $$

Carrickfergus Museum and Civic Centre
✉ 11 Antrim Street ☎ 028 9335 8049; www.carrickfergus.org 🕓 Mon.–Sat. 10–6, Sun. 1–6, Apr.–Oct.; rest of year closes at 5 💷 Free

Flame – The Gasworks Museum of Ireland ✉ Irish Quarter West ☎ 028 9336 9575; www.flamegasworks. co.uk 🕓 Daily 10–5, Jul.–Aug.; 2–5, May–Jun. and Sep.; Sun. 2–5, Oct.–Apr. 💷 Free

Andrew Jackson Centre and U.S. Rangers Centre
✉ 2 Boneybefore ☎ 028 9335 8049 🕓 Open by arrangement. Contact tourist office for information
💷 Free

The Causeway Coast

The most distinguishing feature of the north Antrim coast is the Causeway Coast and the string of such small towns as Ballycastle, Portstewart, Larne and Portrush set along it. Inland from Larne, Ballymena, the county town of Antrim, is proud that one of its sons founded Eaton's Stores in Canada.

The fantastic Giant's Causeway is much more impressive when you walk alongside its basalt columns (there are 37,000!) than any photograph can possibly convey. How they came to be packed so tightly together that they form a sort of bridge from the shoreline out into the sea, submerge, and then surface on the island of Staffa in the Hebrides, is a matter of conjecture. Scientists will tell you that they're the result of a massive volcanic eruption 60 million years ago, when molten lava cooled and formed into geometric shapes. But Irish legend has it that the giant Fionn MacCumhaill (see page 199) built the causeway between Ulster and Scotland and it was his Scottish counterpart, Finn Gall, who destroyed all but the bit you see today.

You will not want to miss this mass of symmetrical basalt columns jutting out into the sea from the foot of a steep cliff. The visitor center houses a 12-minute audiovisual show telling the story of the formation of the Causeway, together with fascinating pictoral exhibits, a tourist information office and book store and tearooms. A minibus service from the visitor center to the foot of the cliff is a decided bonus if you don't want to walk.

Generations of imaginative guides have embroidered stories and created names for the remarkable formations – the Giant's Organ, the Giant's Harp, the Wishing Chair and Lord Antrim's Parlour. One story absolutely based on fact is that of the *Girona*, a fleeing Spanish Armada galleon, wrecked in a storm one night in October 1588. A diving team retrieved a treasure hoard from the wreck in 1967, and it's now on display in the Ulster Museum in Belfast (see page 166). The wreck still lies under cliffs in Port na Spaniagh, one of a magnificent array of bays and headlands on the Causeway. The Giant's Causeway is maintained by the National Trust, which has spent in excess of £18.5 million restoring the headland and building a new visitor center, which opened in summer 2012.

Portrush, west of the Giant's Causeway, is a typical seaside resort that flourished with the rise of the railroads. It has three good bays, with broad stretches of sand, ranges of dunes, rock pools, white cliffs and a busy harbor. Nearby, there could hardly be a more dramatic sight than the craggy headland crowned by the great lump of ruined 13th-century Dunluce Castle sitting on the very edge of the cliff. Back in 1639 a storm actually picked up and dumped the kitchens, the cooks and all the pots into the sea below.

The Dunluce Centre in Portrush town center features the Finn McCool Playground, a themed and interactive game environment, and the Treasure Fortress, Motion Simulator and Turbo Tours, which supply unexpected thrills. Panoramic views from the tower are spectacular and there's a shopping arcade. Portrush's indoor water center, Waterworld, features giant water flumes, water cannon, swings, a rope bridge and even a pirate ship.

The neat village of Bushmills close by is the home of the world's oldest legal distillery. Licensed since 1608, it's still turning out the "wine of the country" after all these centuries. There's a marvelous exhibition of its history, and a whiskey tasting nicely rounds off the one-hour guided tour through the distilling process. The water used from St. Columb's Rill, or stream, is said to give the whiskey its special quality.

The Bush River is rich in trout and salmon, and its fast-flowing waters not only supported the mills that gave the town its name, but they also generated electricity for the world's first hydroelectric tramway, which carried passengers to the Giant's Causeway between 1893 and 1949.

Panoramic views of the coast are breathtaking at Downhill, which is perched on the very edge of a cliff overlooking the Atlantic. Mussenden Temple, a beautiful 18th-century rotunda modeled on Tivoli's Temple of Vesta is just one part of this ruined estate that once belonged to the 4th Earl of Bristol, Frederick Hervey. The earl was an eccentric collector and traveler who gave his name to the Bristol hotels throughout Europe. A glen walk leads from the Bishop's Gate to the Mussenden Temple.

✚ C3

Tourist information ✉ The Braid, Ballymena Town Hall Museum and Arts Centre, 1–29 Bridge Street, Ballymena ☎ 028 2563 5900 🕐 Mon.–Fri. 9–5:30, Sat. 10–5, Jul.–Aug.; Mon.–Fri. 9–5, Sat. 10–4, rest of year

Giant's Causeway Visitor Centre ✉ 44 Causeway Road, County Antrim (2 miles north of Bushmills on B146) ☎ 028 2073 1852; www.nationaltrust.org.uk 🕐 Daily 9:30–dusk 🚻 Causeway free; audiovisual $; guided walk $; parking $$

Dunluce Castle ✉ On the A2, 3 miles east of Portrush ☎ 028 2073 1938 🕐 Daily 10–6, Apr.–Sep.; 10–5, rest of year 🚻 $

Dunluce Centre ✉ 10 Sandhill Drive, Portrush ☎ 028 7082 4444; www.dunlucecentre.co.uk 🕐 Daily 11–6, Jul.–Aug.; noon–5, Apr.–Jun. and Sep.–Oct. 🍴 Café 🚻 $$

Waterworld ✉ Portrush, end of Portrush harbor ☎ 028 708 2001 🕐 Mon.–Sat. 10–7, Sun. noon–7, Jul.–Aug.; Mon.–Fri. 10–3, Sat. 10–5, Sun. noon–5, Jun.; ten-pin bowling only Mon.–Sat. 11–8; Sun. noon–8, Easter vacation 🍴 Café 🚻 $$$

Old Bushmills Distillery ✉ 2 Distillery Road, Bushmills ☎ 028 2073 3218; www.bushmills.com 🕐 Mon.–Sat. 9:15–5, Sun. noon–5 (last tour at 4), Apr.–Oct.; tours less frequent Nov.–Mar. 🍴 Coffee shop 🚻 $$ ❓ It's best to come early – tours are popular and cannot be pre-booked

Mussenden Temple ✉ Mussenden Road, Castlerock, County Londonderry ☎ 028 7084 8728; www.nationaltrust.org.uk 🕐 Daily 10–5, Apr.–early Oct.; grounds all year dawn–dusk; call for temple openings 🚻 Temple $

Tourists follow in Fionn MacCumhaill's footsteps on the Giant's Causeway

Yachts and trawlers await the next day's fishing in Killybegs, the largest fishing port in Ireland

Donegal

At the head of Donegal Bay, on the estuary of the River Eske, Donegal is a pleasant town with a splendid central Diamond (square) – a triangular marketplace flanked with buildings and streets radiating from each side. In the center stands a 2-foot-tall obelisk.

Historically, it was the seat of the O'Donnells: Donegal Abbey, now in ruins, was a Franciscan friary founded by Red Hugh O'Donnell and his mother, Nuala O'Connor. *The Annals of the Four Masters* was written here in the 17th century, charting the history of Ireland up until 1616. This important chronicle is now in the National Library in Dublin. Red Hugh also built the west tower of Donegal Castle (1505) on the banks of the Eske beside the Diamond, making it the chief O'Donnell stronghold. Gables and windows were added by Sir Basil

Brooke in 1607, along with a mammoth Jacobean fireplace and a new wing built around the old tower. The remains have been beautifully restored.

The Donegal Railway Heritage Centre consists of a museum and information center that recalls a now redundant scenic line known as "The Wee Donegal." The center has given a new purpose to the original Old Station House where it is housed.

Donegal is an attractive and strategic place for exploring the northwest, and is known worldwide for its shopping. Its main store, Magee's, is one of the best known places to buy tweed, a quality fabric still produced in the town. Other crafts are showcased at the Donegal Craft Village, just outside Donegal on the Ballyshannon road, where workshops include a glass-blower, hand-weaver, jeweler, sculptor and stone carver.

On a much larger scale is the Belleek Pottery, east of Ballyshannon. Their intricate "basket weaving" has to be seen to be believed. A small museum and visitor center conducts guided tours to let you see craftspeople creating and decorating the world-famous porcelain. The shop features tableware, vases, clocks, ornaments and a host of other products. On the road to Ballyshannon is Murvagh Beach, a beautiful mile-long stretch of beach backed by sand dunes and the Murvagh Forest.

The drive to Glencolmcille (Gleann Cholm Cille) travels west of Donegal through lonely mountain country with occasional glimpses of the sea. It is a journey that goes back as far as 5,000 years through a culture little changed since the days of Bonnie Prince Charlie.

Try to get to the picturesque little harbor town of Killybegs (west of Donegal on the R263) in the late afternoon, and go down to the pier to watch the fishing fleet come in. It's a memorable experience – hundreds of seagulls swarm and screech overhead and half the town gathers together to greet the fishermen.

Modest in size, Glencolmcille Folk Village is one of Ireland's most authentic folk museums, with thatched cottage dwellings that have been furnished to depict the lives of people who lived here from 1700 to the 1900s. Guided tours explain the workings of each cottage. The home of a 1720 cotter is earthen-floored, and its open hearth has no chimney; by the 1820s the cotter's home had a flagstone floor, chimney and oil-lamp lighting; the 1920 cottage is like many you'll see in today's Irish countryside.

The Old National Schoolhouse from a century ago and a country pub, or *sheebeen* (where the drink on sale was often the traditional but illegal *poteen*), complete the picture of the village.

✚ A2

Tourist information ✉ The Quay ☎ 074 97 21148; www.donegaldirect.com 🕐 Mon.–Sat. 9–6, Sun. 11–3, Jun.–Aug.; Mon.–Fri. 9:15–5, Sat. 11–5, rest of year

Donegal Castle ✉ Donegal (located beside the River Eske) ☎ 074 97 22405; www.heritageireland.ie 🕐 Daily 10–6, mid-Mar. to Oct.; Thu.–Mon. 9:30–4:30 (last admission 3:45), rest of year 💵 $$

Donegal Railway Heritage Centre ✉ Tyrconnell Street ☎ 074 972 2655; www.donegalrailway.com 🕐 Mon.–Sat. 10–5, Sun. 2–5, Jun.– Sep.; Mon.–Fri. 10–5, rest of year 💵 $$

Donegal Craft Village ✉ Ballyshannon Road ☎ 074 972 2225; www.donegalcraftvillage.com 🕐 Mon.–Sat. 9:30–5:30 💵 Free

Belleek Pottery ✉ Belleek, Co. Fermanagh ☎ 028 6865 8501; www.belleek.ie 🕐 Mon.–Fri. 9–6, Sat. 10–6, Sun. noon–6, Jul.–Sep.; Mon.–Fri. 9–5:30, Sat. 10–5:30, Sun. 2–5:30, Mar.–Jun.; Mon.–Fri. 9–5:30, Sat. 10–5:30, Sun. noon–5:30, Oct.–Dec.; Mon.–Fri. 9–5:30, Jan.–Feb. 🍴 Tearoom 💵 $$

Glencolmcille Folk Village ✉ Glencolmcille, Co. Donegal (on outskirts of village) ☎ 074 97 30017; www.glenfolkvillage.com 🕐 Mon.–Sat. 10–6, Sun. noon–6, Easter–Sep. 🍴 Tearoom 💵 $$

In St. Patrick's Footsteps

St. Patrick's birthplace is uncertain, but it was probably Scotland or Wales. Son of a Roman centurion, he was taken into slavery as a young boy. After six years tending sheep on Slemish mountain in County Antrim, he escaped and studied for several years with Martin of Tours in Gaul before fulfilling his wish to bring the message of Christianity to Celtic Ireland.

Legend says that his arrival in County Down was quite by accident – his destination was the Antrim coast farther north, but Strangford Lough's strong tidal currents drew his boat through the narrows and deposited him where the River Slaney flows into the lough. Undaunted, he quickly converted Dichu, a local chieftan, who gave Patrick a barn in which to hold services. For the next 30 years, he traveled the length and breadth of Ireland preaching the gospel to Celtic chieftains and peasants while generating hundreds of legends – there are many "St. Patrick slept here" stories in Ireland. At the end of his life, he returned to his abbey at Saul, northeast of Downpatrick, where he died in AD 461. A round tower adjoining the chancel of the Celtic-revival church at Saul marks the place where he preached his first sermon.

County Down, especially the Downpatrick area, is strewn with reminders of St. Patrick. Perhaps the best introduction to his history is the excellent St. Patrick Centre (see opposite) where his life story is recounted in his own words. In Down Cathedral graveyard, pause by the grave that is said to be his – pilgrims bring daffodils here each St. Patrick's Day – and you'll find an overwhelming sense of reverence that will dispel any importance you may have placed on whether or not the saint's remains actually lie there.

St. Patrick is also linked with nearby Struell Wells, which is said to have healing properties. Fed by an underground spring, it continues to draw those afflicted with eye ailments and other infirmities to collect the waters in the hope of a cure. Near the site there are ruins of an 18th-century church and bath houses for bathing in the holy waters.

Saul ✉ About halfway between Downpatrick and Strangford on A25

Struell Wells ✉ 1.5 miles east of Downpatrick off the B1

The church and tower at Saul, built in 1932 to commemorate St. Patrick's first church in Ireland

Remains of Inch Abbey on the north bank of the River Quoile

Downpatrick

Radiating from the center of Downpatrick are three streets – English Street, Irish Street and Scotch Street – which recall the Elizabethan system of dividing settlements by nationality. Fine Georgian and Victorian buildings line these streets, notably the High Victorian Gothic Assembly Rooms (now Down Arts Centre), with a large clock tower and an arcaded first floor, the Regency-style Judge's House, the Court House of 1834, and Southwell Charity Schools and Almshouses, about 100 years older.

Northwest of the town are the ruins of the Cistercian Inch Abbey, founded in the late 1180s by John de Courcy on a strategic island in the Quoile Marshes within sight of the Hill of Down. Now reached by a causeway, the monastic ruins include an interesting pointed triple window.

Downpatrick, as its name suggests, has links with Ireland's patron saint (see opposite). The present Down Cathedral is a reconstruction of its 13th- and 16th-century predecessors, and a large stone in the churchyard purports to mark St. Patrick's grave (found under a gigantic weeping willow tree). The gravestone is actually a granite monolith placed on the holy spot in 1901 to protect it from pilgrims who persisted in taking away scoops of earth from the grave. It is said that the bones of saints Columbanus and Brigid were transferred here in the 12th century.

St. Patrick's first stone church is thought to have been erected on the historic Mound of Down site that held a Bronze Age fort. The St. Patrick Centre, an exhibition center close to the Down County Museum, explores the legacy of the saint and the work of Irish missionaries in the Dark Ages.

Other attractions of the town include the Downpatrick & County Down Railway, which runs vintage steam trains to Inch Abbey on summer weekends from June until September and all public holidays. Other special events include St. Patrick's Day, Easter, Halloween Ghost Trains and a visit from Santa at Christmas.

Downpatrick is popular for its access to Strangford Lough (see drive page 169), a beautiful inlet of the sea separating the Ards Peninsula (see page 172) and the rest of County Down. Dotted with numerous islands formed by submerged drumlins (rounded hills), it was named Strang Fiord (Violent Inlet) by the Vikings because of the tidal surges up and down the Narrows between the lake and the open sea.

The lough extends for about 12 miles to the north and measures up to 5 miles wide. It's a serene landscape with white farmhouses, and several nature reserves, including Delamont Country Park, which has Ireland's longest miniature railroad. Across the lough is Portaferry Castle, a 16th-century tower house, now just a ruin, and one of a cluster of strongholds built at strategic points on the lake.

🚩 C2

Tourist information ✉ 53a Market Street
☎ 028 4461 2233 🕐 Mon.–Fri. 9–6, Sat. 9:30–6, Sun. 2–6, Jul.–Aug.; Mon.–Fri. 9–5, Sat. 9:30–5, rest of year

Inch Abbey ✉ Northwest of Downpatrick, off A7
☎ 028 9181 1491 🕐 Free access all year ✋ Free

Down Cathedral ✉ The Mall, English Street ☎ 028 4461 4922; www.downcathedral.org 🕐 Mon.–Sat. 9:30–4:30, Sun. 2–5 ✋ Donations

Down County Museum ✉ English Street
☎ 028 4461 5218; www.downcountymuseum.com 🕐 Mon.–Fri. 10–5, Sat.–Sun. 1–5 🍴 Café ✋ Free

St. Patrick Centre ✉ 53a Market Street
☎ 028 4461 9000; www.saintpatrickcentre.com 🕐 Mon.–Sat. 9:30–6, Sun. 10–6, Jun.–Aug.; Mon.–Sat. 9:30–5:30, Sun. 1–5:30, Apr.–May and Sep.; Mon.–Sat. 10–5, Oct.–Mar. ✋ $$

Downpatrick & County Down Railway ✉ Railway Station, Market Street ☎ 028 4461 5779; www.downrail.co.uk 🕐 Call for ride schedules/ fares

Delamont Country Park ✉ Downpatrick (on the A22, 3 miles north of Downpatrick) ☎ 028 4482 8333; www.delamontcountrypark.com 🕐 Daily 9–dusk 🍴 Tearoom and restaurant ✋ Car $$

Portaferry Castle ✉ Castle Street, Portaferry
☎ 028 4272 9882 🕐 Daily 10–5, Easter–Aug. ✋ Free

Dungannon

The county town of Tyrone, Dungannon is built on several hills. It occupies the site of the ancient seat of the O'Neill chieftains, and there are some remains to be seen of O'Neill Castle, an 18th-century house on the site of 16th-century fortifications. Dungannon prospered through its involvement with the linen industry, a history which can be explored in the Donaghmore Heritage Centre (visits are by prior arrangement only).

Sadly now closed, Killybacky's Tyrone Crystal factory used to be a "don't miss" for visitors to the area. However, you can still buy a few pieces in outlets around Northern Ireland but they are fast becoming collector's items.

The town has many fine buildings, including the former Northern Bank building in Market Square, Dungannon Royal School, founded by Charles I in 1628, and the elaborately designed police station in Market Square, which has been known as the "Khyber Pass" since its plans were mistaken for a fortress in India by a clerk in Dublin.

West of Dungannon is the ancestral home of Ulysses S. Grant, victorious Civil War general and 18th U.S. president (1869–77). The maternal great-grandfather of Grant left a two-room farm cottage in 1738 and settled in Pennsylvania. The mud-floor cottage has been restored but retains its period furnishings.

East of Dungannon is Peatlands Park. Peat has been vital in the Irish home for centuries and this park in the southwest corner of the Lough Neagh basin is the place to learn the fascinating 10,000-year history of the peat bogs. Wooded drumlins break through the surface, and small lakes have been formed in boglands that have been cut over. The rides into the bog on the narrow-gauge railroad are powered by a locomotive that once transported the peat.

🚩 B2

Tourist information ✉ Killymaddy Centre, 190 Ballygawley Road ☎ 028 8776 7259 🕐 Mon.–Thu. 9–6, Fri. 9–7, Sat.–Sun. 9–5, Jul.–Aug.; Mon.–Fri. 9–5, Sat.–Sun. 10–4, Feb.–Jun. and Sep.–Nov.; Mon.–Fri. 9–5, Sat.–Sun. 11–4, Dec.–Jan.

Donaghmore Heritage Centre ✉ 26 Market Square, Dungannon ☎ 028 8776 1306 🕐 Hours by arrangement ✋ $

Ulysses S. Grant Ancestral Homestead ✉ Dergina, Ballygawley (off the A4, 13 miles west of Dungannon) ☎ 028 8555 7133 🕐 Daily 9–5 ✋ Free

Peatlands Park ✉ 7 miles east of Dungannon, exit 13 from the M1 ☎ 028 3885 1102 🕐 Park: daily 9–9, Easter–Sep.; 9–dusk, rest of year; center: daily 10–6, Jun.–Aug.; Sat.–Sun. noon–6, Easter–May and Sep.; Sun. only noon–4, rest of year ✋ $

Enniskillen and Lough Erne

Oscar Wilde and Samuel Beckett were both educated in this appealing town, which owes much of its attractiveness to its setting on an island where the two sections of Lough Erne constrict to their narrowest point. Overlooking the lough is Enniskillen Castle, a magnificent 15th-century stone fortress with a unique two-turret water gate. In the vault, lifesize figures depict castle life. Surrounded by great stone barracks, the keep now houses the Museum of the Royal Inniskillin Fusiliers, which features battle trophies of the Dragoons and Fusiliers from the Napoleonic Wars, arms and a host of colorful uniforms.

The county museum features exhibits on the history, wildlife and landscape of this area. Beautiful handmade lace for which Ulster is renowned is displayed in the Sheelin Lace Museum, with some items dating from 1850 to 1900.

The River Erne and its Upper and Lower Loughs are linked to the Shannon river as part of a 500-mile leisure waterway. The river and the loughs are dotted with 154 intriguing and historical islands, many with ancient monastic ruins (see drive page 186). In summer, waterbus cruises ply the Lower Lough (1 hour 45 minutes), departing Enniskillen Round O pier and calling at Devenish Island. Cruising trips of several days are popular – ask at the tourist office. You can rent a boat to get to the heart of the lake, or even see it from the air with the Amphibious Flying Club.

For a more diverse range of sports, head to the Share Village in Lisnaskea, a holiday village with chalets, camping, canoeing, banana boats, a climbing wall and a health club.

You can take the 7-mile drive through Lough Navar Forest for a marvelous panoramic view of Lower Lough Erne, or follow marked trails to scenic overlooks – the best (and steepest walk) leads to a view across the lough to Donegal and Sligo. Stay alert, whether you're walking or driving, and you might be lucky enough to see the red deer or wild goats that roam the forest.

🚩 B2 and A2

Tourist information ✉ Wellington Road ☎ 028 6632 3110 🕐 Mon.–Fri. 9–7, Sat. 10–6, Sun. 11–5, Jul.–Aug.; Mon.–Fri. 9–5:30, Sat. 10–6, Sun. 11–5, Easter–Jun. and Sep.; Mon.–Fri. 9–5:30, Sat. 10–2, Sun. 11–2, Oct.

Enniskillen Castle ✉ Castle Barracks ☎ 028 6632 5000; www.enniskillencastle.co.uk 🕐 Sat.–Mon. 2–5, Tue.–Fri. 10–5, Jul.–Aug.; Mon. 2–5, Tue.–Fri. 10–5, Sat. 2–5, Apr.–Jun. and Sep.–Oct.; Mon. 2–5, Tue.–Fri. 10–5, Nov.–Mar. 🎟 $

Sheelin Lace Museum ✉ Bellanaleck (5 miles south of Enniskillen on A509) ☎ 028 6634 8052; www.irishlacemuseum.com 🕐 Mon.–Sat. 10–6, Mar.–Oct.; by appointment, rest of year 🎟 $$

Lough Erne Cruises ☎ 028 6632 2882 🕐 Call for sailing schedules and fares

Amphibious Flying Club ✉ Unit 7, St. Angelo Airport, Trory, Enniskillen ☎ 079 6221 3976

Share Village ✉ Smith's Strand, Lisnaskea ☎ 028 6772 2122; www.sharevillage.org

Lough Navar Forest ✉ 5 miles northwest of Derrygonnelly, signposted off A46 ☎ 028 6634 3040 🕐 Daily 10–dusk 🎟 Car $$

Statue on top of a tower at Enniskillen Castle

Drive
Fermanagh Lakeland

Duration: 1 day

This 84-mile drive explores the major monastic sites in Ulster, the awesome Marble Arch Cave and a magical boat ride through 300 million years of history.

Start this drive at the tourist center in Enniskillen. Take the A32 toward Omagh for 2 miles until you reach the signpost for the ferries to Devenish.

Note: Ferries from Trory are currently suspended, but if you'd like to visit you can take Erne Tours' Kestrel boat from the Round O Jetty in Enniskillen.

The sixth-century Augustinian abbey founded by St. Molaise is a noteworthy monastic ruin. There is also a 12th-century round tower that has survived the centuries in perfect condition and is regarded as one of the finest in Ireland. Beautifully proportioned with finely cut stones and precise lines is the intricately carved 15th-century high cross in the

graveyard. The small museum focuses on the monastic history of the island. The great treasure of Devenish, the book shrine of Molaise, a masterpiece of early Christian art, is kept at the National Museum in Dublin.

Take the B82 for 7 miles for Castle Archdale and Kesh.

The old estate of the Archdale family contains an arboretum, butterfly park and farm with rare breeds. The ruins of the old castle, burned in the Williamite wars of 1689, can be seen in the forest. Castle Archdale is one of the busiest places around Lough Erne. The focus is the marina, where concrete jetties and slipways, built for flying boats taking off for the Battle of the Atlantic in 1941, have been turned to more peaceful use. Here you can rent a boat with a gillie (a fishing guide).

It is possible to reach White Island from here to see the enigmatic carved stones that for centuries have puzzled experts. In the 12th-century church, they seem to represent biblical figures, with the exception of Sheil-na-gig, a female fertility figure, a strange meeting of Celtic pagan art and Christianity.

Turn left onto the B82. After 2 miles, turn left for Kesh via the scenic route for 4 miles. At Kesh turn left for Belleek, onto

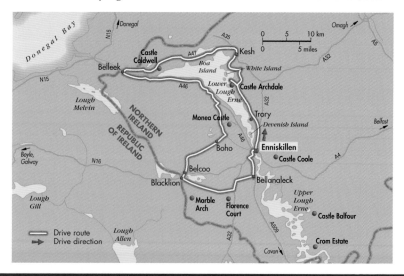

This stone-carved figure of Janus in Caldragh churchyard may be pre-Christian

the A35, then after a mile turn on to the A47 and drive for 8 miles to Boa Island (pronounced "bo").

Two bridges connect Boa Island to the mainland. Just before the bridge at the west end, a track on the left leads to Caldragh graveyard, where there are two pagan idols in stone. One is called a Janus figure – because it is double-faced – and could be 2,000 years old; the other, a small, hunched figure, was moved here from Lusty Beg Island. Long before Christianity began to populate the islands of Lough Erne, the Celts recognized their mystical qualities. Boa Island, with its echoes of pre-Christian Ireland, is said to be named after Badhbh, the Irish goddess of war.

Continue on the A47 for 5 miles to Castle Caldwell.

The Fiddler's Stone at the entrance to Castle Caldwell is in memory of the fiddler Dennis McCabe, who fell out of Sir James Caldwell's family barge in

August 1770 and was drowned. The obituary ends: "On firm land only exercise your skill that you may play and safely drink your fill." The castle, now in ruins, had the reputation of enjoying one of the most beautiful locations of all Irish houses. The fine views are still the same, across water rich in wildlife, with observation shelters that allow an opportunity to catch sight of ducks, geese and grebes.

Continue on the A47 to Belleek (see page 181). Take the A46 for Enniskillen. After 13 miles turn right and, after 6 miles, turn left and follow signs to Monea.

The ruins of this superb plantation castle (pronounced "mon-ay"), built in 1618, sit at the end of a long avenue of beech trees. Its builder, Malcolm Hamilton, became Archbishop of Cashel. Overlooking a lake, the castle has an impressive entrance, twin circular towers with square turrets and interesting corbels. Occupants came and went until 1750, when a fire made it uninhabitable and it was abandoned. There are remnants of the old wall that surrounded the castle, and an ancient crannog, or artificial island dwelling, can be seen in front of Monea.

Turn left leaving Monea, then left for Enniskillen. Turn right, following signs to Boho for 5 miles, then right again for Belcoo.

Belcoo sits neatly between the two beautiful lough Macneans, surrounded by mountains and next to its neighboring village, Blacklion.

To the south of Lower Lough Macnean is the limestone cliff of Hanging Rock, and by the road is the Salt Man, a great lump of limestone, which, it is said, fell off the cliff and killed a man pulling a load of salt. Just north of Belcoo is the Holywell, traditionally visited by pilgrims in search of the curative powers of St. Patrick's Well.

From Belcoo, cross the border into the Republic and Blacklion for a very short distance, then cross back into Northern Ireland, taking the road along the south shore of Lower Lough Macnean. Turn right along Marlbank Scenic Loop and drive for another 3 miles to Marble Arch.

The highlight of Fermanagh is one of the most awesome sights in all of Europe. Experience the mysterious beauty of Marble Arch Cave with a ride on a flat-bottom boat through still, dark waters. Over 300 million years of history are here: The boat travels through spectacular underground rivers, waterfalls, lakes, lofty chambers and winding passages with superb stalagmites and stalactites. Be sure to take a sweater and good walking shoes. Nearby Marble Arch Forest, laced with nature trails, includes a walk along the Claddagh Glen and a beautiful waterfall.

Turn left, then right and drive for 4 miles to Florence Court.

Home of the Enniskillen family, Florence Court is one of Northern Ireland's most impressive great houses.

A three-story 18th-century mansion, with pavilions connected to the house by open, arched walkways, the interior is notable for its fine rococo plasterwork. The dramatic woodland setting is now Florence Court Forest Park, with a landscaped "pleasure" garden as well as the original Irish yew, from which cuttings were first taken to propagate the species, and oaks that were planted around 200 years ago.

From Florence Court, turn right. After a mile turn left on the A32, then after 2 miles turn right for Bellanaleck.

A base for cruising, Bellanaleck gives a glimpse of the winding ways of Upper Lough Erne, as its waters thread through 57 islands between Enniskillen and

The remains of Devenish Priory on Devenish Island in Lower Lough Erne

Galloon Bridge to the southeast. Here are hidden remote treasures such as the ruins of Castle Balfour and the 1,350-acre estate at Crom, a conservation area rich in history and rare wildlife.
Return to Enniskillen via the A509.

Devenish Island ✉ Round O Jetty, Enniskillen (028 6632 2882; www.ernetoursltd.com) ☎ 028 6862 1588 🕐 Daily 10–6, Apr. to mid-Sep. 👆 $
Castle Archdale Country Park ✉ 3 miles south of Kesh on B82 ☎ 028 6862 1588 🕐 Park: daily 8:30–dusk; center: daily 9–9, Easter–Sep.; 9–7, Mar.–Apr.; 9–4:30, Nov.–Feb. 👆 Free
Marble Arch Caves and Marble Arch Forest
✉ Caves: Marbank Scenic Loop Road, Florence Court (off A4/A32, 12 miles southwest of Eniskillen);

forest: near Marble Arch Caves, entrance off main Florence Court–Blacklion road ☎ 028 6634 8855; www.marblearchcavesgeopark.net 🕐 Daily 10–5, Jul.–Aug.; 10–4:30, Mar.–Jun. and Sep. 🍴 Café 👆 $$$
Florence Court and Florence Court Forest Park
✉ 8 miles southwest of Enniskillen via A4 and A32 ☎ 028 6634 8249; www.nationaltrust.org.uk 🕐 House: daily 11–5, Easter vacation and Jul.–Aug.; Sat.–Sun. 11–5, mid-Mar. to Easter and Oct.; Wed.–Mon. 11–5, May–Jun.; park: daily 10–7, Mar.–Oct.; 10–4, Nov.–Feb. 🍴 Restaurant 👆 $$
Crom Estate ✉ 3 miles west of Newtownbutler off A34 ☎ 028 6773 8118; www.nationaltrust.org.uk 🕐 Center: daily 11–5, mid-Mar. to Sep.; grounds: daily 10–7, Jun.–Aug.; 10–6, rest of year 🍴 Tearoom 👆 $$ (car or boat $$)

The Inishowen Peninsula

The Inishowen Peninsula stretches north for 26 miles between loughs Swilly and Foyle, and culminates in Malin Head, Ireland's northernmost point. It's an area of both scenic beauty and ecological importance, and the peninsula's heritage reaches back beyond recorded history, leaving relics of those distant days scattered across its face.

On the 800-foot-high Greenan Mountain sits the Grianan of Aileach, an ancient stone circular fort (*cashel*) affording spectacular panoramic views of this part of Ulster. As far as archeologists can determine, the dry-stone structure was built about 1700 BC and during the Iron Age served as a temple of the sun. High kings of Ireland regarded it as a sacred spot. At the foot of the access road, Burt church is a circular shape, which follows the same design of the fort itself.

A few miles farther north, at the pretty resort town of Fahan, the old graveyard holds a flat, two-faced cross from the seventh century and two curious carved stones.

Buncrana is the principal town of Inishowen. The ruins of 16th-century Buncrana Castle, which are where Wolfe Tone was imprisoned after his capture in 1798, overlook the Crana River. Close by are the ruins of O'Doherty's Castle.

North of Buncrana is Dunree Head where Fort Dunree is located. This restored coastal defense battery commands superb views of Lough Swilly and was in use from the Napoleonic era to the departure of the British militia in 1938.

Magheramore Hill near Clonmany is the home of the huge capstone of a Bronze Age dolmen that is reputed to have been thrown there by Ireland's legendary giant hero, hence its local name of "Finn MacCool's Finger Stone." North of Clonmany is the delightful seaside resort of Ballyliffin where Irish music nights are often held.

The prosperous town of Carndonagh has been an important ecclesiastical center since the fifth century. The striking 1945 Church of the Sacred Heart holds exceptionally fine statuary by the famous sculptor Albert Power, and the nearby Church of Ireland

The bewitching coastline at Ineuran Bay on the Inishowen Peninsula

Ulster and Northern Ireland

occupies a site on which St. Patrick founded one of his churches. If you're picnicking, there's a picnic area in lovely woods on the outskirts of town, on the Ballyliffin side.

A drive to Malin Head takes you as far north as you can go on Ireland's mainland. While this northerly point lacks the spectacular clifftop heights you've seen along the route, it provides marvelous panoramic views of the peninsula and the sea. Southwards takes you through the picturesque village of Culdaff, with lovely sandy beaches, to Moville. This coast is popular with deep-sea divers although the unpredictable tides mean you need to be experienced. The area is also a favorite for fishing and birdwatching.

➕ B3

Grianan of Aileach ✉ Signposted from Burt, 3 miles south of Bridgend, 10 miles south of Buncrana on the N13 Letterkenny/Londonderry road (main access to Inishowen Peninsula) 🕐 Free access

Letterkenny

Overlooking the River Swilly, (said to be named for a 400-eyed monster, Suileach, killed by St. Columcille), is the cathedral town and commercial center of north Donegal. Letterkenny claims to have the longest main street in the country, overlooked by the Cathedral of St. Eunan.

This turn-of-the-20th-century cathedral has a lofty spire, one of the tallest in the country, and stands on Sentry Hill, where secret Masses were held during penal times. Letterkenny is also the home of the Donegal County Museum which, housed in a section of what was the local workhouse back in more difficult times, displays artifacts from the prehistoric to early medieval periods in addition to the folklife of the county and the story of Donegal railroads. Temporary exhibitions cover a wide range of subjects.

If you are using Letterkenny as a base for the countryside of north County Donegal, don't miss the splendors of

the Atlantic Highlands, a landscape of jagged, cliff-filled coastline, rocky mountain pastures and breathtaking mountain passes. Mount Errigal (An Earagait), Donegal's highest peak at 2,466 feet, is an almost straight climb up to an exposed summit that overlooks spectacular views.

Nearby in Dunlewy (Dun Lúiche), there is something for the whole family at Ionad Cois Locha, a charming cottage center beside Dunlewy Lake. There are demonstrations of carding, spinning and weaving of wool, tours, storytelling and boat trips on the lake.

At some point in your Donegal rambles, take in the deeply wooded reaches of Glenveagh National Park. Set between the Derryveagh (Sléibhte Dhoire Bheatha) and Glendowan (Gleann Domhairn) mountain ranges, the park covers 25,000 acres of wilderness, set like a jewel on the edge of Lough Veagh.

At the main entrance near Churchill Village, the Regency-style Glebe Gallery houses the collection of the noteworthy painter Derek Hill, who died in 2000, and also includes works by Picasso, Bonnard and Kokoshka, together with works by Irish and Italian artists.

➕ B3

Tourist information ✉ Neil T. Blaney Road ☎ 074 91 21160 🕐 Daily 9–5, Jul.–Aug.; Mon.–Sat. 9–5, Jun.; Mon.–Fri. 9–5, Sep.–May

Donegal County Museum ✉ High Road (turn right at courthouse in town center) ☎ 074 91 24613 🕐 Mon.–Fri. 10–4:30, Sat. 1–4:30 🎟 Free

Ionad Cois Locha (Lakeside Centre) ✉ Dunlewy. From Letterkenny take N56 and turn left at Termon on to R251 ☎ 074 91 31699; www.dunleweycentre.com 🕐 Mon.–Sat. 10:30–6, Sun. 11–6, Easter–Oct. 🍴 Tearoom, restaurant 🎟 Cottage tour $$; boat ride $$; combination ticket $$$

Glebe Gallery and Glenveagh National Park and Castle ✉ Churchill, about 18 miles northwest of Letterkenny on the Churchill road (R251) ☎ Park: 074 913 7090; gallery: 074 91 37071; www.heritageireland. ie 🕐 Park and castle: daily 10–6; gallery: daily 11–6:30, Jul.–Aug.; Sat.–Thu. 11–6:30, Easter and Jun.–Sep. 🍴 Restaurant (Easter–Sep.), tearoom in castle 🎟 Park free; castle $; gallery $$

Londonderry/Derry

The second-biggest city in Northern Ireland, and fifth-biggest in Ireland as a whole, Londonderry is widely known by its original name of Derry, especially by its mostly Catholic population. Derry's notorious Bogside district has seen much unrest, for it is here that Catholic and Protestant factionalism is most sharply polarized. Catholics, stranded on the Republic's border, suffered much discrimination during the time of Protestant control. However, for all its political ill-feelings, Derry is a fascinating city, retaining intact the 17th-century walls that have played a significant role in its history and successfully withstood several sieges, most notably against Jacobite forces during the Siege of Derry in 1689.

The walls are about a mile in circumference and a walk around them is recommended. They are the only unbroken city walls in the British Isles, and this was the last city in Europe to build protective wall fortifications. The walls measure 20 to 25 feet high and 14 to 30 feet thick, with seven gates.

The old, walled section of modern-day Londonderry is west of the River Foyle, with ancient winding lanes and rows of charming Georgian and Victorian buildings. In the northeastern walls, Shipquay Gate is only two blocks from the river, and the historic old Guildhall, with its turrets and tower clock, is midway between river quays and this gate. Most of what you'll want to see will be within a short walk of these points. Walk them on your own, or join a guided tour from the tourist information center.

Derry's St. Columb's Cathedral was built in the mid-1600s. It's a splendid neo-Gothic structure, but much of what you'll see today has been added since. One of its most important features is the memorial window showing the relief of the siege in 1689.

Learn more about Derry's history at the Tower Museum. The museum houses two exhibitions, the "Story of Derry" with audiovisuals taking the story right up to the 21st century and the "Armada Shipwreck" exhibition, which tells the story of *La Trinidad*

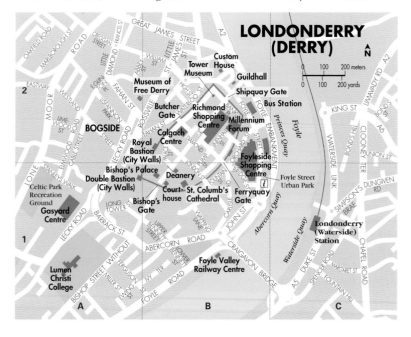

Hands Across The Divide, Derry, a symbol of hope and reconciliation after the city's unrest

Valencera, one of the largest ships of the Spanish Armada. The tower was built by the famous O'Doherty clan, dominant here until the 16th century, as an act of faith in better times to come.

For a poignant insight into the root of Northern Ireland's Troubles, visit The Museum of Free Derry. Here you'll find a civil rights archive of photographs and posters covering recent history and events such as Bloody Sunday.

➕ B3 (regional map on page 152)

Tourist information ➕ B1 ✉ 44 Foyle Street ☎ 028 7126 7284; www.derryvisitor.com ⏰ Mon.–Fri. 9–5, Sat. 10–5, Sun. 10–4, Mar.–Oct.; closed Sun., rest of year

City Walls ➕ A2 ✉ Tours: 44 Foyle Street ☎ 028 7126 7284 ⏰ Tours: contact tourist information for details of times 💲 $$

St. Columb's Cathedral ➕ B1 ✉ London Street (near Bishop's Gate) ☎ 028 7126 2746 ⏰ Mon.–Sat. 9–5, Apr.–Sep.; 9–1 and 2–4, rest of year 💲 $

Tower Museum ➕ B2 ✉ Union Hall Place ☎ 028 7137 2411 ⏰ Tue.–Sat. 10–5 (with seasonal adjustments) 💲 $$

Museum of Free Derry ➕ A2 ✉ 55 Glenfada Park. ☎ 028 7136 0880 ⏰ Mon.–Fri. 9:30–4, Sat.–Sun. 1–4, Jul.–Sep.; Mon.–Fri. 9:30–4, Sat. 1–4, Apr.–Jun.; Mon.–Fri. 9:30–4, Oct.–Mar. 💲 $

Mountains of Mourne

The Mourne Heritage Trust at Newcastle provides lots of information and guided walks. One of the nature trails follows the "Brandy Pad," a notorious smugglers' route that links Hilltown, notable for its many pubs, with the coast south of Newcastle. There is more woodland in the Tollymore and Castlewellan forest parks. Castlewellan is an outstanding feature with a 3-mile trail around the lake adorned with sculptures created from the park's natural materials. There are also gardens and the Peace Maze, tropical birds and the world's longest and largest hedge. To the south the stone-walled countryside is evocatively named Silent Valley.

Slieve Donard, at 2,800 feet, is the highest mountain, and clothing its slopes is the Donard Forest Park. The hike to the summit is the most popular walk in the Mourne Mountains and takes around four hours. Start from Donard Park parking lot in Newcastle, follow the walled path along the Glen River through the woods and emerge in the Glen River Valley and continue to the lower ridge of

Slieve Donard and Slieve Commedagh. Here you arrive at the Mourne wall, where you should turn left up the short but steep climb to the peak. The Mourne Wall is a 22-mile-long circular dry-stone wall built in the early 20th century by the Belfast Water Commissioners, crossing 15 peaks and providing good orientation for walkers. Within the boundaries of the wall, two dams form the Silent Valley and Ben Crom reservoirs, which supply 30 million gallons of water daily to County Down and Belfast. This is worth a visit just for the scenery, which includes lovely parkland before the dams. During July and August, a shuttle bus runs from the Silent Valley Visitor Centre to the southern tip of Ben Crom Reservoir.

Newcastle is a busy seaside resort at the foot of the Mourne Mountains. It first became popular in the Victorian era, as you can see from much of its architecture, but it has recently received a new waterfront promenade that gives visitors easier access to its 7-mile sandy beach and the calm waters of Dundrum Bay. At the north end of the town lies the Royal County Down Golf Club, with one of the world's best championship courses, and the upscale Slieve Donard Resort and Spa (see page 212).

Eastern coastal resorts of Dundrum, Annalong and Kilkeel provide alternative bases to Newcastle. Dundrum Castle, built by John de Courcy in about 1177, is one of Northern Ireland's finest Norman castles. From its hilltop perch, the castle overlooks Dundrum Bay, with splendid views of the sea and the Mourne Mountains. Bird watchers should visit Murlough Nature Reserve, where sea birds and a wide variety of botanical specimens flourish in an outstanding habitat of sand dunes and heath surrounded by the estuary and the sea. You can opt for organized guided walks or follow a self-guiding marked trail.

The wild, steep granite hills of the Mountains of Mourne present the most unforgettable view when seen across Carlingford Lough from the Republic. One of several fortifications guarding the entrance to the lough is Greencastle Royal Castle. In 1316 it was besieged by Edward the Bruce, was sacked twice in the 14th century and was later used as a garrison for Elizabeth I. It fell to Cromwell in 1652 and then fell into disuse. In today's more peaceful climate, the castle offers wonderful views of the lough and the soaring mountains behind.

For a whistle-stop Mourne drive, take the A2 east from Newry via Warrenpoint and Rostrevor along Carlingford Lough with the Cooley Mountains to the south. Turn left at Kilkeel on the B27 Mountain Road, a valley road leading through the heart of the Mournes. You can either turn left, passing Spelga Dam on your way to Hilltown and then return to Newry along the Rostrevor mountain road, or continue onto Bryansford and Newcastle, taking the coast road back to Newry via Kilkeel and Rostrevor.

✚ C2

Mourne Heritage Trust ✉ 10–14 Central Promenade, Newcastle, Co. Down ☎ 028 4372 4059; www.mournelive.com 🕐 Mon.–Fri. 9–5 💷 Free

Castlewellan Forest Park ✉ Main Street, Castlewellan ☎ 028 4377 8664 🕐 Daily 10–dusk 💷 $; parking $$

Silent Valley Mountain Park ✉ Head Road, Annalong, Co. Down ☎ 028 9074 1166 or 08457 440088 🕐 Daily 10–6:30, Apr.–Sep.; 10–4, rest of year 🍴 Café 💷 Parking $$

Dundrum Castle ✉ 5 miles north of Newcastle, Co. Down ☎ 028 9181 1491 🕐 Daily 10–5, Easter–Sep.; Sun. noon–4, rest of year (site always open but only staffed at these times) 💷 Free

Murlough Nature Reserve ✉ 2 miles south of Dundrum on A24, Co. Down ☎ 028 4375 1467 🕐 Reserve always open; center: daily 10–6 (weather permitting), Jun. to mid-Sep.; Sat.–Sun. 10–6, mid-Mar. to May 💷 Parking $ (only when facilities open)

Greencastle Royal Castle ✉ Kilkeel, Co. Down ☎ 028 9054 3037 🕐 Tue.–Sun. 10–6 💷 Free

Opposite: Rocky streams thread through the Mountains of Mourne

Old Irish Street, Ulster American Folk Park

Omagh

Omagh has long been an important center for the extensive agricultural area that surrounds it. The High Street is the heart of the town, with the best shops and architecture, but the Strule River is a major artery, with some fine old bridges and excellent views of the city. The best townscapes include a group of four churches, the most prominent being the Church of the Sacred Heart with its twin asymmetric towers.

To the north of the town are two attractions to give you a taste of the history of Northern Ireland. The well-known Ulster American Folk Park is a unique outdoor museum that has as its main theme the history of 18th- and 19th-century emigration from Ulster to North America. Rural Ulster thatched cottages contrast with log cabins in the New World, and there's a full-scale replica of an emigrant ship at a dock surrounded by buildings from the Ulster ports of Londonderry, Belfast and Newry. Reconstructions include the ancestral home of the Mellon family of Pittsburgh, whose forefathers were from Ulster. They endowed the folk park, as well as the home of John Joseph Hughes, the first Catholic archbishop of New York, who was instrumental in building St. Patrick's Cathedral in New York City.

The An Creagan Visitor Centre is designed to recreate the archeological sites of the area. An exhibition offers information and well-known local stories to transport you back to the Stone Age. Route guides allow you to explore archeological, cultural and environmental sites of the area. There is also a children's play area, a restaurant and a craftshop.

When you have had your fill of history, take a 5-mile drive through the woodlands of Gortin Glen Forest Park, with its off-the-road scenic viewing points. En route, keep an eye out for wildfowl and an unusual herd of Japanese sika deer that inhabit this forest park. The visitor center supplies informative booklets.

Alternatively, given Ireland's unpredictable weather, Aladdin's Kingdom, an indoor children's adventure playground, can be a welcome diversion if you have children. There are pendulum swings, a spiral glide, crawl tunnels, a giant ball pool, rope bridges and even a haunted house.

Omagh's other attractions lie east toward Cookstown. You'll hear all about "scutching," "hackling," "weaving" and

Dense pine forests in Gortin Glen Forest Park, originally planted for timber production

"beetling" at the linen-making demonstrations at Wellbrook Beetling Mill. Beetling, the final part of the process, is when the cloth is beaten unmercifully with wooden hammers, or beetles, to produce a sheen. "Linen-speak" has been used in this water-powered hammer mill since the 18th century, when the phenomenal noise must have been literally deafening for the employees.

Nearby is Drum Manor Forest Park, a haven for nature lovers, featuring a shrub garden, an arboretum, a lake, a heronry, a walled butterfly garden and a self-guided nature trail.

🔶 B2

Tourist information ✉ Strule Arts Centre, Townhall Square ☎ 028 8224 7831 🕐 Mon.–Sat. 10–5:30

Ulster American Folk Park ✉ Castletown, north of Omagh on A5 ☎ 028 8224 3292; www.folkpark.com 🕐 Tue.–Sun. 10–5, Mar.–Sep.; Tue.–Fri. 10–4, Sat.–Sun. 11–4, rest of year 🍴 Café 🎟 $$

An Creagan Visitor Centre ✉ Creggan, Omagh (13 miles east of Omagh on A505) ☎ 028 8076 1112; www.an-creagan.com 🕐 Daily 11–6:30, Apr.–Sep.; Mon.–Fri. 11–4:30, rest of year (craft shop open at weekends) 🎟 Free

Gortin Glen Forest Park ✉ 7 miles north of Omagh on B48 ☎ 028 8167 0666; http://nidirect.gov.uk/forests 🕐 Daily 10–dusk 🍴 Café 🎟 Parking $$

Aladdin's Kingdom ✉ Mountjoy Road, north out of Omagh ☎ 028 8225 1550 🕐 Mon.–Fri. 2:30–7, Sat. 10:30–6:30, Sun. 2–6:30 🎟 $ (varies for activities)

Wellbrook Beetling Mill ✉ 23 miles east of Omagh off A505 ☎ 028 8675 1735; www.nationaltrust.org.uk 🕐 Thu.–Tue. 2–6, Jul.–Aug.; Sat.–Sun. 2–6, mid-Mar. to Jun. and Sep., except Fri.–Tue. 1–6, Easter vacation. 🎟 $$

Drum Manor Forest Park ✉ 23 miles east of Omagh on A505 ☎ 028 8676 2774 🕐 Daily 10–dusk 🎟 Parking $$

The Sperrin Mountains

Nobel Prize-winning poet Seamus Heaney grew up on the edge of the Sperrin Mountains, and their softly rounded beauty figures in much of his work. The range, bounded by the towns of Magherafelt, Omagh, Cookstown and

Strabane, runs about 40 miles east to west, and the highest point rises only 2,240 feet at Sawel. The hillsides tend to be a bit bare, but you can drive through the wooded valleys for 200 miles.

The tourist office at Strabane has useful information abut the Sperrins, including a series of circular-walks leaflets giving information about the region's geology, archeology and folklore. The long-distance Ulster Way takes in part of the Sperrins.

South of the mountain range is the mysterious complex of stone circles at Beaghmore. The three pairs of circles, a single circle, and stone rows known as "alignments" were discovered in AD 130, but are believed to date from the Bronze Age or earlier.

West of the mountains, near Strabane, is the Wilson Ancestral Home. Judge James Wilson, grandfather of Woodrow Wilson, 28th president of the United States and an early winner of the Nobel Prize, left for America in 1807 from this small thatched whitewashed cottage. Members of the Wilson family still live next door in a modern farmhouse. The cottage, with its traditional hearth fire, holds some of the original furniture, including a portrait of James Wilson and large curtained beds.

To the northern boundary of the Sperrins, just 3 miles south of Dungiven, is Banagher Glen and Forest, a National Nature Reserve and Special Area of Conservation. There are some superb walks here and the chance to see buzzards, wildflowers and butterflies.

✚ B3

Tourist information ✉ The Alley and Conference Centre, 1a Railway Street, Strabane ☎ 028 7138 4444 ⊙ Mon.–Sat. 9–5:30, Jul.–Aug.; Mon.–Sat. 9–5, rest of year

Beaghmore Stone Circles ✉ Between Cookstown and Gortin, Co. Tyrone (signposted off A505) 🚪 Free

Wilson Ancestral Home ✉ Dergalt, 2 miles southeast of Strabane, off the Plumbridge road ☎ 028 7138 4444 ⊙ Tue.–Sun. 2–5, Jul.–Aug. or by arrangement 🚪 Free

Banagher Glen and Forest ✉ 3 miles south of Dungiven off the B74 ☎ 028 7776 0304 ⊙ Open for pedestrians all year round. Parking lot daily 9–9, Jul.–Aug.; Sat.–Sun. 9–9, Jun. and Sep. 🚪 Free

The prehistoric Beaghmore Stone Circles, in the Sperrin Mountains, date from between 2000 and 1200 BC

Fionn MacCumhaill

If there's anything the Irish love it's a good story. It seems only natural, then, that gaps in their long history are quickly filled with stories that evolve into legends. At the top of the list is that of Fionn MacCumhaill, "The Fair One," whose name has several spellings, the easiest of which is simply Finn MacCool. Was he a real man who lived in the third century, or a figment of the lively Irish imagination whose exploits were first written about in the seventh and eighth centuries? That weighty question matters not one whit to the Irish – he is their hero, real or fanciful fiction, and that is that.

Descended from the gods through his mother, he was of gigantic stature, noble of nature, and fearless in battle. He also possessed infinite wisdom and accumulated the knowledge of the ages. The story goes that while cooking the Salmon of Knowledge, Finn burned his thumb and stuck it in his mouth to ease the pain, whereupon the salmon's wisdom became his own. From that time forward, he had only to put his thumb in his mouth to find the answer to any perplexing matter.

Finn was also a romantic who rescued his beloved wife Saba from an enchantment that had turned her into a fawn. They had seven supremely happy years together before she fell victim to a wicked spell while she was carrying Finn's son Oisin, and the story of the boy's birth and return to his father through a magical sequence of events forms an important element of Finn's legend.

One of his most significant acheivements was the gathering of his Fianna band of faithful and skilled warriors (this is where the modern-day Fianna Fail political party gets its name) of the highest moral character and courage. Even today you may run across a huge stone in a field believed by locals to have been flung there by Finn or one of the Fianna, and there are those who will tell you that the Isle of Man is actually a sod of Irish soil hurled by Finn MacCool, leaving a great hole that became Lough Neagh. This is where written Irish mythology of Finn the warrior leader of the Fianna has become embellished with oral legends and stories of Finn the giant. The most famous of the giant stories is the one of the Giant's Causeway. According to legend, the causeway would still be above water all the way across had it not been for a ferocious tiff between the Ulster giant, Finn MacCool, and his Scottish counterpart, Finn Gall. Finn MacCool actually built the causeway, but when he went home to rest, the wily Scotsman tripped across, club in hand, to catch his foe unawares. When Finn Gall burst into Mrs. MacCool's kitchen and demanded to know if the sleeping giant was her husband, she – in a master stroke of quick thinking – assured him that it was only her wee baby. Imagining the father of such a gigantic babe put such a fright into the Scotsman that he hightailed it back across the water, destroying the causeway behind him to keep Finn MacCool in Ireland where he belonged. Fact or fiction, either way you'll agree, it is one whale of a story!

To learn more about Ireland's intriguing, legendary figures, look for Lady Gregory's fascinating book *Gods and Fighting Men*, published by Colin Smythe and with an introduction by W. B. Yeats, available in bookstores specializing in Irish publications.

Hotels and Restaurants

■ Connacht   203

■ Leinster   205

■ Munster   207

■ Ulster and
  Northern Ireland   210

Opposite: Many of Dublin's converted hotel buildings boast modern, luxurious interiors

Hotels and Restaurants

The hotels and restaurants in this guide were selected by local specialists and include establishments in several price ranges. Since price is often the best indication of the level of facilities and quality of service, a three-tiered price guide appears at the beginning of the listings. Because variable rates will affect the amount of foreign currency that can be exchanged for dollars (and therefore affect the cost of the room or meal), price ranges are given in the local currency.

Although price ranges and operating times were accurate at press time, this information is always subject to change without notice. If you're interested in a particular establishment, it is always advisable to call ahead to book.

Facilities suitable for travelers with disabilities vary greatly, and you are strongly advised to contact an establishment directly to determine whether it can meet your needs. Older buildings may not be adequately designed or equipped for visitors with limited or impaired mobility.

Accommodations

Accommodations have been selected with two considerations in mind: a particular sense of character or sense of local flavor, or a central location that is convenient for sightseeing. Remember that centrally located hotels fill up quickly, especially during busy summer vacation periods; make reservations well in advance. In-room bathrooms (sometimes referred to as "en-suite bathrooms") may not be available in budget hotels. Room rates normally include a full hot breakfast meal of bacon, sausage, eggs, fried potatoes and toast that should leave you feeling well fed for most of the day. Some hotels offer a price for overnight accommodations that includes an evening meal (an arrangement known as "half-board" in Ireland).

Eating Out

Listed restaurants range from upscale places suitable for an elegant evening out to small cafés where you can stop and take a leisurely break from a busy day of sightseeing. Most Irish meals are meat based, although some enticing vegetarian alternatives are now finding a place on the menus in town and city restaurants. A delicious tradition not to be missed is the popular plate of oysters accompanied by a pint of Guinness. You can sample epicurian seafood delights in Kinsale, often considered to be Ireland's gourmet capital.

Northern Ireland also has a good selection of fish and seafood options.

Elegant dining at the restaurant in Hotel Dylan on Eastmoreland Place, Dublin

KEY TO SYMBOLS

- 🏨 hotel
- 🍴 restaurant
- ✉ address
- ☎ telephone number
- 🕐 days/times closed
- Ⓜ nearest metro/tube/subway station(s)

AX American Express
DC Diners Club
MC MasterCard
VI VISA

Hotels

Price guide: double room with breakfast for two people

$ less than €110
$$ €110–€180
$$$ more than €180

Restaurants

Price guide: dinner per person, excluding drinks

$ less than €25
$$ €25–€50
$$$ more than €50

Three Square a Day

Traditionally, the Irish have always had their heartiest meal at midday. That's primarily because, as an agricultural nation, those working in the fields felt the need for sustenance to see them through a long afternoon. Lunch ("dinner" to the Irish) was the main meal, and the early evening "tea" was often as light as soup and brown bread or sandwiches. That still holds true today, and a full restaurant or pub lunch will provide as much to eat as most evening meals. However, Irish eating habits have changed, and if you are simply not ready for a full meal at noon after that sumptuous breakfast, just look for the nearest pub offering "pub grub," order a cup of hearty soup to go with a sandwich or leafy salad plate and save your main meal for the evening.

CONNACHT

BALLYNAHINCH, CO. GALWAY

🏨 **Ballynahinch Castle $$–$$$**

The castle stands at the foot of Ben Lettery on the banks of the famous Ballynahinch salmon river: The extensive grounds offer woodlands and scenic walks. The individually designed bedrooms are comfortable and spacious, and the restaurant offers game and fresh fish. Facilities include shooting, fishing and cycling.
✉ From N59, take Roundstone exit – the hotel is 3 miles from turnoff ☎ 095 31006 🕐 Closed mid-Dec. to Dec. 28 and Feb. AX, MC, VI

CASHEL BAY, CO. GALWAY

🏨 **Cashel House Hotel $$**

A family-run country hotel, standing at the head of Cashel Bay and set within a 50-acre garden. All accommodations have modern comforts, some with sea or garden views. Guests can relax in the gardens, walk along the seashore and dine on Connemara lamb, venison or quail in the fine-dining restaurant.
✉ N59 Galway–Clifden, turning left 1.5 miles after Recess. Hotel 3 miles on right ☎ 095 31001 🕐 Closed Jan. to mid-Feb. AX, MC, VI

CASTLEBAR, CO. MAYO

🏨 **Garden Gates $$**

In the countryside between Castlebar and Westport, this B&B offers homey comfort, king-size beds, power showers and a kitchen-diner where guests can chat over breakfast and hot tea with the owners.
✉ Rinaseer, Islandeady ☎ 094 902 3110 MC, VI

CASTLEREA, CO. ROSCOMMON

🏨 **Clonalis House $$$**

This 19th-century manor, the ancestral home of the O'Conors, direct descendents of the High Kings of Ireland, offers a slice of history – from the library stocked with 16th-century tomes to family portraits on the walls. Sink into a four-poster bed in the main house or enjoy self-catering in one of the cottages in its vast parklands.
✉ 1 mile along N60/Ballyhaunis Road from Castlerea ☎ 094 962 0014 🕐 Closed Oct.–early Apr. VI

CLIFDEN, CO. GALWAY

🏨 **Alcock and Brown $**

This town-center hotel offers contemporary rooms, a revamped restaurant serving fresh seafood, salads, steaks and vegetarian options, and an inviting bar with regular live music.
✉ N59 Galway–Clifden road ☎ 095 21880 AX, MC, VI

🍴 **Mitchell's Seafood Restaurant $$–$$$**

A good choice of quality food is available throughout the day from this popular Clifden restaurant. Hearty Irish stew is a specialty, with good portions of seafood and steaks.
✉ Market Street ☎ 095 21867 🕐 Closed Nov.–Feb. AX, DC, MC, VI

🏨 **Quay House $$–$$$**

The Quay House is Clifden's oldest building, constructed around 1820. It has 14 individually furnished rooms, some with balconies and working fireplaces. It also has a wonderful collection of Georgian furniture and family portraits. Fishing, golf and pony rides are all nearby.
✉ Beach Road ☎ 095 21369 🕐 Closed Nov. to mid-Mar. MC, VI

COLLOONEY, CO. SLIGO

🏨 **Markree Castle $$–$$$**

This magnificent castle dates back to 1640. Restoration work has transformed the grand building into a hotel with the imposing Knockmuldowney Restaurant. Facilities include horseback riding.
✉ Off N4 at Collooney crossroads just north of the N17 exit, 7 miles south of Sligo ☎ 071 916 7800 🕐 Closed Dec. 24–27 AX, DC, MC, VI

CROSSMOLINA, CO. MAYO

🏨 **Enniscoe Guest House $$$**

A delightful country house set in parkland by the shores of Lough Conn. Specializes in fishing holidays and for those who enjoy nature. Some outbuildings are converted into a heritage center. Excellent meals.
✉ 3 miles south of the village of Crossmolina on the R315 route to Castlebar ☎ 096 31112 🕐 Closed Nov.–Mar. MC, VI

GALWAY, CO. GALWAY

🏨 **Aaron House B&B $**

This modern bed-and-breakfast offers a central location, spacious rooms with contemporary furnishings and WiFi access. There's a social area where guests can relax by an open fire in winter, and breakfast includes vegetarian options. Other dietary requirements are catered to.

KEY TO SYMBOLS

- 🏨 hotel
- 🍴 restaurant
- ✉ address
- ☎ telephone number
- 🕐 days/times closed
- Ⓜ nearest metro/tube/subway station(s)
- AX American Express
- DC Diners Club
- MC MasterCard
- VI VISA

Hotels

Price guide: double room with breakfast for two people

$	less than €110
$$	€110–€180
$$$	more than €180

Restaurants

Price guide: dinner per person, excluding drinks

$	less than €25
$$	€25–€50
$$$	more than €50

Changing Tastes

There is little doubt that tourism has had a notable impact on the cuisine in Ireland. Until recently there was hardly any tradition of eating out. Patterns of diet were conservative, based on "meat and two veg," potatoes (of course) and large quantities of dairy fat. Now demands for predictable, inexpensive fast food are met, as everywhere, with burgers and pizzas – a better bet being fish and chips (fries). The restaurant scene reflects the country's broadening cosmopolitan population, and French, Italian, Chinese, Russian and Indian restaurants have blossomed throughout the country. Sophisticated tastes have also introduced organic and vegetarian restaurants – once unheard of. In fact it seems hard to imagine the grim days of the 19th century when so much of the population was starving and food preparation amounted to little more than boiling a potato.

✉ 25 College Road ☎ 091 563 315
🕐 Closed 24–26 Dec. MC, VI

🍴 Aniar $$–$$$

You can expect mouth-wateringly creative Irish cuisine at this modern, relaxed eatery. Chef Enda McEvoy makes use of local ingredients in main courses such as wild brill with celeriac, clams and lovage or wild venison, red cabbage, apple, beetroot and elderberry and desserts like seabuckthorn panna cotta.
✉ 53 Lower Dominick Street
☎ 091 535 947 MC, VI

🏨 g Hotel $$

This modern, designer hotel in the industrial outskirts of Galway offers the ultimate in contemporary style, luxurious guest rooms and therapeutic spa treatments.
✉ Wellpark ☎ 091 865 200
🕐 Closed Christmas week AX, MC, VI

🍴 The Galleon $

Small, cozy restaurant with varied menu emphasizing fresh seafood, grills, and Irish and vegetarian dishes at reasonable prices.
✉ Salthill ☎ 091 522 963 MC, VI

🏨 Glenlo Abbey $$$

Standing in a landscaped 138-acre estate, this restored 18th-century abbey overlooks a beautiful loch. Bedrooms are in a modern wing along with a library, restaurants, cocktail and cellar bars. Leisure facilities include golf, fishing, archery and clay-pigeon shooting.
✉ Bushypark – 2.5 miles from Galway city center on N59 ☎ 091 526 666
🕐 Closed Dec. 24–26 AX, DC, MC, VI

🍴 Oscar's Seafood Bistro $$–$$$

Whether you prefer fish and chips or seafood specials such as French-style mussels or bamboo-steamed hake, there are fish dishes to suit all tastes here. There are also several decent meat options, too.
✉ Dominick Street, Galway ☎ 091 582 180 MC, VI

KILCOLGAN, CO. GALWAY

🍴 Moran's Oyster Cottage $$$

Internationally famed seafood restaurant in a 200-year-old thatched cottage. Oysters are a specialty, with smoked salmon and mussel soup a favorite as well.
✉ The Weir, 10 miles south of Galway town, off N18 Galway–Limerick road
☎ 091 796 113 🕐 Closed Good Friday and Dec. 24–26 AX, MC, VI

ROSCOMMON, CO. ROSCOMMON

🏨 Abbey $–$$

Set in its own grounds just outside Roscommon, this fine manor house dates back more than 100 years. Bedrooms are well decorated, with period-style rooms in the original house; those in the newer wing are more contemporary. The brasserie-style restaurant serves traditional meals made with local ingredients.
✉ Just outside Roscommon on N63 Galway Road, opposite railroad station
☎ 090 662 6240 🕐 Closed Dec. 24–27 AX, DC, MC, VI

ROUNDSTONE, CO. GALWAY

🏨 Eldons $$

This distinctive building stands on the main street of a picturesque fishing village. Guests receive a warm welcome and good service. The seafood restaurant, Beola, has a good choice of dishes.
✉ Off N59 through Toombedla to Roundstone village ☎ 095 35933
🕐 Closed Nov.–Feb. AX, DC, MC, VI

SLIGO, CO. SLIGO

🍴 Bistro Bianconi $–$$

Pleasant informal restaurant with emphasis on Italian and spicy international dishes.
✉ 44 O'Connell Street (on main street) ☎ 071 91 41744 🕐 Closed Good Friday and Dec. 2–26 MC, VI

🏨 Sligo Park $$–$$$

In 7 acres of rolling parkland to the south of Sligo, this hotel is an ideal base for exploring Yeats country. Offering excellent "executive" rooms, the hotel also has a heated indoor pool, tennis, aerobics, sauna, solarium and hot tub, with good beaches nearby.
✉ Pearse Road, on N4 ☎ 071 91 90400 🕐 Facilities open to residents only Dec. 24–25 AX, DC, MC, VI

WESTPORT, CO. MAYO

🍴 An Port Mor $$

You can savor fresh Innisturk crab with seaweed tagliatelle or aged Kelly's of Newport sirloin steak at this town-center restaurant. There's also an early-bird menu offering two or three courses for a reduced rate.
✉ 1 Brewery Place ☎ 098 26730
🕐 Closed Mon. MC, VI

🏨 Ardmore Country House $–$$

A picturesque country house hotel ideally placed close to the heart of town. Most of the large individually decorated bedrooms have great views over Clew Bay. No children under 12. ✉ The Quay ☎ 098 25994 ⏲ Closed Nov. to mid-Mar. AX, MC, VI

🏨 Knockranny House $$–$$$
Overlooking Westport with Clew Bay in the distance, this family-run hotel offers a spa, luxurious lounge and bar. The restaurant, La Fougère, serves excellent seafood. ✉ N5 Westport–Castlebar road, close to Westport ☎ 098 28600 ⏲ Closed Dec. 21–26 AX, MC, VI

LEINSTER

ARDEE, CO. LOUTH
🏨 Smarmore Castle $$–$$$
One of Ireland's oldest buildings, this castle was the ancestral home of the Norman Taaffe family. Guest rooms include the Viscount's room in the castle tower, featuring a four-poster bed. There's an Italian restaurant and leisure club onsite. ✉ R170 west of M1, N2 south from Ardee, then R166 west and first left to Smarmore ☎ 041 685 7167 ⏲ Closed mid-Dec. to mid-Jan. unless prior bookings AX, MC, VI

ARTHURSTOWN, CO. WEXFORD
🏨 Dunbrody Country House and Restaurant $$–$$$
You'll find tranquility and hospitality in this elegant Georgian manor house. There is an award-winning restaurant, golf, horseback riding, clay-pigeon shooting, a spa, and beaches nearby. ✉ From N11 follow signs for Duncannon and Ballyhack (R733). Hotel is 20 miles beyond the turnoff ☎ 051 389 600 ⏲ Closed Dec. 23–26 AX, DC, MC, VI

DUBLIN, CO. DUBLIN
🏨 Butlers Town House $$
Inside this Victorian town house hotel guests can read the papers or enjoy a nightcap in the Victorian parlor. Upstairs the rooms are well appointed with period-style furnishings. Breakfast is cooked to order and served in the conservatory. ✉ 44 Lansdowne Road ☎ 01 667 4022 ⏲ Closed Dec. 23–28 AX, MC, VI

🏨 Cassidys $–$$
This comfortable family-owned hotel is located just off the end of O'Connell Street in three converted Georgian houses. The 113 rooms are well equipped; some of the executive rooms have access to the tranquil Garden of Remembrance, perfect for unwinding after sightseeing. ✉ 6–8 Cavendish Row ☎ 01 878 0555 ⏲ Closed Dec. 24–26 AX, DC, MC, VI

🍴 Chapter One $$$
A long-standing favorite for special occasions, this Michelin-starred restaurant is located underneath the Dublin Writers' Museum. Choose from a four-course dinner, the tasting, pre-theater or lunch menus. Sample dishes include black pudding and veal sweetbread *boudin*, brill cooked over charcoal and stuffed loin of rabbit wrapped in pancetta. ✉ 18–19 Parnell Square ☎ 01 873 2266 ⏲ Closed Sun.–Mon. AX, MC, VI

🏨 The Clarence $$$
Set in the heart of Dublin city center within walking distance of many restaurants and theaters, this is an individual and very tasteful establishment with richly furnished bedrooms. For sheer luxury, the two-bedroom penthouse suite is outstanding. The public areas include a long gallery and upscale bar and the restaurant serves excellent cuisine. ✉ 6–8 Wellington Quay ☎ 01 407 0800 ⏲ Closed Dec. 24–26 AX, DC, MC, VI

🏨 Clontarf Castle Hotel $$$
This hotel offers guests the best of both worlds – a country location but just 2 miles from Dublin. The hotel has dramatic interiors that deftly combine its historic architecture with fashionable but classical furnishings. ✉ Castle Avenue, Clontarf ☎ 01 833 2321 DC, VI, MC

🏨 Dylan $$$
The Dylan is a wonderful and luxurious place to stay in the leafy suburb of Ballsbridge, only a short bus ride or 10-minute walk to central Dublin. The interior of the Victorian building has been transformed with a stylish modern design. There is a lovely terrace for drinks outside, and a contemporary restaurant. ✉ Eastmoreland Place, Ballsbridge ☎ 01 660 3000 ⏲ Closed Dec. 25–26 AX, DC, MC, VI

🍴 Gallagher's Boxty House $$
This popular restaurant in the heart of Temple Bar serves up typical Irish fare, from Irish stew to steak, but its specialty is boxty, the traditional Irish potato pancake. If that hasn't filled you up, the desserts laced with Baileys will do the trick. ✉ 20–21 Temple Bar ☎ 01 677 2762 DC, VI, MC

🏨 Harding $
At the heart of the fascinating Temple Bar area, this friendly, renovated hotel offers simple, bright rooms. Darkey Kelly's Bar & Restaurant features traditional Irish and contemporary music, while the Copper Alley Bistro serves classic international dishes. ✉ Copper Alley, Fishamble Street, Temple Bar ☎ 01 679 6500 ⏲ Closed Dec. 23–26 AX, MC, VI

🍴 La Maison Restaurant $$
Opened by Breton chef Olivier Quenet in 2009, this restaurant serves up affordable French cuisine using Irish produce. Try dishes like sauté Dublin Bay prawns with girolle mushrooms, and Connemara lamb with dauphinoise potatoes. ✉ 15 Castlemarket Street, D2 ☎ 01 672 7258 AX, MC, VI

🍴 Pearl Brasserie $–$$
Here you can enjoy quality, locally sourced cuisine that won't break the bank. The à la carte menu can include foie gras, *pata negra* ham, king scallops, halibut in a miso and sake marinade and suckling pig. They also offer a value two-course meal from lunch until early evening. ✉ 20 Merrion Street Upper ☎ 01 661 3572 MC, VI

🍴 Queen of Tarts $
This is one of Dublin's best budget eateries, serving up breakfasts of granola, hot oatmeal, Irish smoked salmon and eggs, or bacon, egg and potato-chive cake. There are also vegetarian breakfasts and lunches of soup, sandwiches and freshly made savory tarts. ✉ Cow's Lane, Dame Street ☎ 01 633 4681 MC, VI

🍴 Sabor Brazil $$
Transport yourself to Brazil with the flavors of grilled meats, black bean stew and tropical Brazilian fruit with cheese. It's a popular choice in Dublin at present, so book ahead. ✉ 50 Pleasant Street, D8 ☎ 01 475 0304 ⏲ Dinner only; Sun. bookings only; closed Mon. MC, VI

Leinster

KEY TO SYMBOLS

⊞	hotel
❚❙	restaurant
✉	address
☎	telephone number
⊘	days/times closed
Ⓜ	nearest metro/tube/subway station(s)
AX	American Express
DC	Diners Club
MC	MasterCard
VI	VISA

Hotels
Price guide: double room with breakfast for two people

$	less than €110
$$	€110–€180
$$$	more than €180

Restaurants
Price guide: dinner per person, excluding drinks

$	less than €25
$$	€25–€50
$$$	more than €50

Irish Cuisine

You may be surprised to learn that the hallowed "corned beef and cabbage" is wholly a figment of the Irish–American image of Ireland. The Irish tradition is boiled bacon and cabbage, along with Irish stew, made with lamb and absolutely delicious. The equally hallowed potato is still a favorite, but these days it comes to the table roasted, baked, boiled, mashed or as french fries (call them "chips"; potato chips are "crisps"). And far from being the main dish, your potato is accompanied by local beef, lamb, chicken, prawns or fish. Salads often include cold meats such as turkey, chicken or ham, and vegetables complete the heaping plates of "mains." Don't-miss foods include locally made cheddar, blue or herb soft cheese. Fish (trout and salmon) can be found throughout the country: Dublin Bay prawns and plaice, a lovely saltwater fish, are specialties and you don't have to be rich to enjoy the oysters.

⊞ The Schoolhouse Hotel $$–$$$
Beautifully converted from a former schoolhouse, this hotel is set in leafy Ballsbridge within walking distance of the city center. Accommodations are spacious, quiet and comfortable. There's also a restaurant and an adjoining pub with outside seating.
✉ 2–8 Northumberland Avenue ☎ 01 667 5014 ⊘ Closed Dec. 24–27 AX, MC, VI

DUNDALK, CO. LOUTH
⊞ Ballymascanlon House $$–$$$
A Victorian mansion whose 130-acre grounds include a private 18-hole golf course. There are luxurious bedrooms, an elegant restaurant and spacious lounge, an indoor heated pool, tennis, sauna, gym and hot tub.
✉ North of Dundalk take T62 to Carlingford ☎ 042 935 8200 AX, DC, MC, VI

DUNLAVIN, CO. WICKLOW
⊞ Rathsallagh House $$$
It's hard to believe that this ivy-clad country house hotel was once a stables. Converted after a fire destroyed it in the 1798 Rebellion, today it is an elegant retreat where quality service is the priority. There's an award-winning restaurant, a golf course and even heated dog kennels.
✉ N81 south from Dublin, right onto R756 at Hollywood, then 2 miles beyond Dunlavin village ☎ 045 403 112 ⊘ Closed Mon.–Thu., Jan. to mid-Apr.; Dec. 24–27 AX, MC, VI

ENNISCORTHY, CO. WEXFORD
⊞ Riverside Park $–$$
In a picturesque setting beside the River Slaney, this hotel is easily distinguished by its terra-cotta and blue color scheme. Public areas, including the dramatic lobby, take full advantage of the views. The spacious, attractive bedrooms are equipped with every convenience.
✉ The Promenade. Center of Enniscorthy, N11 Dublin–Rosslare road ☎ 05392 37800 ⊘ Closed Dec. 24–26 AX, DC, MC, VI

FERRYCARRIG, CO. WEXFORD
⊞ Ferrycarrig Hotel $$
Overlooking the River Slaney near Wexford, this hotel offers tranquillity and easy access to the rest of the county. The bedrooms, family rooms and suites are simple, stylish and contemporary. There is both formal dining and a more casual riverside bar-restaurant with a terrace, as well as a leisure club.
✉ N11 on the north side of the River Slaney from Wexford ☎ 053 912 0999 AX, MC, VI

HOWTH, CO. DUBLIN
❚❙ The Oar House Fish Restaurant $$
As the name suggests, fish features high on the menu. Options can include Dublin Bay prawns and crab claws, followed by seafood linguine, blackened Cajun mackerel, seabass with wine and garlic sauce or catch of the day. There are also steak, chicken and vegetarian options.
✉ West Pier ☎ 01 839 2419 MC, VI

KILKENNY, CO. KILKENNY
⊞ Kilkenny $$$
Set on 5 acres of wooded land on the outskirts of Kilkenny, this hotel has renovated bedrooms and and a modern Irish restaurant serving up Kilkenny-style Caesar salad and Irish fillet steaks. There is also a health club and pool.
✉ College Road. Follow ring road to Callan and Clonmel traffic circle, hotel is on the right ☎ 056 77 62000 AX, DC, MC, VI

❚❙ Kyteler's Inn $–$$
This 13th-century pub oozes traditional charm with stone walls and chunky wooden furnishings. Sup a pint of creamy Kilkenny beer and tuck into hearty plates of boiled bacon, roast beef or fish and chips.
✉ Kieran's Street ☎ 056 772 1064 ⊘ Closed Good Friday MC VI

❚❙ Langton Room $$
One of Kilkenny's favorite restaurants, this spot serves classic, wholesome dishes, some with an Asian twist. The spacious dining room has a rather impressive glass roof. There are also 34 comfortable, modern guest rooms here, all individually styled with custom furnishings.
✉ Langton House Hotel, 69 John Street ☎ 056 77 65133 ⊘ Closed Dec. 25 AX, DC, MC, VI

⊞ Rosquil House $$
The rooms are spacious and comfortable in this modern guest house. It's just a 10-minute walk from the city center and the large breakfasts will set you up for the day.
✉ Castlecomer Road ☎ 056 772 1419 VI, MC

LUCAN, CO. DUBLIN

Finnstown Country House $$
This hotel is set in 45 acres of grounds but still only 25 minutes from Dublin city center. Come for lunch of Irish beef, duck or seabass, or stay in one of the contemporary rooms in the country house.
✉ Newcastle Road ☎ 01 601 0700 AX, MC, VI

NAVAN, CO. MEATH

Bellinter House $$–$$$
A beautifully restored Palladian House, the Bellinter oozes Georgian grandeur from chandeliers to elaborate cornicing. Guest rooms are individually styled with contemporary comforts and a drinks cabinet. There is a restaurant serving locally sourced food plus a drawing room, games room, library and bathhouse.
✉ M3 from Dublin, Blunderstown turnoff, N2 toward Navan, then first left and hotel is 2 miles on the right ☎ 046 903 0900 MC, VI

NEWBRIDGE, CO. KILDARE

Keadeen $$
A family-owned hotel set on 9 acres of landscaped gardens and well placed for Dublin Airport and The Curragh racecourse. The hotel has an indoor pool, sauna, solarium, gym, hot-tub. Massages are available. Public areas include a spacious drawing room and two bars.
✉ M7 exit 10 Newbridge, Curragh, towards Newbridge. Hotel is on left ☎ 045 431 666 ◷ Closed Dec. 24–27 AX, DC, MC, VI

ROSSLARE, CO. WEXFORD

Kelly's Resort $$–$$$
This popular seafront hotel offers a leisure center, tennis courts, a children's play room and gardens. Choose between La Marine Bistro and the award-winning Beaches restaurant. Public rooms are adorned with contemporary Irish art.
✉ Town center on seafront ☎ 05391 32114 ◷ Closed mid-Dec. to mid-Feb. AX, MC, VI

STRAFFAN, CO. KILDARE

Barberstown Castle $$$
For that extra special occasion, dine by candlelight in this original 13th-century castle. The confident modern French and Irish cooking includes tempting main courses such as baked wild salmon with pan-fried oysters.
✉ Clan Celdridge Road, just outside Straffan ☎ 01 628 8157 ◷ Closed Sun.–Wed. dinner, Jan. and Dec. 24–26 AX, MC, VI

The K Club $$$
Stay in elegant bedrooms overlooking the gardens, river or golf course at this beautiful, luxury hotel. Facilities include a golf course which hosted the Ryder Cup in 2006, fishing, horseback riding and more.
✉ From Dublin city center (17 miles) take N4 exit R406 and hotel entrance is on right in Straffan ☎ 01 601 7200 AX, MC, VI

WEXFORD, CO. WEXFORD

Talbot $$
The Talbot is a contemporary style hotel created from a renovated 1905 grain mill that enjoys panoramic views of Wexford Harbour and the River Slaney. Facilities include a pool, and health and beauty spa. Good restaurant and bar snacks.
✉ The Quay. Take N11/N25 to Wexford, hotel on waterfront ☎ 053 912 2566 ◷ Closed Dec. 24–25 AX, DC, MC, VI

The Yard $–$$
One of the newest restaurants in Wexford, The Yard has quickly become popular with locals who come for their mixed international menu and relaxed atmosphere. Try the shredded duck with spicy noodles followed by free-range duck on *pommes boulangère*.
✉ Georges Street ☎ 053 914 4083 MC, VI

BALLYLICKEY, CO. CORK

Sea View House $$–$$$
Sample Irish hospitality at this country house overlooking Bantry Bay. Set in attractive gardens, it has cozy lounges with turf fires, and pleasant bedrooms. Award-winning food is served in plush surroundings. This is a good touring base for west Cork and Kerry.
✉ 3 miles from Bantry, 8 miles from Glengarriff on N71 ☎ 027 50073 or 027 50462 ◷ Closed mid-Nov. to mid-Mar. AX, DC, MC, VI

BALLYVAUGHAN, CO. CLARE

Hylands Burren Hotel $–$$
Expect the warmest of Irish welcomes at this hotel on the edge of The Burren. The guest rooms are tranquil and contemporary. Downstairs are all the comforts you could need after a day's walking, including open turf fires and traditional Irish cuisine.
✉ Ballyvaughan ☎ 065 707 7037 ◷ Closed end Oct.–Easter MC, VI, DC

BALTIMORE, CO. CORK

Rathmore House $
A modern, Georgian-style house, this B&B has beautiful views over Baltimore's harbor and the islands beyond. Breakfasts include Baltimore smoked kippers.
✉ R595 from Skibbereen, just before Baltimore ☎ 028 20362 MC, VI

BANTRY, CO. CORK

The Fish Kitchen $
Tuck into the best of local fish and seafood. Oysters, seafood chowder, breaded mussels and battered haddock feature on the menu alongside a few meat options, or choose the surf 'n' turf option.
✉ New Street, Reenrour ☎ 027 56651 MC, VI

BLARNEY, CO. CORK

Blarney Castle Hotel $$
This hotel might not have all the latest boutique styling but rooms are comfortable and spacious and the hospitality is second to none. It has a restaurant that's open for lunch and dinner, and a bar with regular traditional Irish music and dancing.
✉ Village Green ☎ 021 438 5116 AX, MC, VI

BUNRATTY, CO. CLARE

Bunratty Castle Hotel $$–$$$
This hotel exudes contemporary comfort with modern, spacious guest rooms, a luxury spa, leisure club and bar. There's also a restaurant serving Irish local produce with a good selection of wines from around the world.
✉ Bunratty ☎ 061 478700 ◷ May close over Christmas AX, MC, VI

CAHERDANIEL, CO. KERRY

Derrynane $–$$
Halfway around the famous Ring of Kerry, this modern hotel overlooking the sea is convenient for touring. Eight holiday homes on the site provide good self-catering facilities.
✉ 2 minutes' walk off the main road ☎ 066 947 5136 ◷ Closed early Oct.–Easter AX, DC, MC, VI

CLONAKILTY, CO. CORK

The Lodge and Spa on Inchydoney Island $$–$$$
Luxurious hotel set on stunning coastline, near a sandy beach. Many of the stylish

KEY TO SYMBOLS

⊞	hotel
❒	restaurant
✉	address
☎	telephone number
⊙	days/times closed
⊞	nearest metro/tube/subway station(s)
AX	American Express
DC	Diners Club
MC	MasterCard
VI	VISA

Hotels
Price guide: double room with breakfast for two people
$	less than €110
$$	€110–€180
$$$	more than €180

Restaurants
Price guide: dinner per person, excluding drinks
$	less than €25
$$	€25–€50
$$$	more than €50

The Best-Value Meal
One thing is certain: You won't leave Ireland hungry. A "traditional Irish breakfast" (or the "Ulster fry" north of the border) is, simply put, overwhelming. Even if you're a coffee-and-toast person at home, you're not likely to resist the vast spread before your eyes every morning that includes a brimming plateful of bacon, eggs, broiled tomatoes with soda and potato breads and butter. Room rates are nearly always quoted with a full breakfast included, so you might as well fill up for the day!

---

bedrooms have sea views. Healthy options are available at the Gulfstream Restaurant, with less formal dining in the Dunes Bar and Bistro, and treatments such as thalassotherapy in the spa.
✉ N71 West Cork Road to Clonakilty. Take second exit at the traffic circle and follow signs ☎ 023 883 3143 ⊙ Closed Dec. 25 AX, MC, VI

CLONMEL, CO. TIPPERARY
⊞ **Minella $$**
This family-run mansion on the banks of the River Suir has comfortable bedrooms with good views; some of the bathrooms have hot tubs.
✉ Coleville Road ☎ 052 6122388 ⊙ Closed Dec. 23–29 AX, DC, MC, VI

CORK, CO. CORK
⊞ **Ambassador Hotel & Health Club $–$$**
This distinguished sandstone and granite 19th-century building is a fine hotel with city views. Some bedrooms have balconies. There is a cocktail lounge, bar, restaurant and spa.
✉ Military Hill, St. Lukes, just off Wellington Road ☎ 021 453 9000 ⊙ Closed Dec. 24–25 AX, DC, MC, VI

❒ **Greenes Restaurant $$**
Located in Isaacs hotel beside a floodlit waterfall, this restaurant uses fresh local products to produce a modern Irish menu. There are daily blackboard specials and options for vegetarians.
✉ Isaacs Hotel, 8 MacCurtain Street ☎ 021 455 2279 ⊙ Closed Sun. lunch, Christmas week AX, MC, VI

⊞ **Hayfield Manor Hotel $$$**
The former home of Cork merchants the Hayfield family, this secluded Georgian property was converted into a top-class hotel in the 1990s. The hotel's bedrooms exude comfort and the public rooms retain the elegance of yesteryear.
✉ Perrott Avenue, College Road ☎ 021 484 5900 AX, MC, VI

❒ **Strasbourg Goose Restaurant $–$$**
This restaurant in Cork's Huguenot Quarter prides itself on serving quality comfort food at affordable prices. Options include baby Tuscany bruschetta, fresh mussels or homemade fish cake to start, and steak, chicken and fish options for the main dish. Look for specials like Barbary duck breast.
✉ 17–18 French Church Street

☎ 021 427 9534 ⊙ Closed Mon.; dinner only Tue.–Fri. MC, VI

COURTMACSHERRY, CO. CORK
⊞ **Courtmacsherry $**
This refurbished family-run Georgian house is set on attractive grounds near the beach. Quality meals are served in The Cork Tree Restaurant. A riding school caters to all ages and there are a number of cottage rentals overlooking Courtmacsherry Bay.
✉ M71 to Bandon, then R602 to Timoleague – head for Courtmacsherry. Hotel is by the beach at the far end of the town ☎ 023 46198 ⊙ Closed Oct.–Mar. MC, VI

DOOLIN, CO. CLARE
⊞ **Aran View House $–$$**
A comfortable and welcoming hotel with a convivial atmosphere, situated on 100 acres of rolling farmland with panoramic views of the Aran Islands.
✉ Coast Road ☎ 065 707 4061 or 065 707 4420 ⊙ Closed Nov.–Apr. DC, MC, VI

DUNGARVAN, CO. WATERFORD
⊞ **Lawlors $$**
An ideal touring center, this family-run streetside hotel caters to both leisure and business guests. There is regular live evening entertainment. The hotel restaurant offers an international menu.
✉ Off N25 ☎ 058 41122 ⊙ Closed Dec. 24–25 AX, DC, MC, VI

ENNIS, CO. CLARE
⊞ **Old Ground Hotel $$–$$$**
This former manor house has individually styled bedrooms in restful colors and a few spacious suites. The Town Hall Bistro is the perfect place for a coffee or afternoon tea, Poet's Corner offers regular live traditional music and the O'Brien Room is the hotel's fine-dining option.
✉ O'Connell Street/Station Road ☎ 065 682 81270 AX, MC, VI

FERMOY, CO. CORK
⊞ **Abbeyville House $–$$**
This 19th-century three-story house combines old-world charm with modern comfort and is only a stone's throw from local pubs, shops and restaurants. All six bedrooms are well furnished, with private bathrooms. The drawing and dining rooms are homey. There is WiFi access. A home-cooked breakfast is served.
✉ Abercromby Place. On the N8 Dublin–Cork road opposite Fermoy's

town park ☎ 025 32767 🕐 Closed end Nov.–Apr. MC, VI

GOUGANE BARRA, CO. CORK
🏨 Gougane Barra $$

This family-run hotel is popular for its cuisine. Its relaxing bedrooms, with private bathrooms, all have mountain or lake views. During the summer months guests can see a varied program of performances at the Theatre by the Lake.
✉ Off N22 ☎ 026 47069 🕐 Closed mid-Oct. to early Apr. AX, MC, VI

KENMARE, CO. KERRY
🏨 Lansdowne Arms Hotel $–$$

Historic, elegant 26-room hotel offering good hospitality in the heart of Kenmare. Bar food is served all day, and the dining room offers excellent Irish and international cuisine. There is regular Irish music in the Bold Thady Quill Bar.
✉ Main Street ☎ 064 664 1368 🕐 Closed Dec. 25 MC, VI

🏨 Park Hotel Kenmare $$–$$$

This luxurious country house stands above terraced gardens overlooking the estuary of the Kenmare River with the mountains rising behind it. There's warm professional service and the restaurant offers good food and fine wines. The world-renowned Sámas spa is here; also golf, tennis and croquet.
✉ On R569, beside golf course ☎ 064 664 1402 🕐 Closed Jan. 3 to mid-Feb., Mon.–Fri. mid-Feb to 1 Apr. and in Nov. AX, MC, VI

KILLARNEY, CO. KERRY
🏨 Aghadoe Heights $$–$$$

A luxurious and hospitable haven with an award-winning restaurant. Other facilities include an indoor heated pool, tennis, fishing, sauna, solarium, gym and spa.
✉ 10 miles south of Kerry Airport and 3 miles north of Killarney. Look for the sign off the N22 Tralee Road ☎ 064 663 1766 🕐 Closed Dec. 31–Jan. 2 AX, DC, MC, VI

🍴 Chapter Forty $$

A restaurant with imaginative vegetarian options such as mushroom risotto with squash and duck egg, Chapter Forty also serves a range of meat and fish options. Save space for dessert – donuts with pistachio ice cream or damson and lime cheesecake are good choices.
✉ New Street ☎ 064 667 1833 AX, MC, VI

🏨 Killarney Park $$$

On the edge of town, this charming hotel has rich colors, open fires and welcoming staff. There's a spa, and a health and fitness club.
✉ Kenmare Place ☎ 064 663 5555 🕐 Closed Nov. 28–Dec. 15 and Dec. 24–26 AX, MC, VI

🏨 Lake $$$

This former mansion stands among mountain views and woodland walks. Some bedrooms have balconies and four-poster beds.
✉ Muckross Road. Kenmare road from Killarney ☎ 064 663 1035 🕐 Closed mid-Dec. to Feb. 1 AX, DC, MC, VI

KINSALE, CO. CORK
🍴 Man Friday $$

Popular long-established restaurant with a garden terrace and views over the marina. Seasonal à la carte menus feature seafood from local waters, along with duck, lamb and steak.
✉ Scilly (a 10-minute walk from town center) ☎ 021 477 2260 🕐 Dinner only. Closed Sun. AX, MC, VI

🏨 Trident $$–$$$

The redeveloped Trident Hotel has fabulous views over Kinsale Harbour. There is a good choice of food at the Pier One Restaurant and the Wharf Tavern.
✉ Worlds End. Take the R600 from Cork city to Kinsale; the hotel is just beyond the pier ☎ 021 477 9300 🕐 Closed Dec. 25–26 AX, MC, VI

🏨 The White House $$

This Georgian property is now a contemporary, stylish hotel with an international restaurant and a lively bar where you can also dine on seafood chowder and steaks.
✉ Pearse Street ☎ 021 477 2125 AX, MC, VI

LIMERICK, CO. LIMERICK
🍴 Brasserie One $$–$$$

Located inside the immaculately restored Georgian hotel No. 1 Pery Square, this restaurant serves simple, classic and rustic food. Make the most of specialty tasting menu nights with wine pairings.
✉ No. 1 Pery Square Hotel and Spa ☎ 061 402402 🕐 Dinner only; closed Mon. AX, MC, VI

LISDOONVARNA, CO. CLARE
🏨 Sheedy's Country House Hotel $$–$$$

Well-run family hotel with an award-winning restaurant, renowned

for its excellent breakfast. Set in gardens close to The Burren region. Eight rooms and three junior suites.
✉ Town center, close to the sulfur wells ☎ 065 707 4026 🕐 Closed Oct.–Apr. MC, VI

LISMORE, CO. WATERFORD
🏨 Ballyrafter House $–$$

A welcoming country house with a bar and conservatory, where locals gather alongside guests. Bedrooms are pleasantly furnished in pine with in-room facilities. There is salmon fishing on the Blackwater river, and horseback riding is available locally.
✉ 0.5 miles from Lismore ☎ 058 54002 🕐 Closed Dec.–Mar. AX, DC, MC, VI

MALLOW, CO. CORK
🏨 Longueville House $$–$$$

Set in a wooded estate, this elegant 18th-century Georgian mansion has bedrooms overlooking the river valley and the courtyard maze. The restaurant has a long-standing reputation for excellence. Specialties might include pan-fried escalope of cod with citrus and tomato confit and crème brulée with garden red currants. Dinner reservations recommended.
✉ 3 miles west of Mallow on N72 to Killarney ☎ 022 47156 🕐 Closed Jan. 6 to mid-Mar. AX, MC, VI

MIDLETON, CO. CORK
🏨 Barnabrow Country House $$

This is a 17th-century family-run country house set on 35 acres of parkland adjacent to the village of Cloyne. A blend of old-world charm with an exceptional restaurant.
✉ Cloyne, Midleton. Take N25 from Cork to Midleton, then turning for Cloyne village ☎ 021 465 2534 🕐 Closed Dec. 23–27 DC, MC, VI

🏨 Midleton Park Hotel & Spa $$

This hotel has fine, spacious suites, while the comfortable restaurant offers good food and attentive service. Wide range of treatments in the health club.
✉ From Cork, turn off N25, on the right. From Waterford, turn off N25, over bridge until the intersection, turn right, hotel on right ☎ 021 463 5100 🕐 Closed Dec. 25–26 AX, DC, MC, VI

ROSCREA, CO. TIPPERARY
🏨 Damer Court Hotel $

An attractive Georgian townhouse hotel opposite the 13th-century castle and Heritage Centre. Rooms are pleasantly furnished in warm

KEY TO SYMBOLS

🏨	hotel
🍴	restaurant
✉	address
☎	telephone number
🕐	days/times closed
Ⓜ	nearest metro/tube/subway station(s)
AX	American Express
DC	Diners Club
MC	MasterCard
VI	VISA

Hotels

Price guide: double room with breakfast for two people

$	less than €110/£70
$$	€110–€180/£70–£110
$$$	more than €180/£110

Restaurants

Price guide: dinner per person, excluding drinks

$	less than €25/£15
$$	€25–€50/£15–£30
$$$	more than €50/£30

Themed Foods

Throughout Northern Ireland, look for the green and white "Taste of Ulster" sign, which guarantees the best of fresh local ingredients. Special events at the Ulster American Folk Park (page 196) near Omagh often offer the chance to taste various traditional delicacies, either of the Old Country or the New World. At the Frontier Festival Weekends in summer, guests can enjoy pioneer cooking, while at the end of October, Halloween fare accompanies fun and dramatic antics around the park.

---

colors and the relaxing oak-paneled lobby lounge has deep leather sofas and armchairs. Restaurant and bar. ✉ Castle Street. Off N7 Dublin–Limerick Road. Turn off for town center and follow signs to hotel ☎ 0505 23300 🕐 Closed Dec. 25 AX, MC, VI

ROSSCARBERY, CO. CORK
🏨 Celtic Ross $$

This striking landmark on the west Cork coastline overlooks a lagoon on the edge of a peaceful village. Light and spacious public areas have richly textured fabrics and highly polished Irish elm, yew, bog oakwood and cherrywood. Facilities include the new Druids Restaurant, Kingfisher Bar, a swimming pool and a leisure center for therapies and beauty treatments. ✉ On the N71 Bandon–Clonakilty road. Follow signs for Skibbereen ☎ 023 884 8722 🕐 Closed mid-Jan. to mid-Feb. MC, VI

TRALEE, CO. KERRY
🏨 The Brandon $–$$

This modern hotel is a golfer's paradise, within 30 minutes' drive of six superb courses. Other facilities include an indoor heated pool and state-of-the art gym and spa. ✉ Prince's Street ☎ 066 712 3333 🕐 Closed mid-Dec.–28 Dec. AX, MC, VI

WATERFORD, CO. WATERFORD
🏨 Dooley's $–$$

A comfortable family-run hotel, near the quayside. The bedrooms and public areas are stylish, and guests are very well cared for in a warm and friendly atmosphere with Irish music a regular feature. Try the New Ship Restaurant. ✉ 30 The Quay ☎ 051 873 531 🕐 Closed Dec. 24–28 AX, MC, VI

🍴 Fitzpatrick's Manor Lodge Restaurant $–$$

Housed in a charming old coach house, this highly recommended restaurant specializes in seafood. There is also Irish beef and a good range of vegetarian dishes. Early-bird menu available nightly 5–9:30 p.m. (Sat. to 7 p.m.). ✉ Manor Court, Cork Road ☎ 051 378 851 🕐 Closed Mon. MC, VI

🏨 Granville $–$$

This charming quayside hotel has comfortable bedrooms and the public areas and restaurant are furnished to a luxurious standard.

✉ The Quay. Take the N25 to the waterfront city center, opposite the clock tower ☎ 051 305 555 🕐 Closed Dec. 24–26 AX, DC, MC, VI

🍴 La Bohème Restaurant $$–$$$

In the vaults of an historic Port of Waterford building, La Bohème offers classic French cuisine. Owner/chef Eric Thèze offers a menu of modern delicacies and heritage recipes. Chief among La Bohème's specialties is Dunmore East lobster. ✉ 2 George Street ☎ 051 875 645 🕐 Closed lunch. Table d'hôte Tue.–Fri. (early bird 5:30–7 p.m.); à la carte Tue.–Sat. MC, VI

🏨 Waterford Castle Hotel and Golf Club $$$

Set on a private island, accessible only by a chain-linked ferry, this 16th-century castle is now an elegantly restored, internationally acclaimed 19-bedroom hotel. It has an 18-hole championship golf course, clay-pigeon shooting, archery, croquet and tennis. ✉ The Island, Ballinakill ☎ 051 878 203 🕐 Closed Dec. 24–26 AX, MC, VI

ULSTER AND NORTHERN IRELAND

BALLYBOFEY, CO. DONEGAL
🏨 Kee's Hotel & Leisure Club $–$$

This former coaching inn is a comfortable hotel with 53 well-furnished bedrooms and good facilities. There is a bistro as well as a conservatory lounge and popular restaurant, plus indoor heated pool, sauna, gym and salon treatments. ✉ 1 mile northeast on N15, in Stranorlar village ☎ 074 91 31018 AX, MC, VI

BALLYCONNELL, CO. CAVAN
🏨 Slieve Russell Golf and Country Club $$$

An imposing hotel set on 300 acres with a championship golf course. Public areas include lounges, three restaurants and a fitness suite. Bedrooms are tastefully furnished. Facilities include the Clúin Spa and Wellness Centre. ✉ From Cavan, head for Enniskillen, at Butlersbridge turn left toward Belturbet. Through village toward Ballyconnell, hotel is on the left after 5 miles ☎ 049 952 6444 AX, MC, VI

BALLYGALLY, CO. ANTRIM
🏨 Ballygally Castle $–$$

Parts of this castle hotel on the stunning Antrim Coast road date to

1625, and the original features are enhanced with antique furniture. There's even talk of a house ghost! Restaurant on site.
✉ Coast Road ☎ 028 2858 1066 VI, AX, MC.

BANGOR, CO. DOWN
🍴 The Boathouse Restaurant $$
Run by two Dutch brothers, this restaurant has gone from strength to strength. Main dishes such as seared Clandeboyne Estate wild pigeon breast or rouleaux of brill and Parma ham are beautifully cooked and immaculately presented. There's a reasonably priced set menu.
✉ 1a Seacliff Road ☎ 028 9146 9523 MC, VI

🏨 Royal $$
This Victorian hotel overlooks the marina and offers modern bedrooms. Quays restaurant provides a formal dining experience. Two bars, the Library and the Windsor, plus the more traditional Crown Bar.
✉ Bangor seafront ☎ 028 9127 1866 🕐 Closed Dec. 25–26 MC, VI

BELFAST, CO. ANTRIM
🍴 Beatrice Kennedy $$–$$$
The dark-wood floors and furnishings of this townhouse restaurant give it both a classical and rustic feel. Set in the university district, it has a seasonal menu that features dishes such as pork belly and monkfish cheeks with champ, wild garlic and cauliflower gratin, and pan-roasted Fermanagh dry aged rib-eye with smoked bacon rosti.
✉ 44 University Road ☎ 028 9020 2290 🕐 Dinner only Mon.–Sat. AX, MC, VI

🏨 Culloden Estate & Spa $$$
An elegant baronial mansion converted to a modern hotel with great views. Day rooms include a bar and lounge areas. Facilities include indoor heated pool, tennis, Jacuzzi, steam room, gym, spa, beauty salon and aromatherapy. The restaurant serves very accomplished dishes.
✉ Bangor Road, on A2 ☎ 028 9042 1066 AX, DC, MC, VI

🍴 James Street South $$–$$
An elegant restaurant on the ground floor of a refurbished linen mill. Owner and head chef Niall McKenna uses only the best of local seasonal ingredients. A typical meal may include asparagus soup laced with

crème fraîche, roast turbot with razor clam and lobster bouillabaisse and white chocolate brûlée with mixed berry compote for dessert. There is an extensive wine list.
✉ 21 James Street South ☎ 028 9043 4310 🕐 Closed Sun. lunch and Dec. 24–26, Jan 1. AX, MC, VI

🏨 Merchant $$$
The Merchant is a stylish boutique hotel with just 26 luxurious bedrooms and suites. Located in Belfast's renovated Cathedral Quarter, you will find a good choice of restaurants in the vicinity, in addition to the first-class eateries within the hotel, such as the formal Great Room restaurant.
✉ 35–39 Waring Street ☎ 028 9023 4888 🕐 Closed Dec. 24–25 AX, MC, VI

🍴 Molly's Yard $$
Tucked down an alley, Molly's Yard creates modern Irish dishes and has a seasonal menu. Starters can include slow-roasted *porchetta* or terrine of Irish game, with main dishes of seabass and vegetarian options such as roast butternut squash or sage and chestnut cannelloni.
✉ 1 College Green Mews, Botanic Avenue ☎ 028 9032 2600. 🕐 Closed Sun. MC, VI

🍴 Mourne Seafood Bar $$
Fish lovers flock to this small restaurant next to one of the city's oldest taverns. Come early for lunch or join the long line of people waiting to eat fresh seafood and fish cooked with modern style. Accompany your meal with a fresh glass of white wine or specially brewed Mourne stout.
✉ 34–36 Bank Street ☎ 028 9024 8544 🕐 Lunch only Sun.–Mon. MC, VI, AX

🍴 The Square Cafe & Restaurant $$–$$$
This restaurant wants everything just right, from pressed linen cloths and polished glassware to perfectly presented portions of food. Try dishes like smoked haddock and leek in puff pastry, three-pepper crusted sirloin with brandy butter, and white chocolate and raspberry cheesecake.
✉ 89 Dublin Road ☎ 028 9023 9933 🕐 Closed Sun. AX, MC, VI

🏨 Tara Lodge $
A long-standing Belfast favorite, this bed-and-breakfast offers simple, yet

stylish, rooms in a central location and at budget prices.
✉ 36 Cromwell Road ☎ 028 9059 0900 MC, VI

CAVAN, CO. CAVAN
🏨 Kilmore $$
This refurbished hotel set on a hillside on the edge of Cavan has a good restaurant. Golfing, fishing, boating and horseback riding are available nearby.
✉ Dublin Road. About 2 miles from Cavan on N3 ☎ 049 433 2288 AX, MC, VI

DERRY, CO. LONDONDERRY
🍴 The Gaslight Grill $$–$$$
This light and airy restaurant, with its relaxed atmosphere and quality cuisine, is one of Derry's finest. The wide-ranging menu includes starters such as Asian-seasoned tian of crab with chilli salsa, main dishes like char-roast breast of duck with rosti potato, and warm chocolate ganache for dessert.
✉ 31–33 Foyle Street ☎ 028 7126 0708 🕐 Dinner only Mon.–Sat. AX, MC, VI

🏨 Tower Hotel Derry $–$$
Set within the city walls. Stylish rooms fully equipped, and those on the upper floors enjoy superb views. The Mediterranean-style restaurant offers a contemporary menu.
✉ Butcher Street, off the Diamond ☎ 028 7137 1000 🕐 Closed Dec. 24–27 AX, MC, VI

DONEGAL, CO. DONEGAL
🏨 Harvey's Point Country Hotel $$$
Superbly located on Lough Eske offering spacious public rooms and a warm Irish welcome. Excellent cuisine and a range of facilities including tennis and fishing.
✉ Lough Eske. From Donegal take the N56 then first right marked Loch Eske and Harvey's Point. The hotel is about 10 minutes' drive ☎ 073 972 2208 🕐 Closed Mon.–Tue., Nov.–Feb. MC, VI

DUNFANAGHY, CO. DONEGAL
🏨 Arnold's $$$
Overlooking Sheephaven Bay, this hotel has sandy beaches on its doorstep. Public areas offer comfortable seating with a good restaurant (open weekends only during the winter), bars and live music in the summer. Tennis, fishing and horseback riding are available.

KEY TO SYMBOLS

🏨	hotel
🍴	restaurant
✉	address
☎	telephone number
🕐	days/times closed
Ⓜ	nearest metro/tube/subway station(s)
AX	American Express
DC	Diners Club
MC	MasterCard
VI	VISA

Hotels

Price guide: double room with breakfast for two people

$	less than €110/£70
$$	€110–€180/£70–£110
$$$	more than €180/£110

Restaurants

Price guide: dinner per person, excluding drinks

$	less than €25/£15
$$	€25–€50/£15–£30
$$$	more than €50/£30

Afternoon Tea

In properties owned by the National Trust conservation organization, the on-site tearooms are well known for the quality of their cakes and cookies, and those in Northern Ireland have the added benefit of the Ulster tradition of home baking. Recipes include a sumptuous variety of breads, potato cakes, soda breads, *barm brack* (a fruity tea cake) and cookies. To finish off a visit to one of the magnificent stately homes with afternoon tea is a treat not to be missed.

✉ On N56 from Letterkenny. Hotel is on left entering the village ☎ 074 91 36208 🕐 Closed Nov.–Apr. AX, MC, VI

ENNISKILLEN, CO. FERMANAGH

🏨 **Killyhevlin $$–$$$**

This hotel commands superb views over Lough Erne from the public rooms. Attractive rooms and a modern health club and spa.

✉ Dublin Road. 2 miles south, off the A4 ☎ 0286 632 3481 🕐 Closed Dec. 24–25 AX, MC, VI

GLASLOUGH, CO. MONAGHAN

🏨 **Castle Leslie $$–$$$**

This castle hotel is nestled on vast grounds with its own riding school, spa and fine-dining restaurant. Rooms in the castle itself each have a story to tell, having once been the bedrooms of the Leslie family. Guests can also opt to stay in the Hunting Lodge or one of the self-catering houses in the village.

✉ Glaslough ☎ 047 88100 🕐 May close over Christmas AX, MC, VI

LETTERKENNY, CO. DONEGAL

🍴 **The Lemon Tree Restaurant $$**

In the center of the town, the exterior is bedecked with flowers and terra-cotta tiles. Serves modern European food, locally grown and prepared in an open kitchen.

✉ 39 Lower Main Street ☎ 074 91 25788 🕐 Closed lunch, Christmas AX, MC, VI

LIMAVADY, CO. LONDONDERRY

🏨 **Radisson Blue Roe Valley Resort $$$**

In a stunning spot, this country-house offers superb sporting and leisure facilities and two restaurants and a bar.

✉ On the A2 Londonderry–Limavady road, 1 mile from Limavady ☎ 028 7772 2222 AX, DC, MC, VI

MAGHERAFELT, CO. LONDONDERRY

🏨 **Laurel Villa $–$$**

This award-winning guest house is a Victorian villa with pristine period decor and uniquely decorated rooms based on a literary theme; each contains poems and quotes from the writers for which they're named.

✉ 60 Church Street ☎ 028 7930 1459 🕐 Closed first week Jan. AX, MC, VI

NEWCASTLE, CO. DOWN

🏨 **Slieve Donard Resort and Spa $$–$$$**

The hotel, with a restaurant, bars and a spa, has views over Dundrum Bay and the Mountains of Mourne, as well as access to the beaches of Newcastle and the championship Royal County Down golf course.

✉ Downs Road ☎ 028 4372 1066 AX, MC, VI

OMAGH, CO. TYRONE

🏨 **Mellon Country Inn $$**

A hotel with stylish, modern bedrooms, international restaurant and the Heaven on Earth spa in the foothills of the Sperrin Mountains.

✉ Castletown, Omagh. On A5, 6 miles from Omagh, 1 mile from Ulster American Folk Park ☎ 028 816 61224 AX, MC, VI

STRANGFORD, CO. DOWN

🏨 **The Cuan Hotel $–$$**

This award-winning pub-restaurant has accommodation. Guest rooms are simple and contemporary and the restaurant serves mouth-watering dishes such as seafood chowder, local Finnebrogue venison casserole and Northern Irish lamb shank.

✉ Strangford Village ☎ 028 4488 1222 🕐 Closed Dec. 25 AX, MC, VI

PORTBALLINTRAE, CO. ANTRIM

🏨 **Bayview $–$$**

Close to the Giant's Causeway in the heart of a picturesque village, this small hotel of 25 rooms is an ideal destination for a leisurely break.

✉ 2 Bayhead Road ☎ 028 2073 4100 🕐 Closed Dec. 25 MC, VI

PORTRUSH, CO. ANTRIM

🏨 **Ramada Portrush $$**

In the center of Portrush, the hotel overlooks the sea. An ideal location for outdoor pursuits and sightseeing.

✉ 73 Main Street ☎ 028 7082 6100; 🕐 Closed Dec. 25 AX, DC, MC, VI

ROSSNOWLAGH, CO. DONEGAL

🏨 **Sandhouse $$–$$$**

A hotel with good cuisine and marine spa. Rooms have ocean views, and a conservatory lounge is a cozy retreat.

✉ Donegal Bay. On coast road, 5 miles north of Ballyshannon ☎ 071 985 1777 🕐 Closed Dec.–Jan. AX, MC, VI

Essential Information

Information
214

Driving
218

Language
220

U.S. CITIZENS

The information in this guide has been compiled for U.S. citizens traveling as tourists.

Travelers who are not U.S. citizens, or who are traveling on business, should check with their embassies and tourist offices for information on the countries they wish to visit.

Entry requirements are subject to change at short notice, and travelers are advised to check the current situation before they travel.

National flag of the Republic of Ireland

Before you Go

Passports

The most important document you'll need before you travel is a passport. Passport application forms can be obtained from any federal or state court or post office authorized to accept passport applications. U.S. passport agencies have offices in all major cities; check the *Yellow Pages* (U.S. Government, State Department) for the one nearest you. You can also request an application form by calling the National Passport Information Center at (887) 487 2778. (Note: There is a credit card charge.) Comprehensive passport information and application forms are available on the U.S. State Government internet site at www.travel. state.gov.

Apply for your passport early, as processing can take several months from the time of application until arrival. Rush service is available for an extra charge. Before departure, make sure your passport is valid for at least another six months after you are due to travel: some European countries require this.

There are no border formalities between Northern Ireland and the Republic if you are crossing by car, although it is always advisable to take your passport with you.

Travel visas are not necessary for American citizens traveling to either the Irish Republic or Northern Ireland (which is part of the United Kingdom), but if you'll be traveling on to other nations, check their entry requirements before you leave home.

Travel Insurance

Before departing make sure you are covered by insurance that will reimburse travel expenses if you need to cancel or cut short your trip due to unforeseen circumstances. You'll need coverage for property loss or theft, emergency health and dental treatment. Before taking out additional insurance, check to see if your current homeowner's insurance or medical coverage already covers you for travel abroad. If you make a claim, your insurance company will need proof of the incident or expenditure. Keep copies of any police report or medical bills or statements to submit with your insurance claim.

Essential for Travelers

Required ● Recommended ◉ Not required ◉

Passport	●
Visa	◉
Travel, medical insurance	◉
Round-trip or onward airline ticket	◉
Local currency	◉
Traveler's checks	◉
Credit cards	◉
First-aid kit and medicines	◉
Health inoculations	◉

Essential for Drivers

Required ● Recommended ◉ Not required ◉

Driver's license	●
International Driving Permit	◉
Car insurance (for non-rental cars)	◉
Car registration (for non-rental cars)	◉

*See also Driving section, page 218

When to Go

The weather in Ireland is impossible to predict. You can experience all four seasons in one day, but you can be certain that no conditions will last for long, and showers pass quickly. The warmest months are July and August, while rainfall in May, June and September is often lower. May and June are good months to visit, as schools are still in session and there are fewer crowds at major attractions. Temperatures rarely fall below freezing in the winter and you can pick up bargain accommodations deals during the low season, but some sights may be closed.

Important Addresses

Tourism Ireland (Republic and Northern Ireland)
345 Park Avenue
New York, NY 10154
☎ (212) 418-080

Republic of Ireland Tourist Board (Fáilte Ireland)
Baggot Street Bridge
Dublin 2, Republic of Ireland
☎ 01 890 525 525

American Consulate (NI)
Danesfort House, 223 Stranmills Road
Belfast BT9 5GR, Northern Ireland
☎ 028 9038 6100

American Embassy (Republic of Ireland)
42 Elgin Road, Ballsbridge
Dublin 4, Republic of Ireland
☎ 01 668 8777; http://belfast.usconsulate.gov
American Citizens Services: 8:30–11:30 a.m.;
closed Sat.–Sun. and Wed.

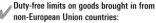

Dublin	New York	Chicago	Denver	Los Angeles	Time zones
12:00 noon	− 5 hrs	− 6 hrs	− 7 hrs	− 8 hrs	

215

Essential Information

Customs

✓ **Duty-free limits on goods brought in from non-European Union countries:**
200 cigarettes or 100 cigarillos or 50 cigars or 250 g. tobacco; 4 L. still wine; 1 L. alcohol over 22% volume or 2 L. alcohol under 22% volume; 60 ml. perfume; 250 ml. toilet water; plus any duty-free goods (including gifts) to the value of €430 per adult and €215 per child under 15 years into Northern Ireland. No limit on the importation of tax-paid goods purchased within the European Union if they are for your own personal use. There are no currency regulations. You can purchase $800 worth of personal goods before returning to the U.S. before a tax is levied; keep sales slips.

✗ **No** unlicensed drugs, weapons, ammunition, obscene material, pets or other animals, counterfeit money or copied goods, meat or poultry.

Money

The Republic of Ireland's currency is the euro (€), which is divided into 100 cents (c). Denominations of euro bills are 5, 10, 20, 50, 100, 200 and 500. There are coins of 1, 2, 5, 10, 20 and 50c and €1 and €2.

In Northern Ireland the currency is the pound sterling (UK£). It must be used in the following counties: Antrim, Armagh, Derry, Down, Fermanagh and Tyrone. The pound sterling is divided into 100 pence (p). The denominations of pound bills are 5, 10, 20 and 50. There are coins of 1, 2, 5, 10, 20 and 50p and £1 and £2. The pound sterling and the euro are not interchangeable.

Credit cards are accepted in hotels, large stores and upscale restaurants; check first in small or rural establishments. Exchange dollars or traveler's checks at a bank, exchange office, post office or large hotel.

Tips and Gratuities

Restaurants (service is almost always included)	12–15%
Cafés/bars	10%
Taxis	10%
Porters	€1/50p per bag
Hairdressers	10%
Tour guides	€2/£1
Cloakroom attendants	€1/50p

Communications

Post Offices

 Buy stamps at post offices, some newsstands and tobacconists, large grocery stores and hotels. Hours for out-of-town post offices may vary. Mailboxes and vans are green in the Republic of Ireland and red in Northern Ireland.

Mail service in the Republic is notoriously slow and expensive. Postcards are cheaper to send than letters.

Telephones

 Older-style public call boxes are blue and cream and marked in Gaelic "Telefón", and red in Northern Ireland, although they are being replaced by glass and metal booths. They take cash (10c/10p, 20c/20p, 50c/50p or €1/£1 coins) or prepaid phone cards bought from newsstands, post offices and local stores.

Calling within Ireland
All Irish phone numbers in this book include the area code; dial the number listed.

Calling Ireland from abroad
The country code for Ireland is 353; for Northern Ireland 44. Note that Irish numbers in this book do not include the country code; you will need to prefix this if you are calling from another country. To call Ireland from the U.S. or Canada, omit the first zero from the Irish number and add the prefix 011 353; for Northern Ireland 011 44. (The number of digits in Irish area codes varies.)
ROI example: 01 122 3344 becomes 011 353 1 122 3344.
NI example: 028 1222 3344 becomes 011 44 28 1222 3344.

Calling from Ireland
To call the United States or Canada from Ireland, prefix the area code and number with 001. Example: (111) 222-3333 becomes 001 111 222-3333.

Emergency Numbers

Police	999 or 112
Fire service	999 or 112
Ambulance	999 or 112

Emergency calls are free from call boxes.

Essential information

Hours of Operation

- Stores Mon.–Sat.
- Offices Mon.–Fri.
- Banks Mon.–Fri.
- Post offices Mon.–Fri.
- Museums/Monuments
- Pharmacies

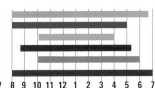

7 8 9 10 11 12 1 2 3 4 5 6 7

In addition to the times shown above, some stores stay open until 8 or 9 for late-night shopping on Thursday or Friday.

In smaller towns and rural areas some stores close in the afternoon on one day of the week.

Some banks in small towns close 12:30–1:30. Nearly all banks are closed on Saturday, and post offices close at 1 p.m. on Saturday.

Hours for museums and tourist sights vary and are subject to change; always check with the local tourist office. Many places close from October to March or have very limited opening times, although most major sights are open all year.

Pharmacies may close earlier on Saturday.

National Holidays

Banks, businesses and most stores close on the following days. Museums also may have restricted hours.

Jan. 1	New Year's Day
Mar. 17	St. Patrick's Day
Mar./Apr.	Good Friday
Mar./Apr.	Easter Monday
1st Mon. of May	May Day Holiday
Last Mon. of May	Spring Holiday (NI)
1st Mon. of Jun.	June Holiday (ROI)
Jul. 12	Battle of the Boyne (NI)
1st Mon. of Aug.	August Holiday (ROI)
Last Mon. of Aug.	Late Summer Holiday (NI)
Last Mon. of Oct.	October Holiday (ROI)
Dec. 25	Christmas Day
Dec. 26	St. Stephen's Day

Restrooms

Identify restrooms in Gaelic-speaking areas by *Fir* (men) and *Mná* (women). A small charge is levied in restrooms at some railroad stations, but most other facilities are free. The standards of hygiene are moderate. You will be welcomed into any local pub if you need to use their facilities, but stop for a drink and a talk while you are there.

Health Advice

Medical Services

Private medical insurance is recommended. U.S. and Canadian visitors can receive treatment in emergency rooms, but are charged if admitted to a hospital bed. A general practitioner also will charge for services. For information on hospitals in Northern Ireland visit www.n-i.nhs.uk.

Dental Services

Dentists charge for treatment. Dental work is expensive, so check to see if it is covered by your medical insurance. Dentists are listed in the *Yellow Pages*, or ask at your embassy, hotel or at a tourist office. Alternatively, a list of dental practitioners can be obtained from the Irish Dental Association (01 295 0072; www.dentist.ie).

Sun Advice

The sunniest months are May and June, with 5–6.5 hours of sun a day (the extreme southwest is the sunniest). July and August are the warmest. During these months you should take sensible precautions against the sun.

Drugs

Pharmacies (also called chemists) sell a range of prescription and non-prescription medicines. If you need medicine outside regular hours, information about the nearest 24-hour facility should be posted on the door of all pharmacies.

Safe Water

Tap water is safe to drink throughout Ireland. If, however, you prefer mineral water you will find it widely available.

Personal Safety

Irish towns and cities are generally relaxed, safe places to be, and are regularly patrolled by police, especially in Northern Ireland. However, it is always best to use common-sense precautions when traveling.

- Keep valuables hidden when you're on the move; a money belt or neck purse is the best option.
- Never leave bags unattended.
- Don't leave valuables on display in vehicles.
- Don't leave vehicles unlocked.
- Avoid walking alone in dimly lit areas at night.
- If you have belongings stolen, report the incident immediately to the police and get a written report to provide to your insurance company as evidence for your claim.
- Security forces on both sides of the border are courteous to bona fide travelers.

National Transportation

Air

Most European flights arrive in Dublin or Belfast; international flights land also in Shannon and Cork. Internal flights and those to the UK are very competitive. Fly with Aer Lingus (www.aerlingus.ie) or Ryanair (www.ryanair.com). Air Arann operates flights from Shannon and Waterford to English destinations. Air Arann Islands (www.airarannislands.ie) operates flights between Connemara Airport and the Aran Islands.

Train

Ireland's rail company is Iarnród Éireann (IÉ). Trains are the fastest way of covering long distances and are generally reliable and comfortable, but the network is limited and one-way tickets cost almost as much as round-trip tickets. Midweek is less expensive than weekends, and there are many special offers on fares. The Dublin to Belfast Express takes 2 hours, and there are eight to nine trains daily (less on Sunday). Round-trip tickets are available; for more information ☎ 01 836 6222; www.irishrail.ie. The Freedom of Northern Ireland pass (seven days of unlimited travel) is available from main Northern Ireland railroad stations (☎ 028 9066 6630; www.translink.co.uk).

Bus

In the Republic, Bus Éireann operates a network of express bus routes serving most of the country, including a service to Belfast (some services run summer only); ☎ 01 836 6111; www.buseireann.ie. In Dublin an exact fare policy is in operation, so have plenty of change with you. The number 41 bus from Eden Quay runs to Dublin Airport. Barratt Tours (☎ 061 384700) in Limerick operates day tours in the summer and on Wednesdays they run a tour combining a trip to Galway City with a cruise on Lough Corrib. In Northern Ireland, Ulsterbus Tours (☎ 028 9033 7004; www.translink.co.uk) has links between Belfast and about 23 towns, and also run ferry and coach tours to England, Scotland and Wales; unlimited travel tickets are available.

Ferry

There are several ferries a day from Belfast and Dublin to ports in the British mainland; taxis, trains and coaches operate a regular service from the ports to the cities. Ferries to Dublin operate from Holyhead on the UK mainland (www.irishferries.com) and to |Belfast from Stanraer in Scotland (www.stenaline.co.uk). Combined train and ferry or bus and ferry tickets can be an inexpensive option from London to Dublin; try National Express (www.nationalexpress.com). A car ferry runs between Ballyhack, Co. Wexford and Passage East,

Co. Waterford (☎ 051 382 480). Another serves Killimer, Co. Clare and Tarbert, Co. Kerry, saving 60 miles over the road trip (☎ 065 90 53124). There are also ferries to several islands; ask for details at a local tourist office.

Ringaskiddy's Ferryport, 10 miles southeast of Cork city, provides passenger and car ferry service to Brittany (Brittany Ferries ☎ 021 427 7801).

Electricity

Ireland has a 230-volt power supply (NI 240 volt). Electrical sockets either take plugs with two round pins or three square pins; American appliances will need a plug adapter and will require a transformer if they do not have a dual-voltage facility.

Photography

The light is frequently poor, so if you are using a film camera you may need fast film. Bring a tripod for landscape work. Film and camera batteries are readily available in Ireland, and you should be able to find good developing and printing facilities in most large towns.

All digital camera requirements and printing facilities are readily available in larger towns.

If landscapes are your interest, there is a large variety to choose from. You'll find a plethora of castles as subject matter, but remember, if the weather is too poor for long shots, zoom in close and study detail. It is generally illegal to take film or photos of the police and military barracks in Northern Ireland.

Media

The main newspapers in the Republic are the *Irish Times* and the *Irish Independent*; both provide great insights into Irish life and politics. The *Irish Examiner* is a respected newspaper, commenting on world affairs. Sunday papers include the *Sunday Independent* and *Sunday Business Post*. British papers are available the same day in major cities and in Northern Ireland. The local *Belfast Telegraph* is a popular evening paper. In the mornings, you can choose between the nationalist *Irish News* or the loyalist *News Letter*.

Republic of Ireland television broadcasting is operated by a state-sponsored body called RTE (Radio Telefís Éireann). It has four radio and two main television channels plus news and sports channels. You can receive them all over Ireland and Northern Ireland. In much of the Republic, you can pick up BBC (radio and television) and Ulster television.

Driving Regulations

Drive on the Left

 Drive on the left-hand side of the road on both sides of the border and, at traffic circles, yield to traffic approaching from your right.

Seat Belts

Must be worn in front seats at all times and in the rear seats where fitted.

Minimum Age

The minimum age for driving a car is 17. However, rental car firms will often stipulate a minimum age of 25.

Blood Alcohol

The legal blood alcohol limit in the Republic of Ireland is 0.05% for experienced drivers, and 0.02 for all other drivers. In the UK (NI) it is 0.08%. Random breath tests on drivers are carried out frequently, especially late at night, and the penalties are severe.

Tolls

The Westlink and Eastlink bridges around Dublin require tolls of about €2–€3, except the Dublin Port tunnel which ranges from €3–€10, depending on the time of day. Tolls are charged on the M1 (Drogheda bypass), M50 (barrier-free Dublin circular), East Link Toll Bridge (Dublin docklands), Dublin Port Tunnel, M4 (Kilcock–Enfield–Kinnegad motorway), N6 (Galway–Ballinasloe), M7/M8 (Portlaoise–Castletown), N8 (Rathcormac–Fermoy bypass), N25 (Waterford City bypass), M3 (Klonee–Kells) and the Limerick Tunnel.

Additional Information

An International Driving Permit (IDP) is recommended; some rental firms require it, and it can speed up formalities if you are involved in an accident.

A Green Card (international motor insurance certificate) is recommended if you are driving a non-rental car.

Irish Republic roads vary tremendously and the road classification gives no reliable indication of the width or surface quality – some primary roads are little better than country lanes. In Northern Ireland the major roads are fast and well-maintained and seldom congested.

Speed Limits

Regulations

Traffic police can impose on-the-spot fines.

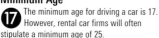 **Limited-access highways** (motorways; blue) 120 k.p.h. (74 m.p.h.)

National roads (green) 100 k.p.h.(62 m.p.h.) Regional (white) 80 k.p.h. (50 m.p.h.) Northern Ireland 60 m.p.h. (96 k.p.h.)
Urban areas 50 k.p.h (31 m.p.h.)

Car Rental

Car Rental

The leading rental companies have offices at airports, railroad stations and large ferry terminals. Hertz offers discounts to AAA members. If you are taking a rented car across the border from Northern Ireland into the Republic of Ireland, check with your rental company to see that you have the appropriate insurance.

Car rental is less expensive in Northern Ireland than in the Republic. A local car rental firm is likely to offer cheaper rates than an international company, but it may not allow different pick-up and drop-off points. Often, the cheapest way to book a car rental is to arrange a package deal in advance with a tour operator (fly and drive or rail and ferry-drive) rather than waiting until you arrive in Ireland. Early booking is advisable if you are traveling during the high season.

The minimum age for renting a car ranges from 18 to 25 depending on the model of the car. Some companies have a maximum age limit of 70. For reservations:

	United States	Ireland
Alamo	(800) 906 5555	0871 384 1086
Avis	(800) 368 3001	021 428 1111
Budget	(800) 527-0700	090 662 7711
Hertz	(800) 826 8782	01 676 7476

Fuel

Fuel

Gas is unleaded and sold in liters; diesel also is easily purchased. Gas stations in villages stay open until 8 or 9 p.m. and usually open after Mass on Sunday. Along main highways on both sides of the border there are 24-hour gas stations.

Parking

In some urban areas, parking is limited to certain times and periods. Where this is indicated you must buy a disk from a newsstand or garage and display it on the dashboard of your car. Multi-story and pay-and-display parking can also be used in cities.

Parking lots in central Dublin are expensive; street parking is in high demand and is recommended. The main attractions in Belfast are close together so there is no need to drive from one to another. Just park once and then you can easily walk or take the sightseeing bus. Central parking lots include Smithfield and King Street.

AAA

 AAA Affiliated Motoring Club
AA Ireland 56 Drury Street,
Dublin 2 ☎ 01 617 9999
  If you break down while driving in the Republic
of Ireland ☎ 1800 66 77 88
  For breakdowns in Northern Ireland
☎ 08457 887766
  Not all automobile clubs offer full services to
AAA members.

Breakdowns/Accidents

There are 24-hour emergency phones at
regular intervals on highways: ☎ 999 or
112. Most car rental firms provide their own free
rescue service; if your car is rented, follow the
instructions given in the documentation. Use of a
car repair service other than those authorized by
your rental company may violate your agreement.
  In the event of a breakdown, the vehicle should
be moved off the highway whenever possible.
Hazard warning lights should be used and, if
available, a red warning triangle should be placed
on the road at least 165 feet before the obstruction
and on the same side of the road.

Road Signs

Driving in Ireland is still, generally speaking,
a pleasure. Out of the big towns the roads are
uncrowded and most drivers courteous. The farther
west you go, the more patience you need: Roads are
narrower, steeper and more winding.

Road signs in the Republic of Ireland give road
distances in kilometers, no longer miles.
These signs are green and white. In Northern
Ireland, the distance signs are always in miles.

Keep left

Vehicles may pass on
either side to reach same
destination

Ahead only

One-way
traffic

No entry
for vehicular
traffic

Yield to
traffic on
major road

Intersection

Double curve,
first to the left

Two-way
traffic
straight ahead

Irish and American English

Although on the surface they are the same language, there are some quirky differences between American and Irish English. The Irish have become familiar with Americanisms through imported American television shows and movies, and on the whole will understand American visitors. However, note the possible misunderstanding if an Irish person directs you to the "first floor" of a building – the American equivalent is actually the second floor. Irish words and phrases are in the left column below; American words appear in the right column.

Hotels

bath	*bathtub*
book	*reserve*
caretaker/ porter	*janitor*
cot	*crib*
duvet	*quilt*
foyer	*lobby*
ground/ first floor	*first/second floor*
lavatory/ loo/toilet	*restroom*
lift	*elevator*

Eating Out

aubergine	*eggplant*
bacon butty	*bacon sandwich*
bacon rasher	*slice of bacon*
bap	*hamburger bun*
bill	*check*
biscuit	*cookie*
chips	*french fries*
courgette	*zucchini*
crisps	*potato chips*
jacket potato	*potato in its skin*
kipper	*smoked herring*
lager	*light beer*
porridge	*oatmeal*
pudding	*dessert*
runner beans	*string beans*
sweets	*candy*
jam	*jelly*
jelly	*Jell-O*

Communications

call box	*telephone booth*
post box	*mail box*
post code	*zip code*
put through	*connect*
reverse charge	*call collect*
ring up	*call*

Money

bank note	*bill*
cashpoint	*ATM*
cheque	*check*
quid (colloquial)	*one pound (money)*
VAT	*value added tax*

Shopping

anorak	*parka*
bank holiday	*public holiday*
braces	*suspenders*
briefs	*jockey shorts*
carrier bag	*shopping bag*
chemist	*drugstore*
dinner jacket	*tuxedo*
ironmongers	*hardware store*
jumper	*sweater*
nappy	*diaper*
off licence	*liquor store*
pants	*briefs (underwear)*
public convenience	*restroom*
queue	*line of people*
tights	*pantyhose*
trousers	*pants/slacks*
sales assistant	*clerk*

Transportation

coach	*long-distance bus*
left luggage office	*baggage room*
lost property	*lost and found*
return ticket	*round-trip ticket*
single ticket	*one-way ticket*
timetable	*schedule*
underground	*subway*

Driving

boot	*trunk (of a car)*
bonnet	*hood (of a car)*
car park	*parking lot*
caravan	*house trailer*
dual carriageway	*divided highway*
estate car	*station wagon*
filling station	*gas station*
flyover	*overpass*
gear lever	*gear shift*
layby	*pull-off*
lorry	*truck*
manual	*stick shift*
motorway	*highway*
pavement	*sidewalk*
petrol	*gas*
roundabout	*traffic circle*
zebra crossing	*pedestrian crossing*

Gaelic Place-name Spellings

Gaelic is the first language in an area of the west of Ireland, known as the *Gaeltacht*. Many English place-names have been changed to the Gaelic spelling, and this process is ongoing. Below is a list of place-names that have already been changed.

English	Gaelic
Achill Sound	*Gob an Choire*
Aran Islands	*Oileáin Árann*
Arranmore	*Árainn Mhór*
Ballydavid	*Head Ceann Baile Dháith*
Ballyferriter	*Baile an Fheirtéaraigh*
Ballyskelligs Bay	*Bá na Scealg*
Barnatra	*Barr na Trá*
Belderg	*Béal Deirg*
Belmullet	*Béalan Mhuirthead*
Binghamstown	*An Geata Mór*
Blasket Islands	*Na Blascaodai*
Brandon Head	*Pointe an Choma Dhóite*
Bunbeg	*An Bun Beag*
Burtonport	*Ailt an Chorráin*
Caherdaniel	*Cathair Dónall*
Carrick	*An Charraig*
Carrowmore	*An Cheathrú Mhór*
Clear Island	*Oileán Cléire*
Cloghane	*An Clochán*
Clonbur	*An Fhairche*
Cloonboo	*Cluáin Bú*
Deenish Island	*Dúinis*
Dingle	*An Daingean*
Dingle Bay	*Bá na Daingin*
Dingle Harbour	*Cuan an Daingin*
Dingle Peninsula	*Corca Dhuibhne*
Dungloe	*An Clochán Liath*
Dunlewy	*Dún Lúiche*
Dunquin	*Dún Chaoin*
Doogort	*Dumha Goirt*
Glencolmcille	*Gleann Cholm Cille*
Glendowan	*Gleann Domhain*
Gortahork	*Gort an Choirce*
Gorumna	*Garumna*
Great Blasket Island	*An Blascaod Mór*
Gweedore	*Gaoth Dobhair*
Inishglora Island	*Inish Gluaire*
Inishmaan	*Inis Meáin*
Inishmore	*Inis Mór*
Inisheer	*Inis Óirr*
Kilronan	*Cill Rónáin*
Kinvarra	*Cinn Mhara*
Lettermullan	*Leitir Mealláin*
Lettermore	*Leitir Moir*
Little Skellig	*An Sceilg Bheag*
Maam Cross	*An Teach Dóite*
Maum	*An Mám*
Moycullen	*Maigh Cuilinn*
St. Macdara's Island	*Oileán Mhic Dara*

Place-names

Scariff Island	*An Scairbh*
Skellig Michael	*An Sceilg Mhicil*
Slea Head	*Ceann Sléibhe*
Ventry	*Ceann Trá*

Gaelic Words and Phrases

The following is a list of words that you may come across during your visit.

Bord Fáilte (Irish Tourist Board)	*bord fallcha*
Céilí (traditional dance night)	*kaylee*
Gaeilge (the Irish language)	*gale-geh*
Gaeltacht (Irish-speaking country)	*gale-tackt*
Garda (police)	*gawrdah*
Fleadh (traditional music evening)	*flah*
Taoiseach (prime minister)	*teeschock*

Meeting people

fáilte (welcome)	*fallcha*
le do thoil (please)	*lay-do hull*
lá maith (good day)	*law moy*
dia hduit (hello)	*gee-ah ditch*
á (yes)	*thaw*
níl/ní hea (no)	*neel/nee*
oíche mhaith (good night)	*okee moy*
cé mhéid? (how much?)	*ka vade*
go raibh maith aguth (thank you)	*go-rah moy agut*
Conas taio? (how are you?)	*konus-taw-too*

Eating and Drinking

bialann (restaurant)	*bee-lun*
teach tábhairne (pub/bar)	*chock tavernya*
bricfeásta (breakfast)	*brick-fasta*
lón (lunch)	*loan*
dinnéar (dinner)	*din-air*
freastalaí (waiter)	*fras-taul-ee*
uisce (water)	*ishke*
ascailte (open)	*oscail-te*
dúnta (closed)	*doon-thaw*

Here are a few terms that may be used in descriptions of many archeological sites, monuments and ruins in Ireland.

Dolmens Standing stones (usually three) surmounted by a massive capstone.

Passage graves Great stone tombs with a large burial chamber, entered through a long passage.

Court cairns These are the earliest megalithic chambered tombs.

Crannogs Artificial islands built in lakes or marshy places.

Clocháns Known as "beehives," these remarkable stone buildings were erected without mortar as tiny oratories.

Index

A

Abbey of Duiske 101
Abbeyleix 102–103
accommodations 22
  see also hotels and restaurants
Achill Island 31, 55–56
Aillwee Cave 134, 135
air travel 217
Albert Memorial 160
American connections 176
American Embassy and Consulate 214
An Creagan Visitor Centre 196, 197
Andrew Jackson Centre 177
Antrim Coast Road 175
Antrim, County 152, 153, 174–175, 178–179
Aran Islands 29, 38–39
Ardmore 124, 126
Ards Peninsula 172
Armagh 172–173
Armagh, County 152, 153
Armagh Planetarium 173
Ashford Castle 43
Athlone 90
Athy 102
Atlantic Drive 55
Atlantic Highlands 191
Avoca 91
Avoca Handweavers 91
Avondale House and Forest Park 91

B

Ballina 56
Ballintubber Abbey 31, 57
Ballybunion 146
Ballycastle 174
Ballyferriter 131
Ballyliffin 190
Ballymagibbon Cairn 43
Ballymaloe Cookery School and Gardens 117
Ballymena 178
Banagher Glen and Forest 198
Bank of Ireland 70
banks 216
Bantry 126
Bantry House 126, 127
Beaghmore Stone Circle 198
Beara Peninsula 127
Beckett, Samuel 10, 88, 185
Behan, Brendan 88
Belcoo 188
Belfast 155–171
Belfast Castle 160–161
Belfast Zoo 161
Bellanaleck 188–189
Belleek Pottery 181
Belvoir Park Forest 161
Blarney Castle 117–118, 122
Blasket Islands 131–132
Blennerville Windmill and Steam Train 145, 146
Boa Island 187
Bonamargy Friary 174, 175

Book of Kells 85, 96
Botanic Gardens, Belfast 161
Boyle 40–41
Boyne, Battle of the 92, 93, 96
Boyne Valley 92, 94–96
Brian Ború 16, 61, 128, 172
Brownshill Dolmen 102
Brú Ború Heritage Centre 130
Brú Na Bóinne Visitor Centre 92, 93
Buncrana Castle 190
Bundoran 51
Bunratty Castle and Folk Park 142, 143, 144
The Burren 134
buses 217
Bushmills 178
Buttevant 123

C

Cahersiveen 138
Cahir 128–129
Cahir Castle 123, 128, 129
Cairns Hill Forest Park 52
car rental 218
Carlingford Lough 195
Carlow 101–102
Carlow, County 60, 62
Carndonagh 190
Carrick-a-Rede rope bridge 174, 175
Carrick-on-Suir 129
Carrickfergus 177
Carrowmore 49, 52
Cashel 103, 129–131
Cashel Folk Village 130
Castle Archdale Country Park 186, 189
Castle Caldwell 187
Castle Ward 171
Castlebar 41
Castlecove 139
Castledermot 102
Castlerea 42
Castlewellan Forest Park 193, 195
Causeway Coast 178–179
Cavan, County 152, 153
Cave Hill Country Park 161–162
Céide Fields 56, 57
céilís 11, 144
Celtic Tiger 18, 64
Charles Fort 141
Chester Beatty Library and Gallery of Oriental Art 70
Christ Church Cathedral, Dublin 70–71
Christ Church Cathedral, Waterford 149
City Hall, Belfast 162, 168
Claddagh rings 33
Clare, County 112, 134–135
Clare Heritage and Genealogical Centre 134, 135
Clare Island 54
Cleggan 44
Clew Bay 54

Clifden 44
Cliffs of Moher 134–135
climate and seasons 8, 214
Cloghy Rocks 171
Clonalis House 42
Clonmacnoise 62, 90
Cobh Heritage Centre – The Queenstown Story 118–119
Colin Glen Forest Park 162
Cong 29, 31, 42–43, 57
Connacht 26–57
  Galway city 32–37
  hotels and restaurants 203–205
Connemara 29, 44–45
Connemara Heritage and History Centre 44
Connemara National Park 45
Coole Park 46
Corca Dhuibhne Regional Museum 131, 132
Cork 114–121, 125
Cork Butter Museum 119
Cork City Gaol 118
Cork, County 112
Craggaunowen Project 134, 135
Crawford Art Gallery 120
credit cards 215
Croagh Patrick 31, 54
Croke Park Stadium and GAA Museum 71
Crom 189
Crown Liquor Saloon 162
Cuchulainn 154
cultural heritage 10–11
The Curragh 102
Cushendall 174–175
Cushendun 174–175
Custom House 71–72
customs regulations 215

D

Dalkey 91–92
Dalkey Island 91
Delamont Country Park 183–184
dental services 216
Derrynane House 139
Derrynane National Historic Park 139
Desmond Castle 141
Devenish Island 186, 189
Dingle 132
Dingle Peninsula 131–132
Donaghmore Heritage Centre 184
Donegal 180–181
Donegal, County 152
Donegal Craft Village 180, 181
Donwpatrick 183–184
Doolin 132–133
Doolin Cave 133
Dooney Rock Forest 52
Douglas Hyde Gallery 72
Down Cathedral 183, 184
Down, County 152, 153
Downpatrick 171
Downpatrick & County Down Railway 183, 184

Dowth 95
drinking water 216
driving 22–23, 214, 218–219
Drogheda 92–93
drugs and medicines 216
Drum Manor Forest Park 197
Drumcliff 50
Dublin 64–89
Dublin Castle 72–73, 86
Dublin City (Hugh Lane) Gallery 73
Dublin City Hall 73
Dublin, County 60
Dublin Writers' Museum 74
Dublin Zoo 74, 76
Dublinia and The Viking World 76
Dún Aengus 39
Dun Laoghaire 97
Dunbeg Fort 131
Dundrum Castle 195
Dungannon 184
Dunguaire Castle 46
Dunluce Castle 178, 179
Dunmore Cave 99

E

electricity 217
emergency telephone numbers 215, 216
Emo Court 102, 103
Ennis 134
Enniskillen 185
Exploris Aquarium 170, 171

F

Fahan 190
Fermanagh, County 152, 153, 186–189
Fernhill Gardens 108, 109
ferries 217
festivals 19, 75, 125, 147
Fethard Folk, Farm and Transport Museum 103
Fionn MacCumhaill 131, 178, 199
fishing 13
Flame – The Gasworks Museum of Ireland 177
Florence Court Park 188, 189
food and drink *see* hotels and restaurants
foreign exchange 215
Fota Wildlife Park 118
Four Courts 76
Foxford Woollen Mills 56, 57
Foynes Flying Boat Museum 142, 143
Fry Model Railway Museum 105
Fuerty 53

G

Gaelic football 13
Gaelic language 22, 39, 152, 221
Gaeltacht 22, 113, 152
Gallarus Oratory 131–132
Galway 32–37

Galway Atlantaquaria 35
Galway, County 28, 29
Garinish Island 127
geneaological research 134, 158
General Post Office, Dublin 76
geography 7–8
Giant's Causeway 178, 179, 199
Giant's Ring 163
Glasnevin Cemetery and Museum 76–77
Glebe Gallery 191
Glencar Lake 51
Glencolmcille Folk Village 181
Glendalough 97–98
Glengarriff 127
Glens of Antrim 174
Glenveagh National Park 191
golf 13, 146, 195
Gort 46
Gortin Glen Forest Park 196, 197
Gosford Forest Park 173
Gougane Barra National Forest Park 127
Graiguenamanagh 101
Greencastle Royal Castle 195
Greyabbey 169
Grianan of Aileach 190, 191
Guinness Storehouse 77

H

Harbour Commissioner's Office, Belfast 163
health 216
high crosses 94
Hill of Allen 102
Hill of Tara 96
history 14–17, 20–21
Holycross Abbey 145
Hook 106
hotels and restaurants 200–212
Howth 98
Hunt Museum 142, 143
hurling 13

I

Inch Abbey 183, 184
Inishbofin Island 44
Inishcrone 56
Inishowen Peninsula 190–191
insurance 214
International Museum of Wine 141
Ionad Cois Locha 191
Irish Famine Museum 53
Irish Jewish Museum 77
Irish Museum of Modern Art 77
Irish National Heritage Park 106–107
Irish people 8–9, 154
Isle of Innisfree 51

J

James Joyce Centre 80

James Joyce Tower and Museum 97
Japanese Gardens 108, 109
Jerpoint Abbey 100–101, 103
John F. Kennedy Park and Arboretum 107
Jones, John Paul 176, 177
Joyce, James 10, 36, 75, 80, 88, 97

K

Kanturk Castle 122
Kavanagh, Patrick 152–153
Kearney 170
Keel 55–56
Kells 95–96
Kenmare 139–140
Kennedy, John F. 37, 107
Kerry Bog Village 138
Kerry, County 112, 138–140
Kildare 102
Kildare, County 60, 62
Kilkenny 98–99
Kilkenny, County 60, 62
Killala 56
Killarney 136–137, 147
Killiney Bay 92
Killorglin 138, 147
Killybegs 181
Killyleagh 171
Kilmainham Gaol 80
Kilronan Abbey 40, 41
King House 40, 41
King John's Castle 142, 143
Kinlough 51
Kinsale 141
Knappogue Castle 134, 135, 144
Knock Folk Museum 56, 57
Knock Shrine 31, 56, 57
Knockmealdown Mountains 123
Knowth 92–93, 95
Kylemore Abbey 45

L

Ladies' View 140
Lagan Valley Regional Park 163
language
  Gaelic 22, 39, 152, 221
  words and phrases 220–221
Laois, County 60, 62
Larne 175
Leinster 58–109
  Dublin 64–89
  hotels and restaurants 205–207
Leinster House 80
Leitrim, County 28
Letterkenny 191
Limerick 142–143
Limerick, County 112
Linen Hall Library 164
Lisdoonvarna 134
Lismore 123, 143
Lissadell House 50–51, 52
Listowel 143
literary scene 10, 88–89

Locke's Distillery 90, 91
Londonderry, County 152, 153
Londonderry/Derry 192–193
Longford, County 60, 62
Lough Erne 185
Lough Gill 51, 52
Lough Gur Stone Age Centre 142–143
Lough Key Forest and Activity Park 40, 41
Lough Navar Forest 185
Louth, County 60, 62

M

Macgillycuddy's Reeks 136, 140
Magheramore Hill 190
Malahide Castle 104–105
Malin Head 190
Mallow 122–123
Manorhamilton 51
Marble Arch Caves and Forest 188, 189
Marsh's Library 80–81
Mayo, County 28, 29, 55–57
Meath, County 60, 62
medical treatment 214, 216
medieval banquets 144
Metropolitan Arts Centre (MAC) 164
Minnowburn Beeches 163
Misgaun Maeve 52
Mitchelstown Caves 123
Mizen Head 127
Moll's Gap 140
Monaghan, County 152
Monasterboice 94
Monea 187–188
money 215
Mount Juliet 101
Mount Stewart Gardens 169–170, 171
Mount Usher Gardens 108, 109
Mourne Mountains 193–195
Muckross Abbey 140
Muckross House 137
Muckross Traditional Farms 137
Munster 110–149
  Cork 114–121, 125
  hotels and restaurants 207–210
Murlough Bay 174
Murlough Nature Reserve 195
Museum of Country Life 41
Museum of Free Derry 193
Museum of the Royal Inniskillin Fusiliers 185
museum/monument opening hours 216
music 11, 68, 125, 132–133
Mussenden Temple 179

N

National Botanic Gardens 108–109
National Gallery 81
national holidays 216
National Library of Ireland 81

National Maritime Museum 97
National Museum of Ireland – Archaeology and History 82
National Museum of Ireland - Decorative Arts and History 82
National Stud 102, 103
Navan Fort 172
Nendrum Monastic Site 171
New Ross 101
Newbridge House and Traditional Farm 105
Newcastle 195
Newgrange 92, 95
Newport 55
Newtownards 169
Nora Barnacle House 36
North Mayo Family Heritage Centre 56, 57
Northern Ireland 153–154
Number Twenty Nine, Dublin 82

O

O'Carolan, Turlough 40, 42
O'Casey, Sean 10, 88–89
Ocean and Country Museum 45
O'Connell, Daniel 17, 139
Odyssey 164
Offaly, County 60
Old Jameson Distillery 82–83
Old Mellifont Abbey 94–95
Omagh 196–197
O'Malley, Grace 54, 55
opening hours 216
Ormond Castle 129

P

Palace Demesne 173
Parke's Castle 51
Parknasilla Resort 139
passports and visas 214
Peatlands Park 184
personal safety 216
pharmacies 216
Phoenix Park 74, 76
place-name spellings 22, 221
Portaferry 170
Portaferry Castle 184
Portavogie 170
Portlaoise 102
Portmarnock 104
Portrush 178
postal services 215, 216
Powerscourt Gardens 109
public transportation 217
pubs 78–79
Puck Fair 138, 147

Q

Queen's University 164
The Quiet Man 42–43

R

Radio Telefís Éireann Museum 118
Rathlin Island 174

index

Reginald's Tower 148, 149
restrooms 216
Ring of Kerry 138–140
River Shannon 90, 153
Rock of Cashel 129–130
Rock of Dunamase 102
Rockfleet Castle 55
Roscommon, County 28, 53
Rose of Tralee 146, 147
Ross Castle 137
Roundstone Musical
  Instruments 44, 45
Royal Hospital Kilmainham 77
Royal Irish Fusiliers
  Museum 173
Royal Tara Gift Centre 36
Russborough House 105

S
St. Anne's Cathedral 164–165
St. Audoen's Church 83
St. Declan's Oratory 126
St. Fiachra's Garden 108, 109
St. Fin Barre's Cathedral 119
St. Malachy's Church 165
St. Michan's Church 83
St. Nicholas Collegiate
  Church 36
St. Patrick 15, 31, 84, 95,
  129, 172, 182, 183
St. Patrick Centre 183, 184
St. Patrick's Cathedral 84
St. Patrick's Festival 19, 75
St. Patrick's Trian and Land
  of Lilliput 172, 173

St. Stephen's Green 84, 87
Selskar Abbey 106
Shaw, George Bernard 81,
  89, 91, 127, 139
Sheelin Lace Museum 185
Silent Valley 193, 195
Sinclair Seamen's Church
  164
Sir Thomas and Lady Dixon
  Park 164
Skellig Islands 137
Sky Drive 44
Slane Castle 95
Slieve Bloom Mountains 102
Sligo 48–49
Sligo, County 28, 31
Sneem 139
Sperrin Mountains 197–198
sports 12–13
Staigue Fort 139
Stormont 165–166
Strandhill 52
Strangford 170–171
Strangford Lough 169–171,
  183
Strokestown Park House 53
Struell Wells 182
survival guide 22–23
Swift, Jonathan 10, 84, 89
Swiss Cottage 128, 129

T
Tara 96
telephones 215
Temple Bar 67, 86

Thomastown 100
Thoor Ballylee 46
Thurles 103, 145
time 215
Timoleague Abbey 141
Tipperary, County 112
tipping 215
Titanic Belfast 166
tolls 218
Torc Waterfall 140
tourist information 214
trains 217
Tralee 145–146
Tramore 146
traveler's checks 215
Trinity College 84–85
the Troubles 154
Tuam 56–57
Tullyboy Animal Farm 41
Tullynally Castle Gardens
  109
Tyrone, County 152, 153

U
Ulster American Folk Park
  176, 196, 197
Ulster and Northern Ireland
  150–199
  Belfast 155–171
  hotels and restaurants
  210–212
Ulster Folk and Transport
  Museum 166, 169
Ulster Museum 166
Ulster Way 154

Ulysses S. Grant Ancestral
  Homestead 184
University College Cork 119
U.S. Rangers Centre 177

V
Valentia Island 137, 138

W
water sports 13
Waterford 148–149
Waterford, County 112
Waterford Crystal 148, 149
Waterville 138
Waterworld 178, 179
Wellbrook Beetling Mill 197
Westmeath, County 60, 62
Westport 31, 53–54
Westport House 54
Wexford 106–107
Wexford, County 60, 62
Wexford Wildfowl Reserve
  107
whiskey distilleries 82, 90,
  118–119, 174, 178
White Island 186
Wicklow, County 60, 61–62
Wilde House, Oscar 83
Wilde, Oscar 10, 83, 89, 185
Wilson Ancestral Home 198

Y
Yeats, W. B. 46, 49, 89
Yeats Country 50–54
Youghal 123–124

Acknowledgments

The Automobile Association wishes to thank the following photographers and organisations for their assistance
in the preparation of this book. Abbreviations AA - AA World Travel Library

3 AA/C Hill; 4/5 Karl Blackwell /Office of Public Works of Ireland; 7 AA/G Munday; 8/9 AA/C Hill; 10 Illustrated London
News; 11 AA/K Blackwell; 12 Design Pics Inc. - RM Content/Alamy; 13 Paul McErlane/Alamy; 14 AA/S Day; 15 AA/M
Short; 17 AA/M Short; 18 AA/K Blackwell; 23 AA/C Hill; 24 AA/C Hill; 26 AA/L Blake; 28 AA/L Blake; 30/31 AA/C Hill; 33
LOOK Die Bildagentur der Fotografen GmbH/Alamy; 35 Gareth Byrne/Alamy; 36 AA/C Hill; 38 AA/S Hill; 39 AA/S Hill; 40
AA/L Blake; 40/41 AA/L Blake; 42 AA/L Blake; 43 AA/C Hill; 44/45 AA/C Jones; 46 Ken Welsh/Alamy; 47 AA/C Hill; 49
AA/C Hill; 51 Robert Harding Picture Library Ltd/Alamy; 52 AA/C Coe; 53 AA/L Blake; 54 JLImages/Alamy; 57 JLImages /
Alamy; 58 AA/K Blackwell; 61 AA/K Blackwell; 62/63 AA/K Blackwell; 64 AA/K Blackwell; 67 AA/K Blackwell; 70 AA/K
Blackwell; 71 AA/K Blackwell; 72/73 AA/K Blackwell; 74 AA/K Blackwell; 77 AA/K Blackwell; 78/79 AA/K Blackwell; 80
AA/K Blackwell; 81 AA/K Blackwell; 82 AA/K Blackwell; 83 AA/K Blackwell; 84 AA/K Blackwell; 85 AA/K Blackwell; 87
AA/K Blackwell; 91 AA/K Blackwell; 93 AA/M Short; 95 AA/K Blackwell; 96 Bernard O'Kane/Alamy; 97 AA/K Blackwell/
Office of Public Works of Ireland; 98 AA/K Blackwell; 99 AA/P Zollier; 101 AA/M Short; 103 Steppenwolf/Alamy; 104/105
AA; 106/107 Stephen Emerson/Alamy; 108/109 AA/C Jones; 110 AA/S McBride; 113 AA/J Blandford; 115 Neil
McAllister/Alamy; 117 AA/S McBride; 119 AA/K Blackwell; 121 Neil McAllister/Alamy; 124 scenicireland.com/
Christopher Hill Photographic/Alamy; 124/125 George Munday/Alamy; 126 Steve Frost/Alamy; 127 Mike Kipling
Photography/Alamy; 128/129 Enzo Cositore/Alamy; 130/131 AA/S McBride; 131 AA/C Jones; 132/133 nagelestock.com/
Alamy; 135 Eye Ubiquitous/Alamy; 136 AA/S McBride; 138 nagelestock.com/Alamy; 140 Ken Harvey/Alamy; 141 AA/D
Forss; 142 AA/D Forss; 143 Chris Cameron/Alamy; 144 noel moore/Alamy; 145 M. Timothy O'Keefe/Alamy; 146 AA/S Day;
147 INSADCO Photography/Alamy; 148 Travel Division Images/Alamy; 150 AA/C Hill; 153 AA/C Hill; 156/157 David
Cordner/Alamy; 158 AA/C Hill; 160 AA/C Hill; 161 david soulsby/Alamy; 162 AA/C Hill; 163 AA/C Hill; 165 AA/C Coe; 166
PIxel pusher/Alamy; 167 AA/C Hill; 168 AA/C Hill; 169 AA/C Hill; 171 AA/C Hill; 173 David Taylor Photography/Alamy; 175
AA/C Hill; 176 Rex Features; 177 Roger Bradley/Alamy; 179 AA/C Coe; 180/181 Joos Schoeman/Alamy; 182 AA/I
Daswon; 183 AA/I Daswon; 185 AA/I Daswon; 187 AA/G Munday; 188/189 AA/I Daswon; 190 Gareth McCormack/Alamy;
193 scenicireland.com/Christopher Hill Photographic/Alamy; 194 AA/C Hill; 196 J Orr/Alamy; 196/197 Robert Whitworth/
Alamy; 198 David Lyons/Alamy; 200 AA/J Blandford; 202 AA/J Blandford; 214 Central Intelligence Agency; 215t AA/K
Blackwell; 215b AA/K Blackwell.